Up the Swiftwater

A Pictorial History of the
Colorful Upper St. Joe River Country

Revised with new photographs and a new foreword by the authors

Published by the Museum of North Idaho
in cooperation with Sandra A. Crowell and David O. Asleson

Published by
Museum of North Idaho
P.O. Box 812
Coeur d'Alene, Idaho 83814
(208) 664-3448
in cooperation with Sandra A. Crowell and David O. Asleson

Cover design and publication services by
PageWorks
P.O. Box 1893
Post Falls, Idaho 83854
(208) 773-9304

Book design by Douglas Crabtree

Cover photograph courtesy of Lucian (Wayne) Turner

Back cover photograph courtesy of Betty Clark

Printed by Braun-Brumfield, Ann Arbor, Michigan

Negatives prepared by Pre-Press Color, Coeur d'Alene, Idaho

Foreword

A lot of water has gone down the 'Joe since Sam "49" Williams first came up the swiftwater and laid claim to that wide spot on the river near the North Fork. The waters that once offered prime fishing for Indians saw homesteaders and settlers coming up in poling canoes. The banks carried a proud transcontinental railroad and later the cars and trucks of an active economy. So many changes. . . .

Potlatch Corporation operated a railroad from Avery to St. Maries to haul its logs, but that stopped operations in the early 1980s. The transcontinental railroad—the Milwaukee Road—is gone completely, its rails removed. Now the Loop Creek portion of the railroad is going to be a recreational trail frequented by mountain bikers taking the Taft Tunnel from Idaho to Montana, thanks to local boosters and an act of Congress.

Mt. St. Helens blew its top in 1981, blanketing the St. Joe valley along with the rest of eastern Washington and northern Idaho. The mill in Calder burned; the Rainbow Coalition demonstrated against the use of herbicides on National Forest lands; the stretch of road between Avery and Marble Creek was paved beginning in 1986, fueling an exposion in recreational activity in the area. The Red Ives Ranger District consolidated with the Avery District in 1984, and this larger Avery District, comprising almost the entire St. Joe National Forest, consolidated with the St. Maries District in 1994. Burlington Northern's lands became the property of its "daughter" corporation, Plum Creek Timber Company, in 1984. While the story we tell here is one of timber as king, concerns over threatened and endangered species and logging practices have led to dramatic declines in the amount of timber taken from the St. Joe valley.

The old Avery Ranger Station office built in 1908–09 was placed on the National Historic Register, and was formally dedicated during Avery Days in July 1989; it has been remodeled into a residence. Twin Creek Cabin, headquarters for the Roundtop Ranger District, was rejuvenated in 1988–89 by Avery District employees and serves as a popular recreational facility. The former Roundtop and Red Ives Ranger Stations have been almost entirely dismantled. The Marble Creek drainage became a National Historic Site in 1989 as part of the Idaho Centennial, and a kiosk now stands at the mouth of Marble Creek telling some of the same story we tell here. The Log Cabin Bar and Restaurant burned in 1992, but a new general store opened across town at about the same time.

And—as we wrote in 1980 for the first publication of this book—the town of Avery still hangs on, often beset by contemporary problems of sewage disposal and excessive traffic for its narrow roads. Its future potential for growth may lie as much in tourism and recreation as in mining and the ever-present timber industry. Whitewater canoeists and recreationalists now enjoy the swiftwater; the St. Joe River above Avery has the legal classification of a Wild and Scenic River. The town along the banks of the swiftwater still has an individuality to be proud of in this era of urban sprawl.

The first publication of this book was in 1980. Since then, businesses have changed hands or changed names; the mining prospects we saw in the offing in 1980 have not materialized; even the "Dolly Varden" we wrote about is now designated by fish biologists as bull trout instead. But the book still provides an accurate and thorough history of the upper St. Joe valley. Sources were verified and re-verified when we did the original research, and for this reprinting we have added some new photographs and corrected a few typographical errors found in the original printing, making this an even better reference.

Up the Swiftwater is the product of a seven-year dream: a dream resulting from a love for the community of Avery and the St. Joe River. It is indeed a special place, and we hope to convey that message to our readers.

And now it is time for you to join us for a journey *Up the Swiftwater.*

About the Authors

The compilation of *Up the Swiftwater* took the teamwork of a number of individuals. Much of the effort was behind the scenes, from friends who helped so much in so many ways, and their support will never be forgotten. The list is long, and each person should receive a special "thank you." However, to recognize and to remember each contribution would be an impossible task.

It is imperative to mention a few names. Those who especially contributed to the project include: Thelma Cramp, responsible for editing and providing additional information; Harold Theriault, Charley Scribner, and Ruth Lindow, who all shared their many memories and photographs; and Cheryl Bailey, who typed the final manuscript. Since the book was originally printed, Harold, Charley, and Ruth have all left us, as well as several other individuals who contributed to the book. It is in their memory that we are reprinting the book.

Authors Sandra A. Crowell and David O. Asleson in 1993.

Authors Sandra A. Crowell and David O. Asleson are pictured here with the group that aided most in their effort to publish Up the Swiftwater. *Posing in the Avery Community Museum are (left to right): Sandy Crowell, Harold Theriault, Charles Scribner, Thelma Cramp, Cheryl Bailey, and Dave "Norgy" Asleson.*

Sandra Crowell lived in Avery with her family in the late 1970s. A native of Colorado, Crowell graduated from the University of Northern Colorado with a degree in Speech and English. With the wild beauty of the St. Joe at her doorstep, she became intrigued with preserving the area's colorful past. Crowell now lives in southwestern Washington, where she directs educational programs and teaches writing at the community college level.

David "Norgy" Asleson came to the St. Joe country in 1966 as a seasonal employee for the Forest Service; his first job was as a lookout on Dunn Peak. Throughout his college years as a History/Geography major at Moorhead State College in Minnesota, he continued to return each summer to the Avery Ranger District. Asleson later obtained a Master's degree in Geography from the University of Wyoming in 1975 before returning to make Avery his home. He began collecting research materials and photographs about the St. Joe in 1974, and played a major role in preserving local history. He left Avery in 1985, and currently works on the Priest Lake Ranger District in Idaho, after living in Washington, Montana, and Oregon.

To Harold,
our third partner whose life story this is and whose
keen memory has made the recording of it possible.

Table of Contents

Before...A Prologue

The St. Joe River struggles out from its headwaters, in the Bitterroot Mountains, over rocks and around logs. It plunges through narrow channels and winds in rugged curves. As it builds power, the path it has cut through the mountains straightens and finally meanders lazily into Lake Coeur d'Alene. The impact of water—washing and working, pushing and eroding—has determined the character of the land as we know it. Its slow, erosive action formed the craggy hillsides, set the quality of the minerals and soils, established the course of its own waterways. The history of St. Joe country began with water.

The first water was nothing like the scenic river we know now. A shallow sea covered most of the western United States about three billion years ago in the Pre-Cambrian era. Before vegetation or animal life could survive, the surface of the land showed ripple marks, mud cracks, and rain drop patterns that mark it even yet. The sediments from ancient seas gathered and dried when exposed to the air, eventually sinking and depositing many thousands of feet of sedimentary material. These sands, silts, and clays, known to geologists as the Belt Series, were cemented by pressure and heat, and some were recrystallized. Made up of quartzite and argillite, the rocks are characterized by layering or bedding in flat and wavy slabs. This foundation was not enough; nature continued to work on its creation, shifting and lifting, fracturing and folding until the sediments were forced upward into mountains. Water began its work on the sedimentary rock and left Shefoot Mountain as an example of Belt Series bedrock. North of the St. Joe River the bedrock shows weathered outcroppings of rusty brown and forms the topography of the northern part of the Avery Ranger District.

During the next several million years, the earth's crust continued to change but left us no evidence of its work. The signs of the uplifting and submersion eroded away with the passage of time. The next period, however, marked the land with a tangible imprint. The area's granite was formed in what is known as "the age of dinosaurs," about 130 to 150 million years ago. A large body of fiery molten material, known as the Idaho Batholith, burst dramatically from the earth's core into central Idaho. This intrusion of granite below the surface spread from Boise as far north as the St. Joe-Clearwater divide, 250 miles in length and 40 miles wide, seeping into smaller intrusives, dikes, and sills throughout North Idaho. If Roundtop Mountain were to erode

away, its core would show the intrusion of granite that came as an offshoot of the Batholith. The pressure and heat of this geologic event was so intense that previously formed quartzites and argillites for miles around changed in mineralogy and texture. To become more stable in the environment of higher temperatures, the grains first melted, then recrystallized and segregated to form mica, feldspar, quartz and garnet. North of the St. Joe River the rocks were relatively unaffected, but south of the river, the impact of the Batholith can be seen everywhere. Road-builders on the north of the river find good, hard materials for solid roads; to their chagrin, the area to the south has mica in its soil, making the roads soft and slick. With the exception of the Durham Creek area which has Belt Series rocks, most rock south of the river is schist, gneiss, or mica.

The course of what was to be the St. Joe River was probably formed during the time of Batholithic activity. With a combination of heat and movement, the restless energy strained and cracked the earth's crust. These constant forces within the earth uplifted northern Idaho into the mountains as we know them today. As the earth released stress, the rocks were warped by folds and cracked by faults whose adjustments extend for miles. The St. Joe fault splintered through the core of the mountains, and when water collected later and ran toward the sea, it followed the westerly course along the broken and sheared rock of the fault zone. Most of the tributaries of the St. Joe chose similar weak zones for their channels. In addition, the faulting action created the complex faults of the mining districts of the Silver Valley. Mineral bearing waters then seeped in to form metallic deposits of gold, silver, lead, copper, and zinc. Water had again changed things.

Then between thirty million and ten million years ago, hot lava bubbled up over the land from the Columbia River Basin. Almost like melted wax in an irregular mold, the lava spread out in layers. It turned into gray basalt in column-like blocks now seen in lower portions of the landscape and in flat plateaus between higher, older mountains. Subsequent erosion cut the basalt down and left caps on ridgetops, especially around Big Creek on the lower St. Joe and near Clarkia.

When the lava flows stopped, winds blew across dried-up lake beds on the west side of the basalt flows. The silt from the lakes had been enriched by coastline volcanoes, and the winds blew it far into

Washington and northern Idaho with choking dust storms. This loess generously frosted the rolling hills of the Palouse and covered many ridgetops of the St. Joe with a depth of one to four feet of fertile soil.

Water in its liquid form did not do all the work of erosion, nor was the land always sculpted by drops of water. In the Ice Age 100,000 years ago, glaciers moved from British Columbian ice fields into the valleys of the northwestern United States. As they melted they left behind debris which dammed up valleys to form Hayden Lake, Liberty Lake, and Lake Coeur d'Alene. The water of Lake Coeur d'Alene during glaciation was five hundred feet higher than it is presently and probably extended up the St. Joe River past Avery. The St. Joe valley was not touched by the huge continental ice sheet. However, small, isolated alpine glaciers did leave their mark as they retreated: on the Mallard-Larkins, Snow Peak, the Buttes, Cedar Mountain, and St. Joe Lake. The largest area was along the Bitterroot Divide as evidenced by the small alpine lakes and Ü-shaped valleys near the headwaters of the St. Joe.

Certainly the formation of glacial lakes in this portion of the Northwest led to some of the most spectacular floods in geologic history. Glacial Lake Missoula was the largest of these glacial lakes with a depth of 950 feet where the University of Montana now stands and 2200 feet depth at Flathead Lake. As the massive ice tongues moved southward from British Columbia, one plugged the Clark Fork valley like a cork. The water backed up nearly 2,000 feet deep at the ice dam, or twice the depth of Lake Superior. As the other glaciers melted and joined the moisture of snow and rainfall, the lake level rose—and rose. The inevitable happened—the ice dam collapsed, and the contents of the lake were released. The result was a huge, awesome flood with a rate of flow about ten times the combined flow of all the rivers in the world. Even more impressive than that, the Spokane Flood occurred at least four different times and perhaps even seven times! The floods carried 300-ton basalt boulders 500 miles to the Columbia Basin and formed giant ripple marks as much as 30 feet high, 300 feet apart and two miles long in Montana. Sweeping through Pend Oreille Lake, an arm passed through Lake Coeur d'Alene and churned up the St. Joe, again probably as far as Avery. The rest of the water washed on to erode down to the bare rock and form the Scablands of eastern Washington.

Did early man see the fearful devastation of the floods? The latest dates on the last flood are 13,000 to 12,000 years ago, and evidence near Twin Falls shows that people were living in our state then. If they were living in the north as well as the south, they could have gotten pretty wet!

1 The First Ones

Three thousand years before the birth of Christ, the ancient Egyptians were building pyramids in their part of the world. India and China were just beginning to feel the stirrings of their civilization, and in Europe, the ancestors of many Americans were still using stone tools to scratch out an existence. On the St. Joe River at about the same time, Indians were setting up camps and surviving off the resources of their land, too. History has recorded events in Egypt, India, China, and Europe, but we know so little about the people who lived in North America then. With our misconceptions about these "natives," we assume that the only local history worth recording is that of the last century. Yet evidence indicates that human beings have occupied the St. Joe corridors and survived here for at least *five thousand years!* They camped temporarily or used game drives at 48 identified sites (and probably many more exist) along the Bitterroot Mountains between Idaho and Montana. In the last one thousand years the people used two other known sites between Shoshone and Clearwater Counties, and another 21 sites show the presence of Indians between the headwaters of the St. Joe and its mouth.

It is difficult to picture people so long ago in a land so remote and impenetrable by our standards. But they were here, men and women nameless to us now, in a land of rivers, lakes, and mountains. They had to rely solely on themselves and what the land had to offer. Who were they? How did they live? How did they use the St. Joe? Where did they travel? Why?

Let us try to reconstruct a picture of these first occupants with the puzzle pieces we have. The picture is not yet filled in for those years between 5,000 B.C. and 1800 A.D. when white men first arrived. By that time the people living in the area had become a distinct tribe within a larger group sharing similar languages and customs. The tribes within the approximate range of the Inland Empire, including the Coeur d'Alene, spoke Salish, while the Nez Perce tribe to the east and south spoke a tongue related to Sahaptian languages. Before smallpox struck them, the Coeur d'Alene tribe was estimated to have had a population of one thousand in 1800, but it dropped to five hundred in 1853. We know that the tribe was shrewd to deal with. In fact, their name was earned by their "stinginess" in dealing with French-Canadian traders who said they were "awl-hearted," or in French, *Coeur d'Alene,* after the shape of the small, pointed tool. (Another interpretation for their name was "strong-breathed" or long-winded, in recognition

An early photograph shows a man Leo, cousin of Andrew Aripa, of the Coeur d'Alene tribe (St. Joe Clan) posing in his native dress. Hanging from his shoulders are ermine hides. The Coeur d'Alenes, a Salish-speaking tribe, were known as proud, handsome people. (Aripa)

of their strength as tireless runners.) They called themselves the "Skitswish" or "Camas People." By whatever name, they continued to be "awl-hearted" by refusing to allow the white men to penetrate the boundaries of the land.

The four million acres claimed by the Coeur d'Alenes stretched north of the Steptoe Butte in Washington, to the southern tip of Lake Pend Oreille, east to the Bitterroot Mountains, and south to the St. Joe-Clearwater Divide. Natural geographic differences in the land led to the formation of three separate bands of people with social and political differences. One band had their main winter villages on the Spokane River, another lived on the Coeur d'Alene River, and a third called the banks of the lower St. Joe their home. They named the shadowy stream the Gentle River.

Between the present town of St. Maries and the mouth of the St. Joe River the people lived in six permanent winter villages, ranging in size from 15 to 100 occupants. Although no year-round villages were located above slackwater, tent poles at Siwash Creek and temporary camp sites have been found at Goat Rock (Spring Creek), Hoyt Flat, the townsite of Avery, Turner Flat and Bird Creek. Campsites were chosen for good grazing for horses, firewood and convenience to hunting and fishing, and were always near waterways.

The earliest families whom we know inhabited the St. Joe valley were given Christian names by the Catholic missionaries in 1844. The Coeur d'Alene language does not include some of the English sounds, so the names were changed somewhat. Unable to say "Edwards," one Coeur d'Alene family called themselves "Aripa." Another family named "Saint John" by the priests became known as the "Sijohn" family. The "Chroyu-Tuus" family adopted the name Nickodemus, although the original name is still used within the tribe. The Augusta family also called the St. Joe their homeland. The families were interrelated, and the organization of the clan was based on families more than anything else.

The Nez Perce, neighbors of the Coeur d'Alenes to the southwest, also knew the St. Joe. While their territory spanned the Snake and Clearwater Rivers, their treaty of 1855 claimed all land whose waters flowed into the Clearwater. This included the Little North Fork of the Clearwater, a part of the present Avery and Red Ives Ranger Districts. The Nez Perce, probably the largest tribe in aboriginal Idaho, were fabulous horsemen known for developing the appaloosa and were major carriers of trade products in the Northwest. They passed through parts of the St. Joe in their travels.

Our modern civilization is geared to the availability of all sorts of products, jobs, and travel. A way of life without any outside influences is difficult to visualize. Mere survival on what Nature has to give us? A hard thing to imagine. The Indians had rivers with fish, wildlife, and plants. They were dependent on the seasons and their immediate environment for subsistence. They built Salishan canoes of stretched skins for transportation on the waterways near their homes, using long cedar poles to ascend rapids in the swiftwater. Before they acquired the horse in about 1730, they trained dogs as pack animals. They became skilled fishermen, building elaborate fish traps of willows in shallow rapids all along the St. Joe. Near the spot known to them later as Mission Point they constructed a fishtrap some 400 feet in length. A dike made of sod from the river bottom stood 18 inches high and was planted with five willows. As these grew, more willows were woven in crosswise until water

could go through, but no fish. The fish were then speared.

In the spring the Coeur d'Alenes moved south and west of their territory to fish for salmon. They traveled to Forty-nine Meadows and near Pole Mountain for bull trout and salmon. Both the Coeur d'Alenes and Nez Perce harvested salmon in Spotted Louie Creek and the Little North Fork of the Clearwater. Even the Flatheads from Montana occasionally came as far as the headwaters of the Clearwater to fish.

The Coeur d'Alene word for trout is *ath'too'mis*, and the people tell the story about a wonderful swimmer with the same name. Long ago, the Coeur d'Alenes participated in the St. Maries Fourth of July celebration (*ju'ju'li'emsh*) in a variety of contests, such as horse-racing and swimming. The Indians bet that Ath'too'mis (the man) could outswim any of the whites and proceeded to back their bets with quite a pile. Ath'too'mis was lounging in the sun along the bank of the St. Joe when his tribesmen pushed him in the water. "Swim!" they shouted. So he leisurely and lazily swam across the river, meeting the whites returning from the other side about halfway across.

Men such as Louie Aripa, son of Andrew, and Moses Moses spent their childhood hunting and fishing on the St. Joe. The influence of white men changed their life style as this rare, informal photograph show. (Aripa)

When he finally climbed out of the water, the Indians were furious with him. "We could kill you!" They gave him such a hard time that he dove into the water and swam all the way across the river without coming above the surface. Coming back, he dove and shot through the water, arching his back, looking for all the world like the trout for which he was named.

Fish was a main staple of the Indian diet, but the people also relied on camas. Eating the nutmeg-like bulb was only half the story. They traveled from far away to the camas fields, joined members of other tribes, and from all indications had a heck of a good time during the camas season! The women used a special crutch-like digging stick to dig the plant at its prime in June and July, no doubt chatting in the company of their friends. They cooked the product in pits in the ground until it was pulpy and could be formed into licorice-tasting cakes and stored in baskets. The men took off on fishing and hunting jaunts into the high country of the Clearwater and St. Joe tributaries during the day. Social activities such as gambling, horse-racing, swimming and smoking drew the Indians to camas fields, in the area just south of what is now DeSmet, Idaho, the area around Moscow, and the area around Clarkia. The Coeur d'Alene, Nez Perce, Palus, Spokan, and a few Kutenai all enjoyed the roots at Clarkia as late as the 1930's.

After the camas season it was the time of year to pick huckleberries. While the residents of Avery today still appreciate the big, purple berries, the Indians turned out in force to harvest the crop. Imagine the whole town of Avery out with specially-made berry baskets, picking berries for days! One favorite spot was south of the southern St. Joe tributaries and east of Clarkia. They named the place Huckleberry Butte, but the name did not carry over to the modern-day maps. Nez Perce, Palus, and Coeur d'Alenes all used the area. The berries they picked were made into cakes to be used for trade and turned into pemmican, a brick made of berries, animal fat, and fish. One-half pound of this mixture provided a day's nutrition for a grown man. Long after Avery was settled, the Aripa family and others came to Roundtop for huckleberries. The berries were picked onto blankets and rolled into containers; the blankets caught the leaves and debris.

The social season on the camas fields and huckleberry fields ended in September when large bison hunting parties were formed among the tribes to go to the Montana plains. The Coeur d'Alenes traveled often with their neighbors, the Spokan, who shared a similar language. Large groups leaving such places as Clarkia, passing through the Bitterroots, and crossing the St. Joe River made a colorful procession. Picture a group such as this one heading to the bison grounds: in October of 1853, fifty Nez Perce riders and two or three hundred good horses, sixty Coeur d'Alene men, women, and children with two hundred horses, and one hundred Spokan with three hundred horses passed by. Horses were packed with lodge poles, bison and deer hides for tepee coverings, household gear, bales of skins and meat, and riders. Along the way, groups

like this one trapped beaver on the St. Joe and other streams for trade in Helena.

The fall was also the time to hunt deer, and the Indians had developed an ingenious method for doing that. They scouted out the area where deer were, then surrounded them with a circle of people and scarecrows or pieces of smoked leather. Often one part of the circle was a rock wall, a pit, or a blind. The deer panicked but were afraid to bolt past the odor of people. The circle closed in, and the animals were easily slaughtered with bows and arrows as they bunched together. Governor-appointee of Washington Territory, Isaac Stevens, reported in 1853 that in one such drive the Pend Oreille tribe killed eight hundred deer and the Coeur d'Alene bagged four hundred! The people had the wisdom to burn underbrush and create winter forage for their deer population long before white settlers had thought of it. Drives were conducted all along the St. Joe and Coeur d'Alene Rivers; some of the identified archeological sites along the Bitterroot crest are game drive pits. After the people acquired rifles, hunting became more individualized and the Aripas and other families acquired game easily along the banks of the St. Joe.

One hunting trip took Andrew Aripa and members of his clan far up into Goat Mountain country. They had put in a long hard day, and as it neared dusk, the hunters became thirsty. The only water they could find was far down a steep ravine, so they lowered one man down with a rope. He filled his container full of water—and also with many bright, shiny specks, the likes of which the Indians had never seen before. They carried the stuff back to their priest who told them it was gold. The word went no further, for neither the priest nor the Indians wanted an influx of whites in the area. Years later when the Indians realized what their discovery meant, they went back to search for the spot. The ravine was gone; the spot was obscured forever by a flood that changed the course of the creek. The gold was never re-discovered.

When the fall hunt was over, the people returned to their permanent villages for the winter (though some Nez Perce wintered near the bison hunting grounds with the Flatheads). Winters were not much fun; food was not always plentiful, and in severe winters the people were known to eat horse and pine moss to stay alive. That was rare, however, for they still hunted and ice-fished. Some of the warriors even crossed the Bitterroots on snowshoes for hunting and trapping expeditions.

These people traveled and moved in a consistent pattern during part of the year, mainly in search of food. But there was movement for other reasons, too. All the tribes of the Northwest interacted constantly in a variety of ways: warfare, trade, intermarriage. They allied together to ward off mutual enemies such as the Blackfoot tribe and other eastern Indians. At the battle sites they coated themselves with red clay warpaint found in the Rockford, Washington, area and used arrows dipped in rattlesnake venom. Most importantly, in this movement they traveled through the St. Joe country.

One source describes three main trails used by the Nez Perce and their neighbors. One was the famous Lolo Trail, and another was a trail crossing the Bitterroot Mountains at Nez Perce Pass near the northwesterly part of the Salmon River. The third passed the southern end of Lake Coeur d'Alene and followed the St. Joe River to cross the Bitterroot Divide near the headwaters.

Two other local trails, however, were equally important. One trail originated near the camas fields by Moscow, passing east toward Montana. Through the hilly land, it turned northeast to cross the St. Joe River at what is now known as Conrad's Crossing. It climbed north over the Bitterroot Divide into the St. Regis River valley. Then following the Clark Fork River, it came to a rendezvous point near Missoula known as "Horn" by the Indians. Later this route was named the Father DeSmet Trail or the Old Montana Trail. The second trail passed from the site of Elk River, generally trending eastward. A branch of this trail terminated at Chamberlain Meadows, another rendezvous point.

Other trails joined these; still others ambled across the country from one spot to another without established routes. Most were high, Stanislaus Aripa explained, because the Indians could spot game easily that way. While important trails were marked by elkhorn wedges, the descriptive Coeur d'Alene placenames served as a map or a set of directions. Unfortunately, none of the names have been passed down.

All of North America was criss-crossed by a network of trails and trade in aboriginal times. Each tribe was linked to its neighbor by a unique trade relationship that benefited everyone. The exchange of goods was truly remarkable. Indians on the Missouri River traded their substantial garden crops for salmon products from the Dalles in Oregon, over a thousand miles away. (Dalles natives prepared over a million pounds of salmon annually to transport inland.) The trade system extended so far that Russian-made bells traded with coastal Alaskan Indians found their way into the possession of the Coeur d'Alenes. A Sioux moccasin was discovered near Spokane Falls in Coeur d'Alene territory, far from its place of origin. Besides such "luxury" items, the Coeur d'Alenes needed fish products and produce. In return, they offered camas, beargrass, berry cakes, fresh water shells, cooking and berry baskets, and bows. The Nez Perce traded their beautiful horses, buffalo and deer hides, conical hats, mountain sheep bows, and products of the hunt. The Nez Perce were major carriers of the Missouri-Coastal trade, exchanging corn and beans of the Missouri for the fish products of the Northwest.

Trading was so common among the various tribes that a special trade jargon named Chinook developed, being in use long before white men entered the area. It incorporated words from several tongues, cut across one hundred different language areas, and greatly improved trade from the California seaboard to the Alaskan coast. Chinook left its mark on placenames in

the Avery Ranger District. W. F. Daugs, Avery's second ranger, got an 1876 edition of the Chinook dictionary and attached words from that jargon to unnamed creeks. The name *Wa-Wa* Creek came from the Chinook word meaning to speak, talk or declare. *Siwash* means Indian or savage, sometimes in a derogatory way. *Mowitch* Creek refers to deer, venison, or any animal. *Calipeen* Creek got its name from carbine or rifle. One creek was once called *Dago* Creek, the Chinook name for gnats, but because of unpleasant slurs on the Italian race, it was changed to Italian Creek! Although the name was given before Daugs arrived, Skookum Creek also has a Chinook derivative. *Skookum,* meaning strong, powerful (originally a ghost or evil spirit), is one of the most widely used words in Chinook jargon. It has been used so much in the Northwest that it has become a regional English word and has nearly lost its Indian significance. Coeur d'Alene families returning to the St. Joe after the turn of the century told their children the placenames in their language. The kids, being kids, were more interested in candy bars bought at St. Joe City and eating huckleberries than in the wisdom of their elders. Sadly, the names were not remembered or recorded, and the stories they might have told us about the past are lost.

Intertribal trade festivals and fairs were big events in the trade network where everything was swapped from tools, trinkets, folk tales, and dances to brides and disease. Locally, each year the Nez Perce and Coeur d'Alene met the Flatheads to trade at their rendezvous point at Chamberlain Meadows just south of the St. Joe headwaters. It would be a safe assumption that trading also occurred at the camas fields near Clarkia. Values in trading were based on deerhides and horses; "expensive" products were, of course, those most in demand. At one time, eagle feathers had such value that the Coeur d'Alenes would trade a horse for one, while one hundred elk teeth were equal in value to one horse. Sexual exchanges and marriages were a part of the trade system, too. For example, Nez Perce outmarriages took place in the Yakima, Umatilla, Warmsprings, Cayouse, Colville, Okanagon, Klamath, Palus, Spokan, Flathead, Pend Oreille, and Coeur d'Alene tribes. That was within the Northwest; Nez Perce marriages extended into 26 other tribes as far away as the Seneca in New York!

The Coeur d'Alene people were less horse-oriented, and their strong sense of territoriality made them less open to strangers than the Nez Perce. It is doubtful that outmarriages were as common. However, one legend has been passed down about a marriage with a Flathead or a Pend Oreille girl that led to an internal feud. It seems that a long time ago a Flathead (or Pend Oreille) chief sent his daughter to marry a Coeur d'Alene chief named *Waxene'* and told her how to descend the Coeur d'Alene River. The girl made a mistake and came down the St. Joe where she met a man called *Cililtesq'wa'ilix.* She wore a leather dress painted red, and he knew she was a stranger. By signs she communicated her intention to marry *Waxene'.* He told her he was glad, because he was *Waxene'.* After a few days of marriage the girl noticed that her new husband was called *Cililtesq'wa'ilix* and questioned the chief's daughter about it. As it turned out, the chief was *Waxene'* and not too pleased about the loss of his bride. He waited until wintertime when most of the tribe was out on an elk hunt, then he arranged to kill What's-his-name. That night *Waxene'* also killed the man's brothers and uncle at the elk hunting camp and left the men's father to starve. Because all the men were dead in *Cililtesq'wa'ilix's* family, the deaths went unavenged.

The St. Joe was a part of Coeur d'Alene legend and myth. The Coeur d'Alenes believed that mysterious powers lurked in mountain peaks, waterfalls, lakes and sometimes trees of the St. Joe. These mysteries took the form of half-mammal, half-human or half-fish. People who saw them died soon afterward. Once long ago some women were gathering serviceberries at a place called *Golxe'estem,* a long way up the St. Joe River. Among them were four sisters who decided to swim in the water. One sister saw what she thought was a fish and suggested that they swim to it. The four sisters reached the spot where the fish was, but it sank--and so did they. They were seen no more. The people knew that it had not been a fish but the tongue of a water mystery. Near this spot on the St. Joe is a high mountain lake called *Tuxe'stem.* After the sisters drowned, some people were up on this mountain and discovered the hair of the sisters on the shores of this lake. The people knew then that there was a passage between the river and the lake up on the mountain. At another lake near the head of the St. Joe which the Coeur d'Alenes had named with a word meaning "swallowing," an older brother ordered a younger one to get him a drink of water. This was a lake of mystery, and the young man balked but finally did as his brother ordered. The water followed the younger brother up the hill, overtook him, and drowned him. Land mysteries could be found at the high summits where trails passed by in the mountains of the eastern part of the Coeur d'Alene territory (presumably on the Old Montana Trail). In order to placate these mysteries, each passerby put down a stone until great heaps of stones were build up. Coeur d'Alene youths underwent rituals seeking certain visions. As proof of their manhood, they too erected rock cairns, some of which still can be found on St. Joe Baldy Peak.

While our culture does not recognize these mythical "mysteries," we have our own mysteries to deal with about Indians on the St. Joe. Some studies have turned up limited information, but a whole world is still waiting to be uncovered. Why, for example, has an arrowhead been found on Illinois Peak, the highest point on the St. Joe? What was the person doing who dropped the arrowhead on Bad Tom Mountain? If some of the camp sites discovered on the Bitterroot crest were only temporary camps, then why were grinding and pounding tools discovered? Are these sites where stone tools may have been made?

One of the biggest mysteries of all appeared in the

Wallace *Daily News,* December 20, 1890. "Sacred Altars: A Mullan Man Finds Them in the St. Joe Mountains," says the headline. An old mining trail fifteen miles southeast of Mullan on a tributary of the St. Joe goes to a "wild, weird . . . place (where) the morning sun kisses the chapel of the past through a pass in the Bitterroot Range and leaves its last beams dancing on these pyramids to unknown gods." The article describes six basaltic altars, seven feet in height, with a deflection or sink, on each square top. Hieroglyphics and a crescent were on the face of each. A square amphitheater stood in the middle, worn smooth as polished marble, with narrow trails leading out to the mountains. No other sign of man exists in the area. Is this a hoax written to draw people to an undeveloped area? Perhaps . . . but an oldtimer told of seeing it after the 1910 fire. A prospector stumbled on it in the 1930's, and an article published in the 1960's also described the place. A hoax . . . or a mysterious shrine covered now by overgrowth?

These mysteries offer some pretty enticing possibilities, but we must temper that curiosity with a word of caution. It is a violation of federal law to disturb archeological sites, and a new law will stipulate severe penalties for destroying them.

Dr. Ruthann Knudson, University of Idaho archeologist, points out that ". . . Archeological sites are a non-renewable resource--once disturbed, they can never be put together exactly that way--and the distribution of artifacts within them, horizontally and vertically, is a frozen statement of the distribution of the original activities of the site occupants that cannot survive destruction." In addition, artifacts may help the Coeur d'Alene tribe piece together its tribal legacy. The St. Joe Valley is one of the few places not greatly disturbed by the great glaciers or the Spokane flood. It offers an exciting opportunity to shed light on early man's special niche in the environment. These mysteries may be solved yet.

The life pattern of these early occupants of North Idaho was destined to change. It started in 1805 with Lewis and Clark, the first known white men to set foot in the area. Of course, their path did not lead anywhere near the St. Joe but passed one hundred miles to the south along the Lolo Pass Trail and out the Snake and Clearwater Rivers. Nonetheless, their written comments revealed much about the untouched Pacific Northwest, the people, and the potential of the land. Most of all, they opened the door to Manifest Destiny and nothing was to be the same again. They were soon followed by Finn McDonald, a British fur trader, and David Thompson, who built a trading post called the Kullyspell House on the shores of Lake Pend Oreille. Their trade with the Kalispel (or Pend Oreille) tribe brought trappers, traders and explorers to the area. It is possible that white people entered the St. Joe during that time, but no records can verify that. Besides, the "awl-hearted" Coeur d'Alenes protected their territory against intruders. For a while, that is. . .

The chief of the tribe around 1830 was named

Stellam, or Circling Raven. As a young man living at Post Falls, Circling Raven had a dream of white man's religion coming to his people. He dreamed that two kinds of people were to come, both white. One was a preacher who was married and had a family; the other was not married and wore a long, black robe. The Coeur d'Alene people, he dreamed, would believe in the man in the black robe who would teach the story of the true God. Circling Raven shared this dream with his people. Meanwhile, in 1832, the Flathead Indians sent a representative to St. Louis in search of the white man's religion. In answer to their plea, Father Pierre-Jean DeSmet, a Jesuit missionary, journeyed west to Montana. He established the St. Mary's Mission in the Bitterroot Valley in 1841. The following year he sent two companions westward, for the Coeur d'Alene tribe had requested the Black Robes after an Iroquois Indian had partially converted them. The priests planted a cross on the north bank of the river that Father DeSmet named Saint Joseph, and they dedicated the spot of a new mission to the Sacred Heart on November 4, 1842. Father Nicholas Point and Brother James Huet stayed at the Mission in the spot known as Mission Point to become the first white settlers among the Coeur d'Alenes. Much to the surprise of the Hudson Bay traders who had tried for years to enter the territory, the fathers were immediately accepted. Circling Raven's dream had come true.

As Father DeSmet traveled bringing Catholicism to the wilderness, he took upon the task of naming places. "How greatly has Christianity contributed to the civilization and welfare, temporal and spiritual, of mankind by simply calling persons, things, places her (Christianity's) own names!. . . How vulgar and trivial are these (names such as Boulder, Dry Gulch, Deadhorse) when compared with the noble and elevating appellations supplied by Religion!" exclaimed a book about Father DeSmet's travels. The good Father changed the name of the Bitterroot River to St. Mary's. He wrote from Idaho in 1844: "I have called the two great streams which form the great Coeur d'Alene Lake . . . by the names Saint Ignatius (Coeur d'Alene River) and Saint Joseph. They in turn are formed by the names of a great number of branches, the four principal ones are known by the names of the four evangelists, and the various mountain streams which form these last bear the names of all the Catholic hierarchy of the United States." Washed away in the course of history were the names of rivers Matthew, Mark, Luke, and John, plus the Catholic hierarchy in the tributaries. Yet many of Father DeSmet's "noble and elevating appellations" have stayed with us. Familiar names are St. Joseph, St. Maries, St. Regis (originally St. Regis de Borgia), St. Ignatius, and DeBorgia. DeSmet, Cataldo, Ravalli and Mission Point commemorate names of priests.

Catholicism was met eagerly by the Coeur d'Alenes. "The savages who lately addressed their prayers only to the animals of the mountains" almost immediately abandoned many superstitions. At the completion of the mission at Mission Point west of St. Maries, the entire tribe received Holy Communion at Christmas in 1844. The priests traveled regularly upriver by canoe to spend Saturday nights with the members of tribes living along the St. Joe and to serve mass on Sunday. In the spring in both 1845 and 1846, about a dozen Nez Perce chiefs came to the mission for religious instruction in the ways of the Great Spirit, although they were hampered by the language barrier.

The Sacred Heart Mission on Mission Point was abandoned after four years because it was flooded each year by waters of the St. Joe, and a new site was chosen near the head of navigation on the Coeur d'Alene River. The Cataldo Mission was a labor of love, designed by Father Anthony Ravalli. The

The Coeur d'Alenes converted eagerly to Catholicism. This picture of Susan Aripa and her youngest daughter, Mary Aripa Red Eagle, was taken in 1931 at DeSmet. Since the time Father DeSmet arrived on the St. Joe River in 1842, the people have been devout Catholics. (Aripa)

beautiful structure had wooden pegs, hand-hewn logs, hand-forged hinges and bolts, and hand-carved panels. Indian fingerprints mark the mud plaster on the walls behind the chapel, mute evidence of loving hands. Old-world paintings adorned the walls when the mission was completed in 1853. Many of the Coeur d'Alenes lived near their mission in log houses and learned to grow potatoes and grain; gone were the days of traveling and roving for their subsistence. In spite of the tremendous influence of the priests, the three separate bands refused to live in one spot. The St. Joe clan still remained on the river, fishing and hunting, but also raising potatoes, grain, and cattle. When the Indian uprising occurred in 1858, the Coeur d'Alenes joined with the Spokan and Palus to fight the whites at Steptoe Butte in Washington. Against the advice of the priest, ancestors of the Aripa family left the St. Joe to fight. Albert, the original Aripa, took his wife Susan who helped load rifles in the battle. Thus, women as well as men played an important role in the war, serving as a kind of Red Cross to care for the wounded. Ajot (Agatha) was another proud "soldier" in the conflict.

The Indians were defeated by Colonel George Wright and returned to live in peace in their territory for twenty more years. The tribe was bewildered and aggrieved when the government forced them to abandon their lovely mission and cultivated fields and move to the reservation in 1878.

"For the consideration hereinafter stated the said Coeur d'Alene Indians hereby cede, grant, relinquish, and quitclaim to the United States all right, title and claim which they now have, or ever had, to all lands in said territories and elsewhere, except the portion of land within the boundaries of their present reservation in the territory of Idaho known as the Coeur d'Alene Reservation," concluded the agreement with the Northwest Indian Commission on March 26, 1887. Within a period of fifty years, the Coeur d'Alenes had changed from a semi-nomadic tribe, traveling through their large territory, to Christian farmers and landlords. One single document confined them to the land chosen for them by the government. The people from the St. Joe moved to the reservation in the early 1880s, leaving their Gentle River. Young Stanislaus Aripa whose childhood had been spent on the banks of the river went to the first Indian school in DeSmet.

The Coeur d'Alenes adjusted very well to their move to the reservation, retaining their self-respect besides earning respect of the whites. In 1902 Peter Moctolme was chief of the St. Joe band of the tribe, and his strong leadership put him in the position of chief of the entire tribe in 1907. His life was marked by frustration and failures in dealing with government legislation, for in 1907 Congress passed legislation directing the allotment of 160 acres to each Indian on the Coeur d'Alene Reservation and then opening the rest to homesteading. This opposed every previous treaty and promise made by the government. In protest a delegation was sent to Washington, D.C., with Stanislaus Aripa as the interpreter, but the trip was in vain. The Indians who had developed large holdings of land lost not only the land but their right to protect their territory from intruders. The allotment act was more influential in the social disintegration of the Coeur d'Alene tribe than any single factor. The Coeur d'Alenes had their own "trail of tears" too.

The travels of Father DeSmet in his ministry of the Coeur d'Alene people had drawn attention to the St. Joe. In his many passages from Idaho to Montana, Father DeSmet used routes that had been developed by the Indians. Because one trail carried his name on maps, it is believed that Father DeSmet passed over the Old Montana Trail. Basically, the Father DeSmet trail follows ridgetops in the high country as most Indian trails did. Starting at St. Regis, it led up Mullan Gulch

LEFT: *Stanislaus Aripa and his wife Emma Stanislaus went to the first Indian school in DeSmet. He helped to form the tribal police force in 1897. In 1909 Aripa went as an interpreter to Washington, D.C. to protest legislation detrimental to the tribe. (Aripa)* **RIGHT:** *The last of the chiefs. They had known the old ways and had experienced the changes in the lives of their people. Left to right, they are Broken Tooth, Peter Moctolme (chief of the St. Joe band and later of the entire tribe), Masaslaw (A Kalispel Indian), Peter Wildshoe and Sol Louie. (Aripa)*

The log jam at Conrads Crossing was nearly a mile in length. It was here that the old Montana Trail crossed the upper St. Joe River. The jam was blasted out by dynamite in 1948. (Boyle)

and laid the course for what was to be the Mullan Road, then it veered off up Deer Creek. Across the Idaho-Montana border, the trail headed about a half mile west of Ward Peak and to the head of Gold Creek, south to Beetle Hump and to Bear Springs. It crossed the St. Joe River at Conrad's Crossing where a large log jam provided easy passage. (Daniel Conrad, for whom the site was named in modern times, was a prospector near there in 1906.) From there the trail followed the divide between Mosquito and the East Fork of Bluff Creek to Junction Peak. The trail forked at this point; one part led on to the mining and boomtown at Moose City on the Clearwater. Once a grand piano was packed over this trail to provide some honky-tonk for the miners in the 1880's! The other part of the trail went on to Bathtub Springs, so named because of a natural oval basin filled by a spring. The temperature of the water is low enough that the dirtiest of travelers would not linger in the bathtub. From there the trail went northwesterly on the divide between Bluff and Spotted Louie Creeks to Mammoth Springs.

An old story passed on by W.C. Evenden tells of the naming of Hoodoo Springs, near the head of Spotted Louie Creek. It seems that news of a gold strike in the Coeur d'Alenes brought fifty or sixty men from Superior, Montana, in 1873. They got lost and wandered to Pole Mountain and Bearskull. Some of the men became sick and died; others were killed in disagreements, and several were left behind to die at Hoodoo Springs. Finally, scouts from the group recognized Monumental Buttes and realized that Palouse country lay just beyond. Part of the group made it out before the approaching winter.

The trail from Hoodoo Springs went to Bearskull to the Little North Fork of the Clearwater to Monumental Buttes. Placenames were given along the trail when a spot had a peculiar marker; for instance, Bearskull was marked by the skull of a bear hanging in a tree. Trimmed-tree Hill was called that because of a knife stuck in a tree. Although the geological formation could justify the name of Monumental Buttes, differing stories add more explanation. One story is that Father DeSmet met a band of Indians on one of his trips on the trail. He held services for the group, and the Indians marked the occasion by erecting rock cairns. Another possible explanation for the rock cairns or monuments had to do with the Indians' land mysteries. On high summits where trails pass, and in passes in the mountains in the eastern part of the Coeur d'Alene territory, each passerby put down a stone. The route was well enough established that a good many stones could have piled up, making the monument on Monumental Buttes a product of Indian mysticism. Additionally, stones placed in certain formations identified travelers who had already passed through.

From there the Father DeSmet or Montana Trail bore southwesterly on the divide between Rocky Run and Foehl Creeks. On Foehl Creek another interesting tidbit grabs our attention--very old foundations. Military records tell the story of an off-shoot religious sect who came to settle in this isolated spot in the 1870's. Their beliefs, whatever they were, did not meet the approval of the establishment, and U.S. troops forced the group to leave.

Jug Camp was the next major spot on the trail, named because of a jug left in a tree near the pleasant spring. Near this location, a badly weathered carving on a spruce tree bore this message: "-------T, August 18, 1854." The first part was probably someone's name, the last part an important historical recording of a white man in the territory long, long ago.

From Pinchot Springs to Hemlock Springs (site of one of the first ranger stations, a tent camp, on the St. Joe), the trail wound its way near Freezeout. The name of a particular camping spot found its way from there to early-day maps. Called Hotel de Miserie, the name was inscribed on a large hemlock tree, a very old carving even at the turn of the century. To add to the puzzle of this ancient stopping-off place, a muzzle-loading cannon and one wheel was found near the tree in 1902, by O.O. Lansdale. A military item found in a place like that poses all sorts of questions. Could the U.S. Calvary have been in pursuit of Nez Perce in this area?

At Marks Peak the trail divided, one part going on to Windy Peak and following the St. Maries River. The other part headed out over Grandmother and

The Old Montana Trail passed on the ridgeline along the Monumental Buttes, the rugged ridge on the right of the picture. This picture looking up Butte Creek, taken in 1939, depicts the heavily forested, mountainous terrain typifying the St. Joe country. (U.S.D.A., Forest Service)

Grandfather Mountains, Elk Mountain, and on to Santa Creek and back to the camas fields where Indians searching for food started the whole thing.

The first white women known to enter the Coeur d'Alene territory may have crossed the Montana Trail. A group of four nuns were on their way to teach at St. Ignatius, Montana, in 1864. Their journey in itself was a testimony of faith. The four Sisters of Providence left Montreal in the spring for New York. There they boarded a boat, journeyed by way of the Isthmus of Panama to San Francisco and on north to Vancouver, Washington. From there they proceeded by wagon to Walla Walla where they were outfitted for the upper country. A month of riding horseback and camping out brought the Sisters to the banks of the Spokane River where they were met by Seltis (thought to be the source of the name Saltese), chief of the Coeur d'Alene. They stepped aboard a specially-built flatboat on the shores of Lake Coeur d'Alene for the 65-mile trip to the Coeur d'Alene Mission. The Indians watched the Sisters with fascination. On October 5, 1864, the "lady black robes" ventured on for the second half of their journey into Montana. According

to Palladino, an Indian couple guided them through the Coeur d'Alene Mountains over "steep ascents, deep ravines, fallen timber, streams and gulches (that) lay in their path, and the difficulties and inconveniences of the travel before them were greater than they had so far encountered. But the brave Sisters were inured by this time to all manner of discomfort, and bore these troubles as they had done the others, not only without complaint, but with a buoyant and sparkling cheerfulness." The group passed Indian camps where they held evening devotions and Holy Communion. On October 15, they arrived at Frenchtown, 18 miles west of Missoula, the first white settlement they had seen since leaving Walla Walla four hundred hard miles behind them. Prospectors along the route predicted direly that "No white woman could ever endure living in such surroundings."

If four nuns in black robes caused a stir in the northern Idaho woods, another sight made a downright ruckus: Manchurian camels. Believe it or not, the long-necked, humpy-backed beasts were used in 1865 and 1866 for freighting from Walla Walla to

Helena. The pack train of seven was loaded with merchandise and freight to supply mining camps and other settlements in Montana, Idaho, and British Columbia. They passed through the Coeur d'Alene Mountains to Hells Gate on the Walla Walla train. Several old-time settlers passed down stories of the string of camels on the Old Montana Trail, in addition to their use on the Mullan Road. In the view that the West was the "Great American Desert," the U.S. Army purchased the first camels in 1855 as an experiment. They were used enthusiastically throughout the Southwest, but when they came to the Northwest, the experiment was not so successful. The Indians were so curious about the beasts that it took considerable persuasion to keep them from shooting the camels for game! The muleskinners hated them from the beginning. Not only did they haul twice as much as the average mule, a real insult, but the scent of the camels caused every self-respecting mule in the country to stampede.
The career of the camel pack string was short-lived, but needless to say, memorable. Many colorful stories were told around camp fires about the strange animals so out of their natural element in the rugged terrain of Idaho and Montana.

The Old Montana Trail was an established route for Indians, prospectors, and future homesteaders. Congress, however, wanted a route for a transcontinental railroad. In 1853 Isaac I. Stevens of the Corps of Engineers and appointed governor of Washington Territory, was assigned the task of making the exploration to the Pacific Coast. His findings have made full books in themselves; let it suffice for our purposes to note that Stevens and his party of topographers pushed to the crest of the St. Joe-Coeur d'Alene Divide. Stevens Peak is a reminder of those first white men known to be in that vicinity. An 1874 map labeled "Gen'l Davis' Route" shows Stevens Peak, Striped Peak, and the Saint Joseph River with Slate Creek mislabeled as the North Fork.

The western expansion had drawn several thousand settlers to the Colville and Walla Walla area by 1859 in spite of a mutual distrust with the Indians. There was no safe travel route for the settlers, miners, and freight wagons. Captain John Mullan was given the responsibility of constructing a military road from the head of navigation on the Missouri River at Fort Benton, Montana, to the Columbia at Walla Walla, a distance of 624 miles. Mullan's journal made the following notation about explorations during a period of time ending August 3, 1859: "During this interval our topographers were engaged in tracing the Saint Joseph River to its sources in the Bitterroot Mountains, marking its tributaries and defining its boundaries, also making a survey of Coeur d'Alene Lake." Mullan found the fathers at the Coeur d'Alene Mission cooperative but not knowledgeable about possible routes for his road. He was forced to travel to the camas fields to ask the help of the Indians who were knowledgeable but typically not cooperative. ". . . On reaching the Indians I found them much averse (sic) to giving me any information regarding the country, and on one pretext or another, declined to serve me in any capacity." The Fathers told him of an easy route which crossed the Bitterroots near the sources of the Palouse River. However, Mullan abandoned the idea of finding a route further south than that by the Coeur d'Alene Mission. The original road was to pass over from the Coeur d'Alene River to the St. Joe River four miles above the mouth. Mullan constructed two flatboats, one for each river. A ferry later carried passengers across the St. Joe, but spring flooding forced a route change down the Fourth of July Canyon. Little did Mullan know that this was to be Interstate Highway 90 many years later.

One thing Mullan did realize was that there were indications of gold between the St. Joe and Coeur d'Alene Rivers. Years later he recalled in a letter that, ". . . I frequently noticed vast masses of quartz strewing the ground, *particularly on the St. Joseph River,* and wide veins of quartz projecting at numerous points along the line of my road along the Coeur d'Alene, all of which indicated the presence of gold." Mullan's road literally paved the way for what was to happen next.

2 The Strike of a Pickax Away

In the late 1800's an old Coeur d'Alene Indian named Spotted Louie set out from the mining town of Pierce on the Clearwater. He headed for his prospect somewhere in the vicinity of Snow Peak or Pole Mountain off the Little Fork of the Clearwater. When he returned to town loaded with nuggets and surrounded by an entourage of painted ladies, townsfolk immediately got suspicious. Where did the old Indian get his gold? Where was his mine? Was there more gold where that came from?

After Spotted Louie died, the speculation grew into legend. Some people said he had taken his group of women into the mining camps on the head of the St. Joe and North Fork of the Clearwater where the boys donated their nuggets for the pleasure of some female company. Others insisted that he dug out enough gold to last him and his various "ladies" all winter. Still, none of the wags could ever find out where Spotted Louie's prospect was. The legend of the lost mine was told and retold. It sparked the promise of untold riches; somewhere around the St. Joe were nuggets *this* big. Just as the mystery of gold in the St. Joe lives, so also does Spotted Louis' name live on as the name of a creek flowing into the Little North Fork of the Clearwater. The lost mine has never been found, but then neither has much gold. That doesn't mean a lot of people haven't looked, however.

When gold was discovered in the Sierra Nevadas in California in 1849, no one could have predicted the reverberations in Idaho. That strike in '49 set off a contagious lust for gold that sent prospectors and explorers into all parts of the untouched West and Northwest. Among the hopeful was one Irish immigrant named Captain Elias Davidson Pierce. In 1860, he went from Fort Walla Walla into the heart of Idaho's Nez Perce country where he discovered gold at the site now named for him. That was the beginning of settlement in Idaho. Two years later, in 1862, some 20,000 miners had flocked to the Pierce area. They spilled into the surrounding river valleys of the North Fork of the Clearwater, and perhaps into the St. Joe, in search of the big bonanza.

Prospectors such as these were the first white men to penetrate and explore the territory. "To the south of the Coeur d'Alenes, there had been a stampede by Montanans to St. Joe River country during the 1860's. Placer diggings (south of Mullan, Idaho) were found but not worked very long. Prospectors from the Murray goldfields also went in there on snowshoes in the winter of 1887-1888. . .but the pay was too light

to satisfy them and (the diggings were) abandoned," says Richard Magnuson. In 1873, John P. Vollmer of Lewiston and Frank E. Peck of Boston headed a prospecting trip from Lewiston to the Coeur d'Alenes, exploring the St. Joe and Clearwater on their return trip.

Then a major strike was made in Pritchard, just over the mountain from the St. Joe, in the fall of 1883. The St. Joe Mountains on the north side opened up a treasure of gold, silver, lead, zinc, and copper, and mines in the entire Silver Valley that still prosper after nearly a century of work. Geologically, the St. Joe river basin is similar to the Coeur d'Alene side. It is only logical that some of the veins must continue to the south side of the mountain, right? That theory has drawn prospectors by the hundreds into the 'Joe, starting long before other folks thought much at all about the land.

Many placenames in the area pay tribute to the efforts and frustrations of those early prospectors, names such as Hardpan, Prospector, Gold, and Bluff Creeks. A whimsical story lies behind the naming of Nugget Creek. It seems that late in the 1800's, Con

Claims such as the Bluebird Mine on Bird Creek dotted the St. Joe country, especially in the decades following the Coeur d'Alene strikes in the 1880's. Stockholders in the Bluebird Mine pose in front of the shaft during the winter of 1911. Standing (left to right) are William Rock and Ralph Debitt, both Forest Service employees; Jesse Turner, and Charles Danke. The only other identified person is Eugene Turner, kneeling on the far right. (Turner)

Faircloth and his partner were panning on that stream. After a week of effort and still no sign of "colors," they decided to name the stream Nugget Creek. It would be the best place, they agreed, to find nuggets if there had been any! Maybe they thought it would be a good joke on some other poor suckers who would try panning there. At any rate, the name was blazed on a tree and found its way to maps drawn up later.

Another creek got its name from an incident involving prospectors. Jimmy O'Brien and Charles Ferguson were working near the head of the St. Joe River in the fall of 1888, when heavy snows beginning on September 8 made it impossible for them to cross the Bitterroots. They started downriver with two horses and a dog. Out of food and nearly exhausted, they finally reached the flat now known as Packsaddle, four miles upriver from Avery. They killed their horses for food, left their outfits in the trees, and built a raft. Rafting downriver, they made it to another prospector's camp near Calder, then went on to Fort Sherman at Coeur d'Alene for the winter. Neither one would ever tell what happened to their dog, but one of the packsaddles remained in the tree for so many years that the tree grew around it. From that came the name of Packsaddle Creek. A thoughtless camper sawed the tree down in 1918.

Frank Heller, for whom Heller Creek near Red Ives Ranger Station is named, was reportedly one of the lucky ones as far as gold strikes went. It is rumored that he took out $30,000 worth from one rich pocket on his claim. Though that may be doubtful, the area is still the richest spot for gold, and Heller certainly found enough to keep his hopes alive. He staked his first claim in 1909, his last in 1933. He built a conglomerate of cabins, a blacksmith shop, a sawmill run by water, and a log flume. He had his share of troubles, too; a bout of flu turned into pneumonia in 1937, and all the advice the doctors gave to his companion over the radio-phone did no good, and he died. Heller was buried next to the creek which he had worked for so many years, and his grave and a commemorative marker are now a part of Heller Creek Campground.

Other prospectors' names mark Miller Creek for "Blackjack" Miller and Adams Peak for Geoffrey Adams. Certainly Adams deserved the honor after he spent his energies putting a 200-feet prospect hole straight down from the top of the mountain! He also worked on Eagle and Entente Creek (a branch of Quartz Creek) in the late 1920's.

Many of the prospectors found nothing but disillusionment, but things panned out better for others. Once these lucky few had made a meaningful discovery, they staked the location and filed a claim in Wallace. Some 3,500 claims have been filed in the St. Joe drainage by prospectors who thought they had something, and prospector cabins popped up everywhere. Filing a claim did have its appeal, however; prior to August 1, 1912, placer claims of 20 to 160 acres could be staked as long as there was one person per 20 acres. Some people used their mining

The St. Joe Quartz Company built the first trail upriver from Avery; it remains visible at several locations along the present road. Often carved from bare rock, the trail was an engineering feat in the early 1900's. Pictured here is a short packstring at Skookum Creek. (U.S.D.A., Forest Service)

claims for homesites, others used theirs for the timber, or even for setting up illegal saloons until they were forced to prove their claim to minerals. Misuse of the claims, of course, was the exception because most people thought their claims offered far more than the land or the timber.

There were two types of claims that could be made: placer or lode. Placer is a surface claim, referring to a mineral broken from the rocks and deposited loosely in gravel. Lode is a mineral vein occurring in place or in a fissure, synonymous with "hardrock deposit." Many of lodes in Northern Idaho were formed by complex fault systems. In the upper St. Joe Valley most of the claims were placer. The gold flecks had settled down into creeks and slack water after centuries of surface erosion. The "pay dirt" was rich enough to make placer mining profitable in such areas.

To eke out the riches of those high, clear streams, the placer miners used water to sift off gravel from the heavier gold. One group dug out a trench by hand that carried water out of the St. Joe into Wisdom Creek for sluicing. Trenches can be followed for nearly a mile there, and they can be seen zigzagging the hills above Heller Creek. The remains of a big house built by placer miners are still visible on Yankee Bar. On California Creek, many cabins were built for the miners; at that spot they used wash mining with a hydraulic nozzle to erode the soil off the hill.

A break dam for sluicing was constructed almost a mile above Wisdom Creek, probably in the late 1880's. That operation ended in a tragedy. In 1894, the dam broke unexpectedly with such force that it drowned two men. One was M. M. Chamberlin, the inventor of a patent medicine. The graves of the men have been marked by a longtime ranger on the St. Joe, Charles Scribner.

In the event that the placer miner was not satisfied with his sluice box and shovel, he used dredge mining. A French family named LaCasse dredged on Cedar Creek, Oregon Creek (on the other side of the drainage), and to a small extent on Wisdom Creek and California Creek. Their investment in several saloons (including Avery's 49 Saloon) worked out so well that the family's wealth helped to build Missoula.

Dredge mining is a thing of the past now. In the 1950's and 60's, the dredge mining of Sherlock Creek and Scat Creek Bar opened up such a Pandora's box of controversy that it was instrumental in the passage of a 1955 state law requiring a permit to dredge mine. That did not quiet the argument, however. The state law was amended in 1977 specifically forbidding dredge or placer mining on the St. Joe River or any of its tributaries, except for the St. Maries River. The classification of the St. Joe from the Spruce Tree Campground to its headwaters as a Wild and Scenic River reaffirms the taboo on dredging.

Not all of the claims near the headwaters of the river were placer claims. There were lode claims located at Copper Creek at the head of the drainage, resulting in a mine shaft of some depth. Tailing piles can be found on Bean and Bacon Creeks (named, perhaps, by a hungry prospector who had exhausted his usual supply of condensed milk?). Iron sulphite crystals as big as ten inches in diameter are still abundant in that area.

The largest number of lode claims and actual mines producing or able to produce ore were located on the northeast end of the Avery district. This type of mining involved not only the search for gold but also for zinc, copper, lead, and silver—the same deposits found in the wealthy Kellogg-Wallace area. One of the earliest operations was the Bullion Mine, operated for a long time by Jim Taylor (later a Shoshone County Commissioner responsible for the Avery-Wallace road). The Bullion road was the first wagon road into the area, built before the Milwaukee Railroad was constructed in 1909. Connecting with the Northern Pacific in Borax, Montana, the road was used by four large ore wagons pulled with six-horse teams. The mine had its own dam to generate power, and it also

had at least two well-developed shafts. Although the lives of eight men, along with buildings, were lost in the 1910 fire, the mine was rebuilt and worked for several more years.

Claims and mines virtually dotted the hills high on the Bitterroot Divide near stateline. Most importantly, they were accessible "by a carefully graded road

The halfway cabin at the mouth of Skookum Creek was an important stopover on the St. Joe Quartz trail. The cabin was torn down when the CCC's built the river road in the 1930's. (Theriault)

between the Monitor Mine and Saltese," states a text published in 1914. The text described the following mines: the St. Lawrence, Richmond, Copper Age, Manhattan, and Monitor. Most of those listed had been developed with shafts of some length, but the only one to ship ore was the Monitor which put out about 500 tons before its hoist and buildings were destroyed in the 1910 Fire. On nearby Kelly Creek (tributary of Loop Creek) were the Alice, the Alpina, and Bald Mountain mines.

One man's dreams for a mine on Turkey Creek, also a tributary of Loop Creek, were ended rather abruptly by a gunshot wound in the head. Ward, a tall, moustached man, was working for the Winton Brothers on the St. Paul Tunnel when he found his prospect. After a trip East to raise money, he named his mine Altoona after a town in Michigan. It was the winter of 1911 and Ward's cook, Jack Frost, decided his paycheck was long overdue. Frost stomped to Ward's cabin under the trestle and shot him through the window. That was the end of Ward, although his name is remembered on Ward Creek. (This is not the same Ward for whom Ward Peak, to the north, is named. Two men named Paddy Ward, one an uncle and the other his nephew, prospected the Ward Peak area and scratched out numerous prospect holes here and there.)

The Big Elk Mining Company on Brushy Creek was one of the few mines to have bags of ore ready to ship out. In operation prior to the passages of the railroad, the Big Elk later listed many railroad officials as its stockholders. Unfortunately, the bags of ore sat waiting to be picked up for so many years that the bags deteriorated and the ore is part of the earth again, another lonely testament to high hopes gone awry!

The Lucky Swede Mine, twelve miles up the North Fork, was operated by the Pearson brothers from Minneapolis and boasted of a shaft nearly a mile in length besides its own generating plant. Despite promising signs of gold and copper, only two carloads of ore were ever transported out. After ten years of labor and a sizable investment by Minneapolis stockholders, the only salvageable commodity was the mine tailings, used as fill for the Avery-Wallace road.

Avery did not exist in 1903, and with the exception of those associated with the Bullion and Monitor mines, no wagon roads had been built in the upper St. Joe. Thus, it was quite an accomplishment for the St. Joe Quartz Company to construct the first trail upriver some 26 miles from Sam ''49'' Williams' homestead through the rugged Skookum Canyon. A stock company owned the St. Joe Quartz Mine; its heavy investments permitted not only the construction of the trail, but also the construction of cabins at Skookum Creek, Bird Creek, Malin Creek (which is named for the employee who ran the halfway cabin), and Haggerty Creek. The name of Halfway Hill marks the midpoint in the original trail. Heavy equipment needed to operate the mine was shuttled laboriously up the river by barge to get the operation functioning. But before anything more than a sample of ore was taken out, the head of the company absconded with the funds and went to Europe. The mine was defunct before it began. The Theriault family purchased the equipment and floated it back down the river to Avery in 1912 and later moved it to the family claim at Harvey Creek. Bobby Stauffer, local trapper and prospector, worked the St. Joe Quartz Mine and did assessment on it. It even produced a little bootleg whiskey during Prohibition, which made it more productive than most mines in the area!

On the Slate Creek drainage, the Sailor Boy completed a wagon road to Wallace but never rebuilt

its buildings after the fire swept them out in 1910. The Franklin claim, also on Slate Creek, successfully shipped out a few carloads of low-grade copper. Another copper mine on Slate Creek uncovered a different sort of treasure in the form of several mastadon bones. The Mastadon Mine donated that find to a museum, and after many years of inactivity, reopened briefly in the 1960's and again in 1980.

Since that first burst of activity, mining has come and gone in waves. It slowly died in the 1920's, only to be revived during the Depression by the jobless seeking gold. After World War II, things were quiet until the threat of recession in the 1960's sparked interest in mining again. Recent improvements in markets and mining processes made mining so attractive that in 1970 and 1971 over 3,000 new claims were filed in the St. Joe. Most of these were along the St. Joe-Coeur d'Alene Divide--harking back to that same old tantalizing notion that the rich veins of the Silver Valley must come through somewhere. Indeed, the idea has some merit. Recent assay tests in the Bullion-Champion area reveal richer soils than some in the Silver Valley mining district.

If a prospector-miner were to come to the 'Joe country today, just what would his chances be? Surely the 90-plus years of searching have produced a good idea of what is a possible resource, as well as what is not.

He probably wouldn't be too wise if he staked his hopes on the gold from the legend of Spotted Louie's mine or any other gold. Placer deposits in the upper river between Scat Creek and Ruby Creek are still the richest in the area, but new laws make mining that impossible. Maybe gold will be discovered in other spots; that isn't too likely, however, as hundreds of frustrated prospectors from the past will vouch.

Other types of placer deposits might offer more opportunity. Garnet used in the metal cleaning industry can be found in several places. Some 850,000 cubic yards of garnet is located on Mosquito Creek drainage, another 10 million cubic yards between Red Ives and Wisdom Creeks, and more upstream from Beaver Creek. Mining on nearby Emerald Creek on the St. Maries River drainage has produced both gemstones and abrasives. The market is limited for the product, however.

The chances for mining lode deposits depend on the market, too. If the demand for copper increased, several deposits with the by-product of silver are waiting to be tapped. The Franklin (currently Stanley Brothers) mine on Slate Creek and another claim on Black Prince Creek could produce, and a higher grade copper has been located on Eagle, Bluff, and Gold Creeks. In fact, one of the few mines currently in operation is at Bluff Creek. While the deposits have not yet been economically feasible, the potential is there.

Marble Mountain is another spot for future investigation. It has about 10 million tons of minable quartzite, some of which has been quarried for building stone in the past. The grade is higher than an

The mining equipment pictured in the foreground was floated down the river from the St. Joe Quartz in 1912 after being used only a short time at the Haggerty Creek mine. This picture taken in Avery also shows the Southside Purity Store which housed Avery's first post office. (Theriault)

existing quarry at Kettle Falls, Washington, but the transportation costs are prohibitive now. The quartzite is also a possible source of silicon ore for future development.

There are other ores around: silver, lead, and zinc have been mined at Gold Hill near Herrick and near Bluff Creek. Other deposits can be found in the Marble Creek-Boulder Divide area. Exploration has been done near Monumental Buttes for kaolite.

Charlie McElroy, an old-time mineral inspector, coined a phrase for the most common mineral of all. "Chlorides of assessment," he'd say, shaking his head. What he meant was a whole lot of sweat. Knowing the history of prospecting in this area, he could well have added "leaveright" to the list: "Leave 'er right where

you found her!"

The many prospectors who have made their way up the Swiftwater or journeyed in over the Bitterroots may not have significantly altered the course of history. Still, they were the first explorers and the ones who opened up the first major roads. They have been the ones with the relentless dream that the next big strike would be theirs. The streams have played their part too, luring the men on with just enough color and "float" to keep the glint of hope alive. Because St. Joe country has always looked like "a good place to find nuggets if there were any," it has attracted various con jobs and many legitimate but futile investments. As always, the hope is there—maybe just the strike of a pickax away.

3 Homesteading

GETTING THERE

If a stone is dropped into the quiet pools of the St. Joe River, ripples will spread until the calm is broken up by circles. History is much the same way; one event can generate a lot of ripples. The discovery of gold and silver in the Coeur d'Alenes in the 1880's made such a change. The mining towns of Eagle City, Murray, Wallace, and Kellogg sprang up overnight in the woods of the Coeur d'Alene country. Miners flocked from everywhere, hastily staked claims, and tried to strike it rich.

The town of Coeur d'Alene became important as a supply depot for these mining camps as well as for the military fort situated there. The town grew steadily, especially after the Northern Pacific Railroad was built, opening the country in 1881-83. Up to that time, the community was infantile and only a few settlers were scattered throughout the area. But the railway officials had spurred settlers with their exaggerated reports of

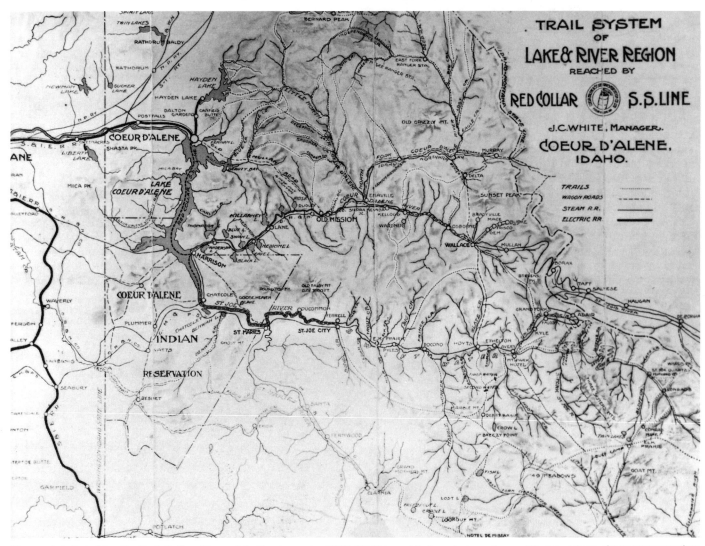

The map printed by the Red Collar Steamship Company in 1907-1908 provided early travelers with a guide to the transportation system in the St. Joe-Coeur d'Alene country. Note the placenames along the St. Joe River; most are described in this chapter. (Theriault)

the mining strikes in the surrounding hinterlands, and now, the country was gaining a spirit of permanence.

Water favored Coeur d'Alene City. The Spokane River to the west connected the settlement with Frederick Post's lumber mill just a few miles downriver and also to the growing city of Spokane and its railhead. To the south was a 22-mile long lake that branched out into two navigable rivers, each with over thirty miles suitable for steamboats. One, the Coeur d'Alene, had a wealth of silver within its grasp, and the other, the St. Joe, led into rich white pine forests.

Other towns grew up along the lake and its network of rivers. In the 1880's a few settlers had made their home on land belonging to the Coeur d'Alene Indian Reservation near the mouth of the Coeur d'Alene River. Supported by the burgeoning mining and timber industries, the settlers petitioned the President and Congress to remove from the Reservation a stretch of land suitable for a townsite. The pressure worked, and in 1889 President Benjamin Harrison signed the bill withdrawing a mile-long strip on the east shore of the lake. Harrison, named after the President, was born and grew so quickly that it soon rivaled Coeur d'Alene for prominence. Harrison during its days of glory was basically a lumbering town. The first mill, a shingle mill, was built in 1892 by Hans Stuve and his brothers, a family of Norwegians. As logging progressed up the Coeur d'Alene River and on Harrison Flats, the rolling hills east of town, Harrison City boasted two large sawmills, several smaller ones, and several shingle mills. By 1900 the population had grown to thousands, making Harrison one of the larger cities in Idaho. But it was part of the general boom on the area, and it declined sharply following a disastrous fire in 1917 which wiped out half the business district.

Stirrings of settlement were also occurring further south and east on the St. Joe River before the turn of the century. A family named Fisher settled at the junction of the St. Maries and St. Joe Rivers in 1887. Three of the Fisher brothers constructed a small mill at that location, selling their lumber to merchants and miners in Coeur d'Alene as well as to the increasing number of new settlers in the St. Joe country. A fourth brother named Joseph from Michigan joined his family the following year. Recognizing the potential of the site at the junction of the two rivers, Joseph purchased 40 acres from the railroad in 1889 and began platting a townsite. The town of St. Maries prospered on the site, reaching a population of 75 by the turn of the century. Joe Fisher became the first postmaster. He also owned and managed the first general merchandise store and the Mountain View Hotel, an early St. Maries landmark. As a result of the construction of the Chicago, Milwaukee, and Puget Sound Railroad and the growth of logging in its upcountry, St. Maries had grown to a population of several hundred by 1910.

Before the Fisher brothers had moved from Michigan to the St. Maries area another enterprising fortune-seeker, William W. Ferrell, had carefully chosen a site twelve miles upstream. Ferrell arrived in

The waterfront at St. Maries in the early days was usually an active place with steamboats and logs anchored to the docks. The sloping ramp on the left was built to accommodate the changing water level. Saloons and hotels stood on pilings above the dock with Old Town in the background. This mill, one of the town's first, was located near the mouth of the St. Maries River. (Theriault)

Coeur d'Alene in the fall of 1883 and spent his winter contructing a flat-bottomed rowboat to carry him up the St. Joe River. Ferrell refused to wait for the ice to melt off the lake the following spring. He impatiently mounted his boat atop a sled and pulled it across Lake Coeur d'Alene and up the St. Joe on the ice, a twelve-day adventure. The trip was worth the hardship, however. His homestead in the lush meadowlands ringing the banks of the St. Joe right below the swiftwater proved to be profitable, and Ferrell was able to buy a boat and barge to haul boatloads of hay to sell at Fort Sherman. Ferrell's business acumen and blind ambition led him to acquire over a thousand acres of land in the valley and made him the founder of his own community.

Ferrell, named after its virtual overlord, was a colorful boomtown. The town's existence resulted from its location below swiftwater, a jumping-off place for the homesteaders, tourists, wild women, lumberjacks, and a scattering of hopeful prospectors who soon flooded the valley. The town bragged about being the highest mountain town on the highest navigable river in the world. W. W. Ferrell erected a general store and a hotel on the banks of the river around 1900. He carved his land into plots, and the town grew, especially after rumors began circulating in 1906 about a proposed transcontinental railroad. During its heyday Ferrell contained a population of over a thousand people plus three hotels, three stores, two drugstores, a bank, a lawyer, and a floating hospital. A new two-room school was constructed in 1908, serving 68 children in eight grades. But more numerous than legitimate businesses were the saloons and bawdy houses of the town which catered to the railway construction workers and lonely loggers and prospectors. The Olympia, Palace, and Shamrock were all choice saloons with "houses" upstairs. The Maize served mainly a Scandinavian clientele and was well-known for having the largest games in town. But

*Ferrell, Idaho, was a colorful boomtown located just below swiftwater on the St. Joe. Steamboats, like the **Colfax** pictured here, anchored at the docks to unload passengers and freight. The St. Joe Mercantile (on the right), owned by town founder W. W. Ferrell, and Van Dyne's store (center) are in this 1908 photograph. (Theriault)*

the most impressive was the Arcade Saloon and Theatre boasting a large dancehall with troupes of high-kicking showgirls and vaudevillians occupying center stage. Altogether, and estimated three to four hundred prostitutes made their livelihood in Ferrell during its boom period. A number of suspicious characters including cardsharks also were present, but Ferrell seemed to escape the murders and general rowdiness which characterized other boomtowns. Numerous families lived in town as well as on surrounding homesteads; maybe their presence toned down the otherwise rough character of the community.

The town of Ferrell began a rapid decline following the construction of the railroad, ironically the basis for its boom. The reason for the decline stemmed from the founder himself, regarded locally as "a man to watch out for" in business. When the railroad surveyors in 1907 planned a right-of-way through his property, Ferrell held out for the $100,000 he was sure he could get. His intransigence led to the railroad being located on the southern banks of the river opposite his town. The railroad attracted businesses and people across the river, and the rival community of St. Joe City grew quickly, shadowing Ferrell in the process. A ferry, necessary to shuttle people back and forth between the two towns, was operated by Civil War veteran Nugget Joe. A high school was built in 1909, and the floating hospital was replaced by one on the hill behind the depot. Added stability came when "Judge" Flewelling built a sawmill in 1908. Logging continued to be the mainstay until 1928 when the old Winton-Rosenberry mill (Flewelling's mill) burned to the ground. The fortunes of St. Joe City faded with the

burning of the mill, and only a scattered number of residences mark the location of a once hopping community. Ferrell, its sister community, fared worse and disappeared entirely except in our memories and in histories.

When the settlers and timber barons were drawn into the timber country, Coeur d'Alene, Harrison, St. Maries, and Ferrell were there to supply them—and the steamboats were there to transport them. The romantic era of steamboats began in the year 1880 when the army hired Captain C.P. Sorenson to construct the 85-foot *Amelia Wheaton* on Coeur d'Alene Lake. The next two decades spawned a flotilla of steamers, making Coeur d'Alene Lake the scene of more steamboating than any other body of water west of the Mississippi. The boats out of Coeur d'Alene, says author Ruby El Hult, "played a part in almost every aspect of life and death--in weddings, births, funerals, crimes, wars, and in every type of pleasure" including excursions and dance barges.

A varied fleet of steamboats vied for the business along the river. W.W. Ferrell built and owned the *Ferrell,* a freighter that operated many years hauling hay, wood products, and other wares between the 'Joe and Coeur d'Alene. Another freighter, built by Joe Fisher of St. Maries, the *Michigan,* was relieved on weekends of its regular duty of hauling freight and was transformed into a dance barge or excursion boat. Two of the largest steamers to float the St. Joe were the *Georgie Oakes* and the *Idaho,* both of which could carry a thousand passengers. Each made daily runs up the 'Joe but the tantalizing menu and luxurious grandeur of the *Georgie Oakes* especially attracted

18

*The lower river received its popular nickname, the Shadowy St. Joe, from the many cottonwoods lining its banks. Another view of the community of Ferrell is depicted in this 1908 photo; Ferrell's Hotel is the large structure on the left. The freighter **Ferrell** lies docked on the north bank of the river, while Jim Peter's swiftwater canoe is manned in the right foreground by youngsters Harold Theriault (left) and a Raney boy (right). (Theriault)*

customers. Passengers promenaded on her three decks or visited the pilothouse (sometimes a lucky boy could even man the wheel for a couple of minutes). The *Oakes* was 130 feet long with a 26-foot beam, making her the most revered boat on the Coeur d'Alene Lake system. The smaller *Colfax, Spokane,* and *Flyer* were three other popular excursion passenger boats plying the 'Joe. Each could haul three hundred passengers. Although the railroad spelled the end of the steamers coming up the 'Joe in 1908, boats continued regularly going up as far as St. Maries until the late thirties.

One man who piloted the queenly vessels became a legend in the area—Eli "Cap" Laird. As a captain for the Red Collar Lines, Laird entertained passengers by the hour with tall tales. His Paul Bunyan stories delighted a whole generation of travelers. For instance, one Laird yarn claimed that Paul Bunyan built his bunkhouse so tall that he had to put hinges on the last ten stories just to let the moon go by! After the demise of the steamboats, Laird spent a good deal of time as a guide for hunting parties in the Avery area, spinning

his famous yarns over campfires. Cap's fame as a marksman and big game hunter made him a sought-after guide by Eastern hunting parties. His friends included the rich and famous; lumber baron Fred Herrick counted as one of his cronies. The two shared the common love of cougar hunting. Laird and Herrick traipsed over the mountains in search of the big cats and were credited with near decimation of the local cougar population.

SETTLING THE SWIFTWATER

Navigation by steamboat on the part of the river known as the Shadowy St. Joe was not always easy, but at least it was feasible. At Falls Creek, however, a natural division point between slackwater and swiftwater made the passage upriver a different matter. That's where early boatmen had to switch to poling canoes. Made of cedar or white pine in Coeur d'Alene, the poling canoes were as long as 28 feet. A three-foot pointed beam allowed greater maneuverability through

Swiftwater canoes provided the only mode of transportation on the upper St. Joe River before the railroad arrived. This romantic photograph of Mrs. Clement Wilkins in a swiftwater canoe was taken in 1907. Note the large cedar trees, which were subsequently burned in the 1910 fire. (Museum of North Idaho)

A good swiftwater man was in great demand because of the skill required in maneuvering canoes in rapids and around rocks. Big Dick in the foreground was one of the best; here, he has a catch of fish atop his canoe shown with his name on it. A drainage on the North Fork of the St. Joe is named after Big Dick who homesteaded at its mouth. (Giles)

the surging rapids and around the hidden rocks of the swiftwater. Instead of oars, steel-tipped poles of about twelve to fourteen feet in length guided these specialized vessels. Getting the long canoes upstream required a good deal of skill and strength, especially with as much as 1500 pounds of freight aboard, and only experienced "swiftwater men" were able to handle the job. Poling became a specialty, for the swiftwater boatmen were much in demand and highly paid; they earned five dollars a day or about twice as much as a laborer of that day.

The boatbuilders decided there must be an easier way to get goods and people up the river. Surely some kind of steamboat would make it. Their first attempt was the *Boneta,* a stern-wheeler 96 by 18. Designed with a shallow draft, she was to make the run to Elk Prairie (Calder). Unfortunately she sat too low in the water and had to be converted to a freight boat. The *Dewey* was more successful, making the jaunt upriver as far as Gordon at Trout Creek for several years until at least 1913. Then the Carscellan brothers of Coeur d'Alene came up with a Stanley Steamer with two engines, and at last a steamboat successful navigated St. Joe swiftwater. Her name was the *Shoshone,* and with ten more feet added to her original fifty, she measured ten by sixty. New engines and railroad irons were added to protect the wheel and rudders. At last a steamboat made it up the 'Joe! Of course, the trip was possible only in the high waters of the spring, so every day for two months, the proud *Shoshone* chugged her way up the rapids as far as Spring Creek with ten or twelve tons of freight. She made a few runs as far as Marble Creek, but one historic day she brought a load of beer clear up to the saloon at Hoyt's Flat! The ride from St. Joe City to Big Creek cost passengers three dollars although if they were ambitious they could get there just as fast on foot. Coming back the trip was faster and only cost one dollar. At times as many as 100 men rode the *Shoshone* downriver to partake in the pleasures of St. Joe City. Though bright, the fame of the *Shoshone* was short-lived. In her one spring of operation she earned $6,000 before being sold to finish out her career on the Columbia River.

The boats brought people into the country to settle. Viewing the penetrating stands of timber and the steep slopes on either side of the St. Joe above swiftwater, it indeed may be difficult to imagine that homesteaders once claimed this land as their own. They did not till the soil and plant their crops as had their cousins on the prairies and bottomlands, but instead they settled for a different purpose. Here there was another resource. . .timber. Eastern lumbermen were aware of the possibilities and turned their eyes westward after the depletion of lumber in the upper Midwest. The Territory of Idaho was continuing to grow in population, and newly constructed railroads connected the state with the potential markets in the Mississippi Valley and beyond. Supportive literature was also instrumental in enticing the newcomers. An informational handbook, *Idaho - 1884,* stated, "the most extensive bodies of timber in the great Northwest are found on the waters of the Coeur d'Alene, St. Joseph, and St. Mary's Rivers." Another contemporary article remarked about the same area, "Around Coeur d'Alene Lake, along the St. Joseph and Coeur d'Alene Rivers there were magnificent meadows and agricultural lands." With such advertisements promising a land of opportunity, thousands of people flocked to the St. Joe valley and elsewhere in North Idaho. Population blossomed quickly throughout the territory, and Idaho became the 43rd state in 1890.

Homesteaders in the St. Joe valley filed claims under three pieces of legislation. The earliest law, the Homestead Act of 1862, opened Federal lands to homesteading and encouraged quick settlement of the country west of the Mississippi. A majority of homesteads in the Panhandle of Idaho as well as the earliest claims along the St. Joe River were registered under this act. The Lewiston area, housing the first land office where homestead claimants could record their properties through the 1880's, was the first area in Idaho to be settled.

As a nuclei of settlement in 1863, when Idaho Territory was separated from Washington Territory and included areas of Montana and Idaho, Lewiston became the first territorial capitol. The Indian wars of the 1870's eventually forced the tribes onto reservations, and then settlement shifted northward from Lewiston to the Palouse country and Rathdrum Prairie. A land office located at Rathdrum later moved to Coeur d'Alene as that city gained dominance on the Panhandle. It was from that city that the settlers of the St. Joe registered their claims.

The bulk of settlers on the swiftwater filed under the Timber and Stone Act of 1878. This law, passed originally to allow settlers in the Great Plains woodlots and wood for cabins, granted a claimant 160 acres of non-tillable ground at a cost of $2.50 per acre. The clause which led to litigation and trouble here stated that the claimant needed "in good faith to appropriate it to his own use and benefit: and that he has not, directly or indirectly, made any agreement or contract, in any way or manner, with any persons whatsoever, by which the title which he might acquire from the Government of the United States should inure, in whole, or in part, to the benefit of any person but himself. . ." In violation of this clause, lumber companies struck bargains with the homesteaders

to sell their properties on receipt of the patent.

A third law, the Forest Homestead Act of June 11, 1906, attracted more settlers to the St. Joe and added fuel to the flames of controversy. The act granted homesteaders the right to file on lands, limited to 160-acre parcels, in the newly created forest reserves. Though heavily forested, these lands needed to show potential for agricultural development. Under the guise of filing for agricultural homesteads homesteaders claimed vast acreages of land near the swiftwater. The claimant could buy his land for $1.25 an acre after proving-up (cheap land even in the early part of the century), and later sell it to the lumber companies for a big profit.

And the people came: newly-arrived immigrants; Midwestern families from the old logging areas of Michigan, Minnesota, and Wisconsin; Southerners with accents and handlebar moustaches; and single women or widows who had the courage to face the uncertainties of a mountain wilderness. The valley of the 'Joe was settled early with most homesteads filed before 1900. Marble Creek, largely settled in the 1890's, contained the heaviest cluster of homesteaders. In 1910, there were enough homesteaders in Marble Creek to have their own voting precinct and justice of peace. Other early concentrations of settlers took land in Trout Creek and Big Creek. The June 11, 1901, *St. Maries Courier* reported: "P. I. Gordon of Gordon stated that the country along the swiftwater of the St. Joe is steadily gaining settlers, no less than 12 families having settled on lands in that section this spring." Slate Creek, the North Fork and Loop Creek, and Forty-Nine Meadows were occupied somewhat later but were well-peopled in the early days of the century. Isolated homesteaders existed elsewhere—upriver from Avery, in Lick Creek, and on Foehl Creek.

To illustrate the density of homesteads in the swiftwater country, let's look at township 47N, R5E in the upper reaches of the North Fork of the St. Joe. The 1904 land survey plotted 27 homesteads in this particular township, or nearly one per section. The limited area of tillable land along the St. Joe riverbottom also had a large number of homesteaders. The March, 1901, *Courier* stated, ". . .the country has settled up rapidly, covered with productive farms to and above the swiftwater. . .houses are situated about every mile apart."

A TRIP UPRIVER

The St. Joe valley has undergone changes since the droves of homesteaders poled their way upriver. The same spectacular scenery may exist, but the landmarks, the "spots" have changed. Roads, people, and fire have accomplished that.

The first "spot" to greet the traveler was Falls Creek, where a 30-foot waterfall cascades into the river. The division between swiftwater and slackwater starts here; the valley grows narrow, the water flows swiftly and becomes shallow. Honey Jones, one of the valley's more fascinating characters, also made the location a special place. Jones earned his living as well as his nickname by raising bees and selling the honey to local residents. In earlier years he had been a successful trapper, supplementing his income by building dugout canoes from the large cedar on his property. His well-kept cabin afforded good hospitality and conversation to the visitor; Jones could recite poetry or discourse on a treatise of philosophy. An array of vegetables and fruits were carefully cultured in a magnificent garden, for Jones was also an amateur botanist. His foxgloves still bloom on the spot each year. What made the man even more entertaining was his beard, which he braided and wore under his shirt because it was so long. His neighbors at Falls Creek likewise were colorful. The woman of one household reportedly could spit her chewing tobacco clear across the room and hit the stove!

Another landmark stood a few miles of river later at the Big Eddy, where the river churned into a whirlpool. Here the Milwaukee Railroad established Garcia, a siding on the north side of the river. During railroad construction days in 1907-1908, a large camp of workers lived at the spot. The railroad changed the name of the siding to Zane after a few months, when the discovery was made that two Garcias already existed along their tracks—one on the Coast, the other near Miles City, Montana.

A short mile upriver from Zane at the mouth of Trout Creek was the small settlement of Gordon named for its first resident. Before the railroad came, steamboats fought swiftwater during highwater in the spring to dock at Gordon's piling. The mooring served as a jumping-off point for settlers in the vicinity and in the upper reaches of Trout Creek. The St. Joe's first schoolhouse, constructed after the turn of the century, also was located there. Used for only a short period, the Gordon schoolhouse later functioned as a bunkhouse for men driving logs down the river. (Another school was built on the West Fork of Mica Creek in 1902 or 1903. This building was built so low that teacher and student alike had to duck their heads to enter the split cedar log structure.)

Across the river on its south bank is the mouth of Hugus Creek. On this site, J. C. Hugus had erected his homestead cabin in the 1890's. An old trail started here, rising over Coyote Butte and Evergreen Mountain to the Mica and Marble Country; settlers around the area heavily used this trail. Most came to get their mail at the Remington Post Office, situated not far from the Hugus homestead. The government established the post office in the early 1900's after local settlers demanded better mail service. The March 19, 1901, *St. Maries Courier* reported, "The settlers along the St. Joe River have circulated petitions asking for better mail service than what they are afforded now. At present they are served with two mails a week. The mail has been going up as far as Gordon, a point above the head of navigation. . .About 300 settlers are served on the route. It is asked that the service be increased to a daily mail service as far up as St. Joe, and then a service of three mails a week from St. Joe to Gordon,

Falls Creek, shown here, marked the divison point between slackwater and swiftwater. Honey Jones, who homesteaded along Falls Creek, stands in his dugout canoe with the photographer's wife, Mrs. Clement Wilkins. A peak in the vicinity was later named for Jones, a naturalist. (Theriault)

distant from St. Joe City eight miles. This would give the people of that country a far more satisfactory service than they are now enjoying." Long after the building was gone, the sign "Remington Post Office" remained in a tree overhanging the river until the 1933 flood washed it away.

Four miles upriver from Hugus Creek on a large meadow north of the river were the beginnings of another community, Elk Prairie. A homesteader named Holbrook, his wife, and three daughters located their claim on the meadow, running a small store and dining room with several bunkhouses available for rent. Business boomed after the Chicago, Milwaukee, and Puget Sound Railway surveyed the St. Joe in 1906, deciding to lay its track along the course of the river. The railroad stationed a construction crew there the next couple of years and added a small depot and a good-sized sectionhouse at the location. At first the railroad stuck with the name Elk Prairie, but confusion with similar names and a dislike of two-word stations led to a name-change. Elk Prairie became Calder, named for a railroad executive; the depot sign was redone, but discerning eyes could still distinguish the painted-over name for several years.

Elk Prairie (as it was still called in 1910) managed to escape the fire, but the area north of the settlement burned. Fire-killed timber was salvaged through the next several years, largely by the Milwaukee Lumber Company. More lumberjacks moved into the area again when the Mica Creek drainage was logged in 1916-1920 by the St. Maries Lumber Company. The settlement of Calder grew through this period; families such as the Buells, Lathams, Taylors, and Prays began calling the place home. When Frank Buell was hired in 1912 by the Milwaukee Lumber Company to tend its horses, the community had no school for his children. He asked for an assistant and conveniently chose a man who had eight children so that a school could be started! The residents engaged Mrs. Isabelle as the first teacher. A few years later Holbrook moved an old logging camp building alongside the tracks and converted it into a saloon. As for the Buells, they remained in the area and still own much property in the St. Joe valley. This well-respected family has produced state representatives, county commissioners, attorneys, school board members, and educators.

Calder grew when Albert Nealy and Henry Phaneuf added a post office, hotel-restaurant, and store to the community in 1916; the two men had previously logged on Slate Creek together. The Calder Store continues to be a popular hangout for residents; long time owners have included Zeke Turner, Dorothy and George Moody, and Bill Jones. Calder, consisting today of about 150 residents, is still largely a logging and mill town. One mill has occupied the same site since Carl and Lloyd Buell started the first one there in 1942. One of its more important contracts supplied lumber for the construction of the Farragut Naval Training Center on Lake Pend Oreille during the Second World War. Since the Buells sold it in 1948 to the St. Maries Lumber Company, the mill has been destroyed twice by fire and has experienced a succession of owners. Various concerns have also operated the shake mill after George Moody first opened it years ago.

A collection of buildings sat at the mouth of Mica Creek, three miles upriver from Elk Prairie. This was McCormack's, a summer resort catering to tourists and homesteaders alike. The saloon and bunkhouses housed weary travelers heading upriver. Logging had started early up Mica Creek, and lumberjacks undoubtedly were frequent customers also. The June 11, 1901, *St. Maries Courier* published this item: "Settlers along Mica Creek will commence to clean out the creek in about a week, in order that it can be used to drive out logs."

A mile further on the north side of the St. Joe stood Pyle's Ranch, another summer resort. Like McCormack's, services included a restaurant and saloon plus log cabins to rent. The resort almost resembled a miniature town and specialized in providing services to those early sportsmen who found a paradise on the St. Joe River. Pyle's summer resort closed its doors when the railroad passed through its property. The buildings remained several years and served as housing for sectionmen on the Milwaukee Road.

Just above Pyle's Ranch, the short-lived hamlet of Herrick straddled the mouth of Big Creek. Fred Herrick, pioneer lumberman, originally built a logging camp at the location after buying a large tract of

choice white pine up Big Creek. His men laid rail up the drainage in 1910, but fire swept away both track and white pine that summer. Herrick rebuilt the railroad the following year and salvaged burnt timber for the next several years. His lumberjacks built cabins and the Chicago, Milwaukee, and Puget Sound constructed a two-room depot along the track. A post office soon followed which functioned a few years. The most active business in Herrick, however, was the Old Crow Bar owned by Bill and Gus Saugstad. The Old Crow served its lumberjack customers only a few years when Bill was drowned after being thrown from his horse into the St. Joe's icy waters. By 1927 little remained of the logging town of Herrick; most of its buildings had burned, been moved, or fallen in a state of disrepair.

The town received another breath of life in the 1930's when the government erected a large CCC camp on the flat. Through the decade Ann and George Salchert operated a small hotel in Herrick which they had started in the late 1920's. Another bar was opened in the late 1930's, but it again met with misfortune. On V-J Day (August 14, 1945) while the rest of the nation was celebrating the end of the war, owner Al Timmel and Henry Hibblen plus their murderer were shot dead at Herrick. The three killings were the final death knell for Herrick also; only a couple residences now occupy the mouth of Big Creek.

Another murder marked the large flat across the river from Herrick. Jim Montgomery had improved his property over the years, raising cattle and growing hay on the flat. In the mid-twenties, a railroad transient, eyeing the property, offered to help Montgomery pull stumps over the winter. The tramp did work for awhile but coldly shot Montgomery one day while he was milking a cow. The body was later recovered from a stump where it had been crudely hidden and covered with manure. Harris and Annetta Bellows purchased the flat a few years later. Their dairy ranch supplied valley residents with milk for nineteen years.

Near the mouth of Spring Creek, a big rock promontory named Goat Rock sat as a landmark for passersby. All except a portion of the rock was dynamited out during the construction of the railroad, but the area remains a landmark. In 1908-1909, before the track was completed, travelers could ride on the Goat Rock Stage Line. The line ran daily between Goat Rock and St. Joe City, hauling passengers, mail, and freight. The light coach bounced and bumped its way over the rocky tote road constructed by the railroad, pausing along the route to load or unload its cargo. To the east of the big rock a roadhouse restaurant owned by homesteader Mrs. Ann Randall (Mrs. George Salchert) offered luscious meals to coachriders in the early years. Black Joe Faniff, a swarthy French-Canadian from Quebec, homesteaded the grassy meadow to the west. Faniff earned his living partly by operating a saloon at the location.

Black Joe was well-known for his fiery temperament. Once while on a drinking bout at his saloon he was so angered that he rushed to get a gun to shoot the offender. He fired at his enemy through the door but killed the wrong man. The judge sentenced him to a year or so in prison, after which he lived out his life on his river home.

Although two crab apple trees are the only reminder of Black Joe, one building is left from another era. This spot was once a bustling CCC camp, and the officers' quarters still stand near the present-day A-frame cabin owned by Bill and Johanna Mueller of Coeur d'Alene. Erling Moe added a short-lived mill to the flat in the early 1950's which was destroyed in the early 1970's. Only a concrete pier is left from that enterprise, though the placename Erlmo is attached to the nearby railroad siding. Lumber was hauled from the siding in 1951-1952.

When the railroad surveyors first came to the flat at Marble Creek in 1906, only the cabins of three homesteaders—Bill Campbell, Dick Rogers, and Mrs. Huff—were located there. Mrs. Huff soon opened a boarding house for the survey parties, running the establishment for several months. Construction crews followed and built a large camp; its supply depot issued equipment to the smaller camps along the track. Nearby the camp O. C. Henderson operated a tie mill briefly in 1911-1912. The excitement generated by the railroad soon tapered off, but the foundation for a settlement had been laid.

Logging soon became the mainstay for the hamlet of Marble Creek. Situated at the mouth of the large drainage of the same name, the small settlement sat at the front door of the largest standing body of white pine in the inland Northwest. Lumbermen invaded the drainage in the teens and twenties, and Marble Creek provided services to the jacks. Groceries and miscellany were sold at Art Olson's General Store and the McQuade's Marble Creek Store; the latter business only recently closed its doors. Lumberjacks also could choose among several saloons before Prohibition was enacted in 1919; one, the Happy Hollow Tavern, outlasted the Eighteenth Amendment and Gus Saugstad reopened it during the 1930's in a small draw north of the railroad tracks. Today logging still is important to the several residents of Marble Creek, and a small mill owned by Tom McQuade remains in operation. Its two businesses, Marble Creek Service and Ragan's Golden 20's, now cater both to loggers and the increasing number of tourists.

Tank Creek enters the St. Joe east of the Marble Creek flat. The drainage received its name from a watertank, erected to quench the thirst of the early locomotives. A quarter-mile from its mouth, the small creek flows through a natural arch. A geological oddity in this country, the arch must have been created after centuries of erosion.

Early travelers up the river found another small flat five miles above Marble Creek. Here Charlie Hoyt, a middle-aged, burly homesteader, placed his claim. A resort of sorts grew under his tutelage with a saloon, restaurant, and seven cabins situated at the east end of the flat where the Slate Creek road now crosses the tracks. Tourists made the trek by horseback over the Slate Creek trail from Wallace in the 1890's and early 1900's. The fishermen and hunters found good food at the restaurant operated by "Fishhook" Graham, a

The bridge over Slate Creek was used by settlers, prospectors, and other travelers heading up the St. Joe to Hoyt's Flat. A few months after this photo was taken in 1907, the bridge was replaced with a railroad bridge. The lady is Mrs. Clement Wilkins. (Theriault)

Southerner with a handlebar moustache, and his Negro sidekick, Brown-Gravy Sam, one of the earliest Blacks in the upper St. Joe. A neatly lettered sign proclaimed the name of the restaurant and its proprietors. Not far from the restaurant was a picture-book wishing well with its oaken bucket waiting to draw water.

When the Milwaukee Railroad came through in 1908, the tracks were laid right through the middle of the collection of buildings. Hoyt and Graham abandoned the enterprise and left the area. Brown-Gravy Sam elected to stay nearby and teamed up with Big Nell, the Avery madam, in the operation of a roadhouse restaurant on the east edge of Avery. He finally left the St. Joe in 1911 or 1912, going over the hill to Wallace where he continued work as a well-known cook.

Hoyt's homestead was not to lie vacant for many years, however. Al Stanley re-homesteaded the flat in 1921; his family still owns the major part of the property from the original Hoyt claim. The railroad moved its sectionhouse from Ethelton to the east side of the flat when the Slate Creek road was built. During the thirties a large CCC camp was also headquartered there; the office building would become the new home of the Stanley's when the Corps moved out.

Other cabins lined the riverbanks in those early days, for the area was well-settled along the swiftwater. But Pyle's Ranch, Goat Rock, and the others served as the stop-overs where homesteaders, lumberjacks, sportsmen, and railroaders would stop for a quick whiskey or a clean bed. They could listen to the latest gossip and learn what new opportunity had invaded the valley. These were the spots, several of which remain landmarks even for the contemporary traveler.

HOPE AND CONTENTMENT ON THE CLAIM

Typical homesteaders in the backcountry were totally different from those who settled along the riverbank. Little of their land was suitable (or level enough) to raise either stock or crops. They had no other means of livelihood because so few travelers passed through who required the services of restaurants or saloons. Moreover, no steamboats or railroads ran near their claims. Realizing all of that, these mountain homesteaders knew from the beginning that they indeed were short-timers on their own claims.

Unacquainted with the territory, the would-be claimants of the backcountry needed assistance in finding a suitable piece of ground on which to file. They usually hired "locaters," men who were knowledgable about the country. These men had participated in the original land survey, and hence were familiar with the patches of prime timber and section markers. Two locaters, Matt Miles and Bill Theriault, brought dozens of claimants to their land in the Marble Creek country. Different locaters worked other areas of the St. Joe and helped the claimants find their new homes.

Once settled, the homesteaders had to be a hardy lot. They lived plainly, ate staple foods that could be simply and cheaply transported to their claim, and supplemented their diets by the fish, deer, berries, and other foodstuffs abounding in their locality. Author Carol Ryrie Brink recalled, "We had a lot of wonderful food out there. Fresh trout, that even we could catch with a small fishline tied to a pole and a hook on the end of it, the trout were so plentiful at that time. And then there was always the sourdough bucket with wonderful sourdough pancakes." A few also had vegetable gardens, and grew hardy vegetables such as potatoes and beans which were able to survive the short growing season. An exceptional mountain homestead may have included chickens or a couple cows, but that was uncommon in the upper St. Joe. Life was simple.

This homestead at Turner's Flat was claimed by Jesse and Eugene Turner. It consisted of two cabins connected by an open breezeway for unloading stock. The cabin was later used as a Forest Service patrol cabin. In the foreground is the garden plot necessary to establish proof of agricultural land. (Turner)

The cabins were typically small, crude log structures. Some had floors built from cedar shakes made on the spot since it was so difficult to pack lumber into their claims. Most cabins had skylights, or "lanterns" as the homesteaders labeled them. A single door served as an entry (usually with a single window) and a couple more small windows were cut out on the side of the cabin. Furnishings were simple and homemade—tables out of shakes, mattresses stuffed with beargrass or boughs, pole beds, etc. Utensils and dishes were often improvised. Adornments were few, except perhaps for a calendar or a pretty picture torn out of a magazine and nailed on the wall. All homesteads had platforms suspended on wires from the ceiling to hold supplies and blankets, protecting them from omnipresent mice, packrats, and other "critters." The vast majority of cabins were one-room affairs, though the Engstroms' and the Marshalls' homesteads on Mica Creek boasted two stories and also porches. Out-buildings were few, but practically every cabin had at least a lean-to for wood and tool storage. As described in the lawsuit of homesteader Cornelius Willis on the Clearwater, ''The home of this entryman and its furnishings and supplies were superior to the childhood home of Abraham Lincoln. . .'' But these crude structures were not built to be permanent or long-lasting, and only served the purpose of fulfilling the requirements of the law.

Sometimes settlers elected to remain on their homesteads year-round to improve their claims and to keep out claim-jumpers. Often they supplemented their income by trapping during the winter. Most of the homesteaders, however, came as early in the spring as possible and stayed the required time limits (i.e., six months and a day). They spent the remaining months at a job on the ''outside'' since the homesteads provided little income. Often they had children to educate, but schools were found only near the growing towns.

Life was hardly an idyllic existence. Times were tough, and distances were far to the supply points of Avery, Clarkia, St. Joe City, Wallace, or even to a neighboring cabin. Homesteaders relished contacts, and a trip to town was like a candied treat. Mary Elizabeth Turner often wrote in her diary about the solitude at Turner's Flat. ''Am so tired and lonesome, could cry my eyes out.'' Or ''Still raining. Eugene fished after dinner. Had to have fire all day. Eugene painted some pictures. We are lonely.''

''Hope and contentment on the Claim'' is portrayed in this post card of a typical homestead cabin. The simple fare evidenced here was the mode of the day. (Turner)

Homesteaders relished mail more than any other kind of contact. Neighbors of William Theriault on Eagle Creek, a tributary of Marble Creek, had the luxury of picking up their mail almost daily. Theriault ran a regular fifty-horse packstring between Marble Creek and St. Joe City where he collected mail for distribution to the Marble Creek-Mica Creek country. Other enterprising homesteaders used a rock cave on Marble Mountain for a community mailbox and message drop. The cave was a fifteen-foot shelter where glass jars and tin cans served as mailboxes. Most people, however, did not enjoy regular mail service and had to make the trip to the post office themselves.

The settlers traveled by foot, donning snowshoes in the winter. They could not always get packhorses and when they could, the service was expensive. Only a few trails existed, and they were little more than footpaths. Iona Adair recalled one particularly bad stretch on the trail to Clarkia from Forty-Nine Meadows, ''There was one place that we used to call Little Lake Thelma, it's a different name than that now on the map, and I don't know what it's called now (probably Little Lost Lake). But at any rate, you had to go up a very high, very steep ridge to get up to the top and come over into the Clarkia country, and we always in going up hung onto our horse's tail and made the horse pull us up instead of riding because it was that way, it was so rough you couldn't ride comfortable on it and we always held onto the horse's tail.''

At a time when women were still abiding by Victorian standards and were not permitted to vote nationwide, it is remarkable that so many women homesteaded on the St. Joe. As author Carol Ryrie Brink reminisced, ''They (i.e. women) expected to make some money out of it, and it wasn't so easy for women to make money in those days, and this was a chance they took. My aunt always said that she was a kind of delicate, fearful, sickly young woman when she went in there, but after, I don't know whether it was four or five years of homesteading, she came out feeling more confident, much happier, and according to her own estimate, it had changed her whole character and outlook on life.'' Harold Theriault remembers Iona Adair and Grace Seeley, both single women, and Mrs. Luella Durham traveling the 28 miles from Forty-Nine Meadows into Avery for supplies on Iona's white horse, a long horseback ride by any standards. Miss Adair told the Latah County Historical Society Oral History Project in 1976 how she obtained her homestead: ''Well, in the first place, the locater out through that part of the country had a wife that wanted a timber claim. A sister that wanted a timber claim; two sisters that wanted timber claims. And there was a couple women here in town that wanted timber claims that we all knew. So when the locater had located this particular batch of timber out in what was called the Forty-Nine Meadows country, and he took this bunch out to show them the country and the timber and if they wanted to locate, then we could locate there with him, a certain distance of each other. Practically a little colony by themselves. So that's the way we all happened to go out there. I joined the bunch with Mrs. Torson and Mrs. Durham and Mrs. Taylor and Winifred Calkins. . .''

They weren't the only women in the upper reaches of the St. Joe. Often brother and sister, or husband and wife, would occupy neighboring homesteads. Mrs. Frank Kellom proved up on her homestead on Big Creek while her husband ran a packtrain from St. Joe City and poled swiftwater boats up the river. To the chagrin of her in-laws who considered it frivolous, Mrs. Kellom celebrated the sale of her homestead by purchasing a $35 gold watch and chain; the treasured watch remains in the possession of her descendant, Thelma Cramp.

The women, as well as the men, can only be characterized by their differences. The first black woman to live on the St. Joe, Mrs. Logan, located her claim on Marble Creek. She was highly respected by her neighbors, and no wonder. The story of her determination to settle in such a foreign place would make a good novel. And there was a comely young school teacher, Ella Cavenaugh Mottern, who settled on Eagle Creek, a tributary of Marble Creek. Mrs. Mary Turner, a matron in her sixties, came to Idaho to cook and to care for her two adult sons on Turner's Flat. Luella Durham was a widowed former dressmaker who brought her ten-year old daughter to reside in Forty-Nine Meadows; her name marks a tributary of the Little North Fork of the Clearwater. It certainly took a pioneer spirit for these women to claim the land, inhabit it for over six months a year, improve it, and prove up on their claims after five years. The number of independent woman homesteaders in the St. Joe Valley was significant, especially in this era of women's awareness and their movement into traditional male occupations.

This group of homesteaders display the furs they trapped one winter above Avery. Pictured here (left to right) are Jim Copeland, Eugene Turner, Mrs. Jim Copeland, Mrs. Mary Turner, and Jesse Turner. During her stay at Turner Flat in 1911-1912, Mrs. Turner kept a diary which gives a good insight into homesteading life. Note the holsters and guns tiny Mrs. Turner and Mrs. Copeland are wearing. (Turner)

Theodore Fohl was another homesteader lending his name to a location, Foehl Creek, a tributary of the Little North Fork of the Clearwater drainage. This misspelling of his name should be corrected on future maps. A native of Michigan and Germany, Fohl was for many years a land agent and cruiser for the Clearwater Timber Company and a fire warden for the Clearwater Timber Protection Association. His homestead in the bottom of Foehl Creek included an area of choice old-growth white pine intended for sale to the Clearwater Company. Fohl had filed on another homestead north of Bovill on which he received patent in 1901. His taking of a second homestead in the St. Joe country was illegal—proof of the profitable land speculation which was occurring in the country at that time.

However, Fohl never achieved patent on his second claim, most likely because of the government crackdown on the rampant land speculation.

THE CLAIM-JUMPERS

Lured by the enticement of quick riches, numbers of disreputable characters moved into the country. Among these men were drifters and claim-jumpers interested only in making a fast buck with little intent of doing it honorably or legally. The majority feared and despised them. O. O. Landsdale, who served as a Forest Guard in those years, remarked in 1944, "The Timber and Stone Act and the homesteading were sure a joke in the Reserve. I have packed homesteaders to their claims that did not know (which were) theirs." A situation in Marble Creek characterizes the illegalities perpetrated by these scoundrels. They built a cabin in that drainage with the quarter-section marker in the middle of the floor. Without having to construct four cabins, they were able to file four claims from the one location.

The large timber companies often "put up" claim-jumpers to grab land away from honest homesteaders. For each claim they jumped, they were paid $300 and a grubstake for their troubles. Scrip was a tool they used. Scrip, like currency or another medium of exchange, enabled the bearer to take possession or pre-empt a piece of property. If a homesteader did not remain on his homestead the required time limits, a claim-jumper could place scrip on the property and take control over the claim for the timber companies. The large companies purchased scrip from Civil War veterans back East; veterans had been granted the right of scrip after the War as an early type of GI benefit.

The Northern Pacific Railway also employed scrip to obtain land in the valley. The government, wanting a specific piece of property from the railroad for an administrative site or other purpose, would grant scrip to the company in exchange for the land it wanted. The railroad could then apply scrip on alternate sections up to a forty-mile limit from its mainline. Recognizing the high value of the timbered lands in the St. Joe Valley, the Northern Pacific used scrip they had been granted in the Midwest or elsewhere for properties here. Several homesteaders lost their claim after having filed mistakenly on these Northern Pacific scrip lands.

Claim-jumping occurred in most of the St. Joe area including Big Creek, Slate Creek, and the North Fork drainage. But Marble Creek, where some acres of land supported over eighty thousand feet of white pine per acre, was where events came at loggerheads. Three claim-jumpers were murdered there in two incidents in August 1904—Ed Boule, Fred Tyler, and a third man named either Lindsay or Hendricks. (Discrepancy has arisen concerning the third man. Some authors say Lindsay was injured and died later. Other sources call Hendricks the third man. Others explain that actually four men were murdered.) Boule, the alleged leader of the jumpers in Marble Creek, was a two-gun gangster from Chicago. The lumber companies hired him specifically to scare the homesteaders off and then to jump their claims. Earlier that summer in June, somebody had shot and wounded Boule in the arm; in that attempt on his life a companion was killed. Two months later they finally succeeded in killing Boule.

The *Spokesman Review* first reported the three murders on August 22, 1904. "Two men are dead, and a third is missing as a result of a row over alleged claim-jumping on Marble Creek near St. Maries on August 20. The bodies of E. Bouly (sic) and N. Lindsay were found on the trail between Marble Creek and the St. Joe crossing. F. Tyler is missing. It is said that Bouly's body had twenty-three bullet holes. It is said that Bouly and Lindsay were claim-jumpers. Excitement prevails in St. Maries, as there has been threatening talk about alleged claim-jumpers for the last several months."

O. O. Landsdale, who also served as a Justice of Peace out of Clarkia, later recalled his part in the scenario. "I found Bullie (sic) dead in the trail, then his horse and dog. About a quarter of a mile farther was Hendricks (Lindsay?), also dead. . .It was up to me, acting as coroner, to hold an inquest and bury them. Being all alone, the inquest was easy—just a case of dispensation of Providence. The burial was not so easy. Digging two graves with a piece of cedar board; then, with a rope around their feet, dragging them to their graves with the rope around the saddle horse." Boule's burial spot lies just below Bussel Peak in the Marble Creek drainage; his dog and horse share a common grave. The grave is covered with a mound of rocks and marked by a wooden headstone and a cross nailed to a nearby tree.

So much animosity existed against Boule that the homesteaders must have considered even his saddle contaminated. They left it along with the horse's bridle, lying on a windfall on Eagle Creek. Bits and pieces of it were still there in 1939. The Winton Lumber Company had built a road about 500 feet above Boule's grave. Dooley Cramp, foreman, was making forays out from the road one day and discovered it. Somebody had scratched an epitath inside a square tin can and nailed it to a tree above the grave. The scratches were rusted by time, but the words were clear: "Here lies Ed Boule, good woodsman but a poor neighbor. Here's where he paid the supreme penalty on August 20, 1904."

The inside of the can was protected from the weather and in it Dooley found five or six notes, still legible, written by unrepentant homesteaders who were inclined to wish the very worst for Boule in the hereafter. Dooley left the can and returned to camp to relate his find. He returned to the spot several days later intending to rescue it, but it was gone!

The remains of Fred Tyler were uncovered near the mouth of Eagle Creek by two timber cruisers on June 25, 1905, nearly a full year after his murder. The badly decomposed body had been wedged between two logs on Jack Simpkin's homestead. The victim's mother,

who lived in Wallace, identified the corpse positively by pieces of clothing which she remembered her son wearing. William Theriault, the local Justice of Peace for Marble Creek, and his brother Frank, were assigned their unpleasant task of manteeing and packing out the remains.

With the discovery of Tyler's body, rumors were rekindled among the Marble Creek homesteaders. Harold Theriault recalls the murders as being the main topic of conversation at his dad's homestead when neighbors called—enough so, that he became bored and went back to playing. A reward of $500 was offered for information concerning the murders, but the Marble Creek homesteaders remained close-mouthed to authorities. They all shared the feeling of strong antipathy toward the claim-jumpers and felt that the victims had received their due.

As a small girl during those eventful days, Annetta Kellom Bellows also remembers discussions of the murder among the adults in her family; an occurrence at her family's home in Ferrell, however, was more than just talk. A man came to the Kellom home with a bullet hole through his hand. Annetta asked her father if the man had been shot by a claim-jumper. He replied to quiet her fears, "Oh, no. . .just an accident." As it turned out, the man had been shot in a scuffle with the jumpers and very likely could have been involved in the murders of Boule and Tyler.

Far away in Boise, events concerning the killings were coming to light. Harry Orchard, a Federation of Miners official, was held in Boise and charged with the bombing death of former Governor of Idaho Frank Steuenberg in December 1905. While jailed, he implicated two other Federation officials, Jack Simpkins (on whose claim Tyler's body was found) and Steve Adams, in a number of other crimes. Simpkins, fearing the heat, was long gone; but Adams was located in Oregon and agreed to testify as a prosecution witness against Orchard in return for freedom.

While being held, Adams confessed to Tyler's murder. In a statement Adams recalled how he and Simpkins had gone to the latter's homestead in the summer of 1904 to find that Tyler and Boule had jumped the claim. The two men decided to kill the claim-jumpers after contacting the local "Jumpers Killing Committee." Adams and Simpkins then ambushed Tyler on the trail and imprisoned him overnight before shooting him the following morning. They then dragged the body off the trail, stuffing it between two logs. Adams also related his part in the murder of Boule.

No one was ever convicted for the murders. Adams later retracted his statement and pleaded innocent. However, he was charged with Tyler's murder in a famous trial in Idaho history. First held in Wallace in 1907, the trial ended with a divided jury on account of the support which the Federation of Miners enjoyed in the Silver Valley. A change of venue to Rathdrum was granted. Clarence Darrow served as the main defense attorney; he later was to become internationally famous during the Scopes "Monkey" Trial in 1925. His opponent William Borah would be elected the notable Senator from Idaho. The two lawyers excited spectators by their verbal dramatizations of the case. Much was made of the disappearance of Jack Simpkins and Adam's earlier confession. The skeleton and skull of the dead laid for days on a table in the courtroom, generating additional furor. The trial ended with the jury again divided—four for conviction and eight for acquittal.

The message was clear, however. The days of claim-jumpers on the St. Joe were over.

PROVING-UP

A large number of homesteaders in the St. Joe country proved up on their homesteads. Usually they did not have the financial resources or backing to develop logging on their remote land. Flumes and other means of transporting logs were costly for individuals. Since few would afford to log their own claims, they sold their holdings to Clearwater, Potlatch, Rutledge, or another large lumber company immediately following final payment to the land office. A forest homestead with choice white pine could net upwards of eight thousand dollars for the claimant, a tidy profit in those days. Recognizing the increased value which the railroad brought to the land, a few homesteaders, especially those in the immediate valley,

Both homesteaders and claim-jumpers reached their highest pitches at Marble Creek. Ed Boule, shown here on the left, was a claim-jumper who ended up with 20-odd bullet holes in his back. He was buried on the spot. With him are Ed and Frank Theriault, brothers who staked Marble Creek land. This is the only known photograph of Boule. (Theriault)

retained title to their property. Many of these old homesteads, passed from generation to generation, are still operated by family members.

The vast majority were not as fortunate as the valley ranchers. Huge areas in Trout Creek, Big Creek, Slate Creek, and the North Fork of the St. Joe went up in flames during the summer of 1910. The Forty-Nine Meadows and Monumental Buttes country of the Little North Fork of the Clearwater drainage also had major fires. Only Marble Creek seemed to escape the flames. The cabins of many of the homesteaders vanished in smoke along with their white pine and broken dreams. Several only had a year and some only months before they would have received title to their property. Luckless homesteaders like Fritz Uhlman on Slate Creek had recently received patent but had not had the opportunity to sell the property to one of the timber companies. Two homesteaders, Roderick Ames and Joseph Beauchamp, lost more than their dreams. Their charred bodies were found at Beauchamp's claim on Big Creek where the two had joined government firefighters in putting up a last stand against the flames.

To the homesteaders whose property survived the onslaught of the flames, the government proved as big a foe as the 1910 fire itself. In the couple of years following the fire, government officials packed local courts with case after case in which they charged the homesteaders with abusing the homestead laws. They brought charges against the timber and stone claims when the large timber outfits began buying up the claims in direct violation of the law. The act specifically spelled out that the claimant could only utilize the timber for his own use.

Officials also increasingly enforced the Forest Homestead Law and even the old Homestead Act of 1862. Both acts required the homesteader to improve his land for agricultural purposes. The authorities especially scrutinized those homesteads filed on steep slopes or at upper elevations. The judges and forestry officials required much imagination indeed to visualize the agricultural value of a homestead filed at 5,000 feet, with sixty percent slopes covered by snow six months every year!

Why did this sudden outburst of law enforcement occur after many of the homesteaders had already received patent or had lived on their claim several years? Probably the fact that the Forest Service had been an infant organization up until this time was part of it. Like an infant, it had been struggling to grow up. The unfamiliar responsibility of administering millions of acres of land nationwide had left it little time to enforce the homestead laws. But then the time came when widespread land speculation throughout the Northwest no longer could be ignored by government officials.

Enforcers of the homestead law made few friends. A statement by one old ranger was documented by Betty Spencer in her book, *Big Blow-up:* "We had a swarm of timber homesteaders to check on and most of those so-called claims we knew to be fraudulent, but it was our job to get evidence. In the Little North Fork,

Marble Creek, and Big Creek, we were extremely unpopular as rangers and had to use discretion and diplomacy. We never knew when a bullet might meet us in a thicket or on the trail. . .''

On the other side of the fence, Iona Adair was not so sympathetic. ''They sent out one of these little—we called them patent leather men—from Washington, D.C. Patent leather shoe men, that didn't know a darn thing about timber or living in the woods or even living! and he'd come in and he'd look over your little cabin and say, 'It's not a suitable habitation.' And I had a little garden patch, and I'd raised radishes and lettuce out there and all. He looked at my garden patch and says, 'It's not sufficient cultivation.' ''

Sometimes the courts decided in favor of the homesteaders, as they did in the Myrtle Durham case. The judge chastised the inspector in his brief. ''No fair-minded person can criticize (sic) an officer for doing

his duty as he sees it, and fairly serving his employer, whether that employer be the United States or another; but there are limits beyond which no one is called to go, and we feel that the brief of the plaintiff herein does transgress those limits.''

By the mid-teens most of the lawsuits involving homestead claims had been settled one way or another in the courts. This era of homesteaders was brief, albeit significant in the history of the upper St. Joe. With a spirit of adventure and challenge, the homesteaders had come to forge a new life in this previously untouched part of northern Idaho. A patchwork of land ownership existing to this day marks the areas where they were successful. Their cabins may have fallen down, their small clearings now indistinguishable, their deeds forgotten, but their imprint will remain. Placenames such as Homestead Creek, Adair Creek, Lund Creek, and Hugus Creek will not let us forget.

4 Avery

THE SOUNDS OF SETTLEMENT

Near the spot where the water of the North Fork of the St. Joe meets its mother river, the shores were once covered with thick stands of white pine. Big cedars stood silently in a grove on a flat by the mouth of what was to be known later as Avery Creek. Although heavy timber concealed the land, here was one of the few flat areas in the narrow canyon. An Indian trail, used only by a few prospectors now that the Indians lived elsewhere, wound its way near the water's edge. Homesteaders had staked out land further downriver, but this was uninhabited.

That is, until 1894. In July of that year, the land was claimed by one Sam "49" Williams. Williams, a portly moustached man, chose his site carefully. His claim ran from the mouth of the North Fork one mile west and one-fourth of a mile wide on the north side of the river. The confluence of the North Fork was a logical place for access to other trails and, of course, the St. Joe could be used as a passage for poling canoes and log drives. Many other new towns had prospered near similar forks; possibly Williams had an inkling that the future might bring people here. Besides, who could say what this new land of his might yield? Williams, originally from Arkansas, had sought his fortune in the California Gold Rush and had earned his nickname "49" there. Gold might be waiting here to be discovered, too; and the timber on those hills was nearly as good as gold. A fellow could prospect, trap, drive a few logs down the river, or even farm a little on a homestead like this one. Besides, Williams wanted a place to hang his hat for awhile. He had no close family, only a nephew he scarcely knew far away in Arkansas. Here in Idaho he had his good friends, Jake and Lee Setzer, who settled in 1898 on the adjoining claim that extended another mile downriver.

Soon the sound of saws and hammers broke the stillness of the forest. Williams was at work developing his claim as agricultural land in order to prove up on it. At first he built a $75 cabin and a bunkhouse near the crossing of the North Fork. He plowed and cleared two and a half acres to raise hay and a garden, and later decided to improve his home. Nearer the river he

The first cabin in Avery was built by Sam "49" Williams, on left, in upper Avery in the 1890's. The cedar log cabin was used as a "sporting house" after Williams left the area in 1908, shortly after this picture was taken. The cabin was torn down in 1948 after being the home to several of Avery's residents. Tommy Martin, Avery's first saloonkeeper, is pictured on horseback. (Theriault)

The second bridge to span the St. Joe River at Avery was built by the Theriault family in 1909 after the first bridge had been taken out by an ice gorge the previous winter. It connected the west side of Avery to a 5-acre island which no longer exists. Pictured are Hamm, a carpenter, 11-year-old Harold Theriault, and his mother, Mrs. Mary Theriault. Note the newly constructed railroad roundhouse in the background. (Theriault)

constructed a larger double cabin of two rooms, joined by an extended roof.

During the next fourteen years, until his death, Williams and the Setzers occupied their homesteads. "49" ran trap lines as far away as Forty-Nine Meadows, near the source of the Little North Fork of the Clearwater. The men drove logs in the spring all the way to Harrison and then celebrated their river drive on the return trip at St. Joe City. Williams may have been a trapper, prospector and homesteader, but a boatman he was not. Cliff Theriault remembers that "Sam made a dugout canoe from a pine log 16 feet long, and it was the most water-logged piece of wood I ever tried to move."

Williams died in 1908, leaving his claim to be squabbled over for years and also leaving his name on Williams Creek, Forty-Nine Meadows, and Forty-Nine Gulch. The Setzer name remains on Setzer Creek, west of Avery.

Across the river and west from the Williams' claim, another settler claimed land, although it belonged to the Northern Pacific Railroad by scrip. Gene Thorpe, a half-breed, built a simple cabin on the spot now occupied by the school. Across one end of the small cabin was a rock fireplace with a hook over the fire for hanging black cooking kettles. One day Thorpe deserted the place, probably because it belonged to Northern Pacific, never to return for his kettles and other belongings.

The quiet of the St. Joe Valley was once again interrupted by some new activity in 1905. The first ranger station was built. Its ranger was to be Ralph M. Debitt; his wife Jessie would establish the first post office in the upper valley. Thus, the town of Pinchot, Idaho, officially came into being. Located three miles downriver from Williams' homestead and two miles from the mouth of Fishhook Creek at the spot known as Rocky Riffle, Pinchot consisted of two buildings. One was the ranger station and dwelling and the other was the post office building. The name of the settlement was chosen in honor of the founder of the United States Forest Service, Gifford Pinchot. The Debitts lived a meaningful portion of their lives on the St. Joe; it was here that their eldest daughter Marie died of typhoid. Here too their second and third children, Marjorie and Ralph, were born, the first white babies to be born on the upper St. Joe. A town had also been born, but its name was not yet Avery.

The valley was destined to change. When the Milwaukee Road announced its plans to come through, the settlements of the St. Joe took on a new look. The Pinchot Ranger Station had to be moved away from the path of the new trains, so Sam "49" Williams relinquished claim on a portion of his homestead to provide a spot for the ranger station. And although Williams' address remained officially Pinchot in 1908, a name still had not been definitely decided upon for the place. A few people called it "49 City" after Williams. The ranger station was now called North Fork, and some people knew the settlement as North

Fork City. That name seemed to stick for awhile, and even the railroad adopted the call letters N.F. which are in use to this day. But with Morse Code, two-word names are confusing, and the name was still not right.

In the end, the naming of the little town had nothing to do with anyone or anything local. Far off in a whole different world, the moguls of the Rockefeller dynasty had been expanding their financial network throughout the nation. John D. Rockefeller became one of the country's oil barons while his brother William chose to be a director of many companies outside the oil industry. For forty years William served as a director of the Chicago, Milwaukee and St. Paul Railway Company. William Rockefeller's son, Percy Avery, was named after the Rockefellers' paternal grandmother whose maiden name was Avery. His daughter's name was Ethel. When Percy Avery Rockefeller had his own son in 1903, he named the child Avery.

In those days it was a common practice to name locations along the railroad line after members of the directors' families. Hence, the new division point for the railroad was named for William Rockefeller's young grandson, Avery. The railroad officials went further down the track and named the siding at Hoyt Flat after Rockefeller's daughter Ethel; it is still known as Ethelton. On February 14, 1910, Pinchot, Idaho, became the town of Avery, Idaho, with the official change in the name of the post office. The operators at the depot happily tapped out the new single-word name on the wireless.

Let us backtrack now to look at another development of the town. Families in the late 1800's migrated from one spot to another searching for a place in which to settle. Three brothers born in New Brunswick, Canada, came to Glidden, Wisconsin, in that search. They were Bill, Ed, and Frank Theriault (French pronunciation: "Terry-Oh"), and they worked in the woods and as contractors in that state until the lure of Idaho's timber brought them West. When timberland opened up for homesteading, the Theriault brothers took claims on Marble Creek. Mrs. Mary Theriault, former wife of Bill, and her five sons settled in St. Joe City and operated the Riverside Hotel in 1907.

Then opportunity knocked, and the Theriaults opened the door to a land deal in the upper St. Joe. The land acquired by the Northern Pacific by scrip was for sale: the section of land with Gene Thorpe's cabin on it. It would be the perfect spot for a nice hotel, especially now that the steamboats were offering excursion cruises for tourists throughout the Coeur d'Alene Lake system and up the Shadowy St. Joe. Surely travelers could be enticed a bit further up the swiftwater. And when the train connections actually came through, business would be assured.

So in the spring and summer of 1908, a riffle in the river lulled Ed Theriault and his nephews to sleep at night in their tents next to Thorpe's cabin. During the day, they tore down the old cabin, and in its place they erected a handsome hotel. The building stood

forty feet by sixty feet with three stories and 32 rooms. The top part was lumber, brought in on the second train passing into the valley in September of 1908. The surrounding white pine on the flat gave the place such a park-like appearance that the Theriaults named their new enterprise the Mountain Park Hotel. They built a bridge to the two-acre island, then a walkway on sawhorses connected the walkway to the railroad track.

Soon pictures of the Mountain Park Hotel were seen by potential tourists all over the United States. The Red Collar Line, a steamship operation based in Coeur d'Alene, had printed brochures advertising vacations in Idaho and distributed them nationwide. One picture reportedly hung in Grand Central Station in New York City. In the brochure travelers were advised to take the Red Collar steamer to St. Joe City, then board the train for Avery. "It is at Avery," the advertisement continued, "that tourists are pleasantly surprised to find a thoroughly modern hostelry, the Mountain Park Hotel, which is made headquarters for trips up the North Fork, the main river, Skookum Creek, and the canyons can be secured and utilized for the upriver trip; but the best way is to throw the camp outfit onto a good cayuse and hit the pretty little trail that follows the river closely, and enables frequent stops for trying the luck in tempting riffles."

The Mountain Park Hotel was constructed in the spot now occupied by the Avery School. The log portion was constructed earlier in the summer of 1908 by the Theriault family with the lumber for the upper two stories brought in by the second train into Avery. Pictured left to right are Fred Theriault, Harold Theriault, Osier (carpenter), Mary D. Theriault, Ed Theriault, and Clifford Theriault. (Theriault)

Its setting and services were not the only attractions at the Mountain Park Hotel. There was also one round black bear named Teddy. When a railroad employee told the Theriault boys about a bear for sale, they were delighted with the idea. Teddy arrived on the train and soon proved his worth by wrestling any challenger who happened by. Men from the rails made it a tradition to cross the bridge, wrestle the bear, then go back to eat at Stubbs, the railroad restaurant by the

Rated as a "modern hostelry" in advertising all over the nation, Avery's Mountain Park Hotel was a handsome three-story structure. Pictured behind this hotel is its barn; the barn was remodeled into a home in later years and remains Avery's oldest building. Note in this 1910 photo: a swiftwater poling canoe and wooden wagon. (Theriault)

roundhouse. Until his fame at wrestling began to frighten people and he had to leave town, Teddy was one of the community's first happy settlers.

On a sad day in July of 1912, the lovely Mountain Park Hotel burned completely to the ground. The Theriault family remained in Avery, however, and their name has become intertwined with the history of the area. Members of the family built bridges, owned land and businesses, fought in the 1910 fire, established the school, worked in health care, and devoted their careers to the railroad. The Theriault name not only appears throughout the history of the area; it remains on the source of West Avery's water supply, Theriault Creek, and on Theriault Lake near Marble Mountain.

The Theriault boys enjoyed having Teddy, the bear, to wrestle with in 1909. Here Fred Theriault takes him on. In the background, a tote wagon road is etched out of the hillside, and a foot bridge crosses the river on the left. (Theriault)

Settlers from other places began to call Avery their home, too. Two of the first were the Swansons who moved from Jamestown, North Dakota, and the Craigs who came from Kenova, West Virginia. They set up housekeeping in boxcars until the railroad flats were completed in 1910. More outfit cars were shipped in to house workers who were building the roundhouse, and surveyors set up a tent camp with wooden frames near the site of the Log Cabin Inn and also in the east end of the town. In fact, many of Avery's homes started out as tent frames or boxcars, hurriedly set up to accommodate the growing population. As additional people kept moving in, the town had grown to a population of 250 by 1910. More people lived on the site of the present landing in West Avery in those days than all of Avery's population now, making up a unique part of the town's history.

Other railroads in the past had made use of Chinese labor, but the Milwaukee and Avery had Japanese people to help it prosper. In exchange for the lucrative Japanese silk trade from the West Coast to the East, the Milwaukee agreed to hire Japanese labor. As construction of the railroad and the roundhouse was completed, a Japanese settlement of nearly eighty people bloomed in Avery where the railroad oil tank above the roundhouse is now located. The settlement later moved to the site of the present landing. The Mountain Park Hotel hired women from the settlement to cook for its guests. After working all day in the kitchen, the women dressed up in big flowered hats and the elaborate styles of the times. Then they went to each of the hotel's guests in the dining room and bowed deeply and courteously.

Avery is probably one of the few towns in the United States that can say it celebrated the Japanese Emperor's birthday. To show their appreciation to their new community and their patronage to the Emperor, each year the Japanese invited the rest of the town to a big celebration. Ben Goto, a leader in the Japanese community, planned the event--and what a party it was! There were wonderful varieties of food, candies for the kids, gifts such as embroidered slippers for everyone, and all kinds of liquor. A handcar stood by to haul those people home who had overindulged. For seven or eight years, all of Avery looked forward to the birthday of the Emperor of Japan.

Until the 1950's many Japanese settlers remained in Avery. In fact, some people displaced from their property in other parts of the country during World War II came to Avery to live, and children who had been in concentration camps attended the local school. The history of the community would not have been complete without this ethnic group.

Another event in 1911 was even more exciting than the Emperor's birthday. It was the day the circus came to town! An honest-to-goodness one-ring circus traveled to Avery by train, and people poured in from all over the hills to watch. Homesteaders, prospectors, lumberjacks, railroaders, and townspeople watched the acts with fascination in the spot now occupied by the substation. They saw snakes, trained ponies, clowns

Posing on Avery's third bridge in 1913 are three unidentified men, Gordon Craig, Jimmy Hanrahan, Ed Theriault, and two more unidentified men. The bridge was built in 1911 by Ed Theriault, and approximates the location of the present structure. The Milwaukee Railroad's icehouse is the large structure in the background. (Theriault)

and a highwire act. Best of all was the elephant. It had been trained to switch the engines on the train with its massive trunk!

Settlers in those early days could not always be categorized as typical homesteaders or railroaders. Certainly that was the case with Spike and Bill Kelley,

This view looking across the Kelley Creek footbridge shortly after the 1910 fire shows the Avery Ranger Station and Pearson Merchantile (on left). The train cars and tents along the river served as temporary housing for many of Avery's early residents. (Theriault)

both Yale graduates and wealthy playboys from the East. They were such wild young lads that their father's friend, President Earling of the Milwaukee Railroad, brought them to Avery to straighten them out and save them from their heavy drinking habits. The brothers opened three stores named the Bitterroot Mercantile in Avery, Grand Forks, and Taft. If they intended to clean up their lives, Grand Forks and Taft in 1909 were hardly the best places to start.

At any rate, Spike Kelley, the rowdiest of the two brothers, decided to get married. He chose for his bride a beautiful socialite, the daughter of a judge from California. After the wedding, Spike brought her home to a brand new mansion. . .incongruously, in the middle of the Idaho wilderness on Kelley Creek Canyon opposite Avery. Compared to the average homesteader's cabins scattered throughout the hills, the Kelley Creek mansion must have looked like the Taj Mahal. It was a two-story building with a huge living-dining room, furnished with a valuable collection of antiques. Various hides and trophies from African safaris decorated the walls. The home had special servants' quarters, occupied by a Japanese valet and a Japanese servant. Its value was an incredible $10,000, compared to the average $150 value of most homes in the area at that time.

Marjorie Debitt, the first white child born in the upper St. Joe, stands in front of the Avery Ranger Station in 1909. Her father, Ralph M. Debitt, was the first ranger and her mother, Jessie, served as the first postmistress. Marjorie was born at Pinchot, located three miles downriver from Avery. (Theriault)

railroad had chosen Avery as its division point, and by 1909, a hotel, ranger station, post office, the Kelley brothers' Mercantile, and the 49 Saloon were thriving. Other businesses soon cashed in on the market as well. Stubbs restaurant served railroaders from its location west of the roundhouse. When the new depot added a beanery, John H. Murphy System out of Kansas City replaced Stubbs for the food concession. The Pearson Mercantile with stores in St. Maries and St. Joe City opened a sister store in Avery in 1909 on the hill adjacent to the ranger station. And for railroad employees from Seattle to Mobridge, South Dakota, Avery's Western Commissary offered goods at a reduced rate. Workers from the rails could buy a good sturdy pair of work shoes for $2.44 or about one day's wages. Not a bad buy considering that they wore well for several years.

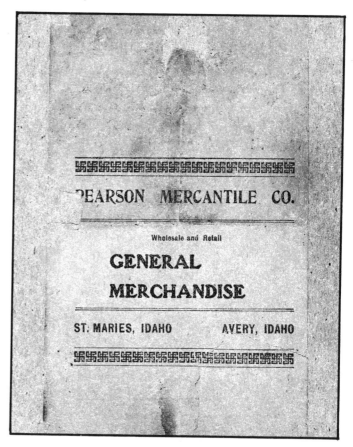

When the new bride arrived in Avery, she came fully equipped for life in Kelley Creek with eighteen trunks! Harold Theriault remembers it vividly; he had to pole them across the river one at a time in a poling canoe. Once they were unloaded at the Mountain Park Hotel, the trunks occupied an entire room. It would certainly be interesting to know how the bride adapted and what she thought of her new environment. All that we really know is that things did not work out well for the Kelleys. Their mansion was the only building to burn in Avery in the 1910 fire, and the Kelleys left the area the following year. Their stores in Taft and Grand Forks burned as well, but the Mercantile in Avery operated for another year under Manager Dick Waters. The building was moved in 1915 to make room for the substation and was converted to a poolroom. Fire eventually got it too, for it burned in 1929.

Meanwhile, opportunity glistened on the new town like the morning dew. The brand new transcontinental

For workers who needed a place to stay, Charlie Grice, a railroad engineer, built another hotel. It was located where the road now curves east of the substation. The Avery Supply House on the first floor sold sporting goods while the hotel occupied the second floor.

Downriver the town of Ferrell was dying as the steamboats stopped their trek to the head of navigation. William W. Ferrell, the founder of the town, kept a shrewd and cantankerous eye out for new business possibilities. He looked upriver and spotted Avery. In 1911 the original homestead of Sam "49" Williams had been tied up in court for several

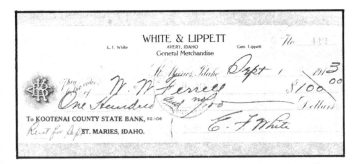

The Pearson Mercantile in Avery sold everything from gloves and suspenders to mattresses, snowshoes and Chamberlain's Cough Remedy in 1910. Ralph Debitt, Garfield Holmes (the storekeeper), and an unknown customer are pictured. (U.S.D.A., Forest Service)

years awaiting a decision about the inheritance of homesteads. Ferrell decided to exercise squatter's rights as he had on his land at Ferrell. Since Williams' homestead included most of the townsite of Avery, it was an attractive chunk of land. Ferrell decided to call it his. Just to make sure things worked out all right, he filed a mining claim on the land too: Claim "49"

Early business flourished in Avery in 1912. Pictured left to right are the Milwaukee depot, the railroad bunkhouse, the doctor's office and express agent's office (two small buildings), and the Bitterroot Mercantile. Directly behind the Bitterroot Mercantile is Avery's first schoolhouse, with the newly constructed Hotel Idaho and Pearson Mercantile to the left. The Grice Hotel, with the Avery Supply House occupying its first floor, is in the right foreground. On the hill in the far right is the Avery Ranger Station. (Turner)

number 3 Lode. Avery with its expanding population could use more businesses, that was clear. Ferrell dismantled a bank building at Ferrell-St. Joe City, shipped the materials to Avery, and built the Hotel Idaho and restaurant in 1911. The Hotel Idaho was a two-story building, a substantial structure. Why he built it to block the entrance to Pearson's Mercantile, only his conscience knew, for there it sat, squarely in the path. Then he added insult to injury by whisking off Pearson's manager, E. F. White, to become the manager of *his* mercantile, the Avery Mercantile. The Pearson Merc was forced to close its doors, though the building remained as a dance hall for several years. The Avery Merc located on the bottom floor of the hotel, did turn out to be a success. Managers White and Shorty Lippitt built up such a reputation for the business that it was listed in Dunn and Bradstreet, a financier's listing of sound businesses. If they had wanted it, the managers of the Avery Merc could have borrowed over a million dollars on their credit rating.

W.W. Ferrell didn't earn as glowing a reputation, however. The railroad was a bit perturbed when he set up his sawmill right next to the depot and directly under foot. He had a long-lasting feud with the Forest Service that resulted in threats to the rangers' lives and destruction of government property. Still, one had to admire Ferrell's ingenuity and ambition. In the year of 1912, he built three additional buildings in Avery—and had six trespass charges brought against him by the Forest Service for building without a permit on a mining claim and then renting the buildings and businesses. After numerous battles with the railroad, the Forest Service and the courts, Ferrell died in 1918.

Tobaccos - - - Fountain - - - Candies - - - Recreation Room

HAROLD E. THERIAULT

AVERY, IDAHO

DRUGS AND SUNDRIES   PRESCRIPTIONS A SPECIALTY   KODAKS AND COLUMBIA GRAFONOLAS

AVERY DRUG CO.

A. T. HUGHES, PROP.

AVERY, IDAHO.

He had amassed quite an estate. His Avery property included one store, one hotel, one restaurant, one barbershop, one public hall with a piano, six cottages, hotel furniture, and mining improvements such as water rights, power plant, boiler, engine compressor, blacksmith outfit, and two air drills. The total value was for that time an impressive $7,575 and earned his widow $350 a month. Much of Ferrell's life had been spent in court with a variety of dubious claims and bankruptcy proceedings. That continued even after he died, for in subsequent court cases his mining claim was ruled non-mineral and invalid, as was his claim to the Williams' homestead. Now the land in Avery reverted to Sam "49" Williams' long-lost nephew in Arkansas who sold it to the Theriault family. The Theriaults then bought the buildings from Mrs. Ferrell, and the Theriault family once again had a hotel in Avery.

SCHOOL DAYS

In 1908 only one child, young Harold Theriault, lived in Avery. Within two years at least one dozen children had moved in. The new town needed a school. Mrs. Mary Theriault worked to resolve that problem. First, she set aside a room in the Mountain Park Hotel for the school, coincidentally in the exact location of the present school gymnasium. Next, she contacted the county superintendent who helped her hire Miss Effie Walker from Lewiston to teach. Her room was to be in the hotel. Then Mrs. Theriault formed the school board to act on an advisory basis and to handle the business matters of the new school district. She was to serve nearly ten years on that board.

One of the first matters of business for the new board to tackle was the construction of a teacherage in 1911. The two-story home had a kitchen and two bedrooms upstairs for single teachers, with roomier accommodations downstairs for the superintendent or the "Professor" as that position was then called. For $8.00 a month rent the teachers were provided with some furniture, oil oven, one rocker each--and their very own washboard.

The class of 1916-17 poses in front of the old schoolhouse in East Avery. Identified in the top row (left to right) are: Laura Kroll (1st), Gordon Craig (2nd), Lee Pears (4th), Jimmy Hanrahan (6th), teacher Nell Mackens (7th), and Harold Craig (8th); third row, Victor Craig (1st), teacher Grace Seeley (2nd), ———Soike (3rd), Eva Theriault (4th), and two Soike boys on far right; second row, ———Townsend, (4th), Clayton Gouyd (6th), Kenneth Gouyd (7th); bottom row, ———Townsend (5th), Virgil Pears (6th). (Theriault)

The school facilities in the hotel were adequate for the upper and lower grades at first. But then the classes grew so large that it was time to build a real school. The following article appeared in the St. Maries *Courier* on March 12, 1912: "J. W. Goddard has the contract for building a schoolhouse at Avery. It will be equipped with the latest in school furniture and will be one of the best district schools in the country." Assisted by his partner Jack Thompson, Goddard erected the building on the slab of cement that is now the floor of a garage west of the Avery Trading Post. And as "one of the best district schools in the country," it even had indoor plumbing in its cupola.

The completion of the school was a good reason for a celebration, so folks from all around gathered for a dance in the new building on April 26, 1912. Mrs. Mary Turner, a homesteader at Turner Flat, reported in her diary that her son Gene attended the event. The long desks with their fold-up seats had been nailed to be shoved aside easily in a swoop. A band from St. Maries played a harp and a banjo, and no doubt, "a good time was had by all."

Avery's first schoolhouse, a single-room classroom, is in the center of this 1915 photograph. Following construction of a new schoolhouse in 1923, the building was moved to become the second-story of the present post office-annex building. Also pictured are the depot and the old Bitterroot Mercantile building. The upstairs of the building on the right housed the Avery Drug Company with a bakery and barbershop located on the lower floor. (Theriault)

As Avery's population sprouted, the new school began to bulge at the seams. When the ninth and tenth grades were added to the school system, the school board paid contractors $3500 to build a high school annex in 1918. It was not long before the board contacted the county superintendent again. Avery had grown to 1100 people and it needed a much larger school. The town agreed by a vote of 66 to 7 to pass a $15,000 bond for the building, and in 1923 contractor W.L. Weld finished the handsome brick building still known as the Avery school. Another occasion was in order, the dedication of the new building. The featured speaker for the event was young Stanford Larson, a ninth-grade student. As for the other schoolhouse, it was used as a community building for several years, and then moved by Ed Theriault to the second story of the present post office. That was no small task for a 24 by 36 foot building.

The Avery School District consisted of more than

one school during its history. Harris Bellows of Herrick was instrumental in starting a school at Herrick for his children Thelma and Ned in 1928. In a building rented from Al Timmel, the Herrick school served children of that area until the end of 1937. The Herrick school was moved to Marble Creek following the shifting school population and existed there until 1944 when it died for want of students.

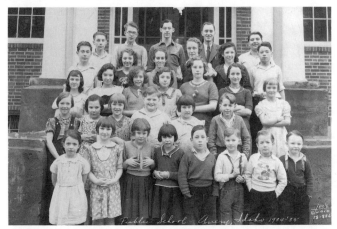

Avery schoolchildren, 1934-35. Identified in the top row (left to right) are: Bill Polasky (1st), Jack Craig (2nd), Herbert Hoover (3rd), teacher Mr. Loren King (4th) and Joe Russio (5th); fourth row, Earl Hiigel (1st), Patty Frank (2nd), teacher Mrs. Roberts (3rd), teacher Mrs. Roe (4th), Betty Fous (5th); third row, Vernice Harding (1st), Beulah Curry (2nd), Dorothy Craig (3rd), Loretta Fous (4th), Beverly Barclay (5th), Maxine Gouyd (6th), Pauline Yates (7th); second row, Edna Eastwood (1st), Jay Cloninger (2nd), Kay Schmalhorst (3rd), Fritz Theriault (4th), Virginia Dietrich (5th), ——— Polasky; bottom row, Vivian ——— (1st), Shirley Barclay (2nd), Carol Hiigel (3rd), Audrey Curry (4th), Gordon Harrigan (7th), Mickey Walker (8th). (Hiigel)

School business for Avery District No. 10 varied somewhat throughout the years. Old school records had a separate column for "Wagon Upkeep and Driver's Salary." The board purchased such things as an electric eraser cleaner and a copy of *Roberts' Rules of Order*. Latin, music appreciation, and manual training were once taught in the school. And an unusual problem faced the board in April of 1932: Mrs. H.E. Theriault, a nurse, was asked to examine the school children "on account of itch being in the school again." The next month school had to be closed three days because of itch. Sulphur sprinkled in the beds conquered that problem though, and things went on as usual. The school budget has also changed. In 1917, the budget was around $1,000; in 1929, it was $12,450; and in 1978, the combined Avery-Calder-Clarkia school district spent $250,000.

Teachers' rights were not a consideration in those early days. In 1917 a teacher was paid $95 a month; later the salary was raised to $140 (at Herrick $130) where it remained for many years. However, one teacher suffered the misfortune of having her salary reduced $10 a month because she could not play the piano! The board once had to pay the return fare home for a teacher who was second choice for a

Dressed in their costumes, Mrs. Thelma Cramp's 1945 class is pictured in the schoolyard before presenting their spring play. Mrs. Cramp's many plays and operettas have been entertaining, memorable events for children and parents alike. The actors in the top were: Dale Wilcox, Philip Stanley, Jim Finley, Joe Dickinson, Dorothy Townsend, George Curry, Deloris Roblinger. Front row: Eiichi Kobayashi, Dick Townsend, Carol King, Helen Higgins. (Cramp)

position, after the first choice came to claim the job. At one point the members of the board protested the late hours kept by the single young teachers. The following month's minutes contained this entry: "the question of Teachers being dated with Gentlemen every nite was discussed." The self-righteous sniffs are nearly audible even yet! As it turned out, Miss Howes, the county superintendent, agreed that social life at the teacherage was not proper and suitable curfews were set up. The trustees later decided that teachers who plan to marry must give 30 days notice prior to their change in status.

This 1914 photograph shows Avery's first teacherage, which was located west of the present school. Left to right are Mary D. Theriault, Fred Theriault, Etta Fountain, Winnie Fountain; back of Winnie are Ed Theriault, Effie Walker (Avery's first teacher) and Eva Theriault, a cousin. (Theriault)

Teachers returning from Christmas vacation in 1939 had a shock when they discovered that the teacherage had been gutted and ruined by fire. They found other places to live in town, but Superintendent Loren King was forced to live in St. Maries the remainder of the year. In 1940 the teacherage was rebuilt into a duplex containing two modern apartments, but in January of

Residents now enjoy ten fewer days of sunshine after the trees have regrown on the hillsides following the 1910 fire. This 1924 photograph shows the newly constructed schoolhouse with the teacherage to its right. (Saunders)

1979 that building burned totally to the ground as bystanders watched helplessly. Destroyed were the belongings of two families, and a small poodle belonging to longtime Avery teacher, Mrs. Dick Crandall.

Avery School District No. 10 consolidated with Calder and Clarkia in 1956 to form School District No. 394. It was during that time period in the late 1950's that Avery School had its highest number of students, related to increased logging and family camps in the area. A staff of seven teachers was necessary to teach the 87 pupils. As the number of people residing at Camp 44 began to taper off and the number of railroad workers declined, the school population also decreased. Presently, the town's high school age students travel by bus daily to St. Maries, and the teaching staff at the Avery School has been reduced to two. The school's low student-teacher ratio and the individual attention students receive continue to be its strong points.

GROWING

The growth of Avery continued throughout the teens and into the '20's until the population reached its peak in 1917 with 1100 souls. Cabins shot up in Kelley Creek for nine or ten families and also in Williams Creek, and in Hoghead Gulch near the roundhouse. As a major Milwaukee installation, Avery needed a variety of goods and services to supply its residents as well as all the Forest Service personnel, prospectors, trappers, and lumberjacks scattered over the countryside. Stores and businesses flourished during this period. Similar to any other prosperous community of the time, local merchants and enterpreneurs provided almost all needed merchandise and services. A Western Union telegraph office tapped out telegrams 24 hours a day, and a justice of the peace was available to handle various legal problems. A dray service operated by H.F. Schmalhorst delivered wood and coal to your back door. You could buy everything from shoes and stockings to soup at one of the three mercantiles. In addition to the Bitterroot and

"Avery, Idaho, The City among the Mountains" says this 1918 postcard. The population at that time was at its height, and cabins were scattered everywhere. Notice the large cluster of houses (across the tracks from the present Potlatch Landing) in what was called "Shacktown." The original Setzer homestead cabin is in the bottom center of the lower flat, with the roundhouse situated on upper flat. (Hiigel)

Avery Mercantiles, the South Side Purity Store operated first by J.E. Ettien and later by C.C. Hamm was located at the site now occupied by the bridge abutments east of the school. For a couple of years, the post office was in the South Side Purity Store. In the late 1950's Joyce and Les Long operated another store near the Log Cabin Inn which later burned down.

Residents could buy an ice cream cone or their medicines or even make a phone call at the Avery Drug, opened in 1916 by Al Hughes who moved his business from St. Joe City to Avery. After the drugstore was running smoothly, it was sold to Eugene Heath. Heath had grown up in Avery and was disabled on his first job working for the railroad. He went away to take a six-month pharmacy course and became Avery's only registered pharmacist. The drugstore's telephone booth provided residents a link to the outside world via lines over Dunn Peak and Cedar Mountain to

Wallace. After fire, Avery's eternal enemy, destroyed the drugstore in 1930, Byron "Doc" Theriault and his brother Harold realized that the drugstore was needed and opened another one in the Hotel Idaho the same year.

Guests at the Hotel Idaho in the early 1920's had a pleasant, almost European, view of the well-maintained downtown square. Popular attractions to local children were the tennis court (one of two in town), the playground and the fishpond. Older residents often danced by the light of Japanese lanterns next to the substation on summer evenings. (Spencer)

Herb Spencer poses thoughtfully in front of the Avery Drugstore in 1929. The drugstore was a popular hangout for train passengers and residents alike. (Spencer)

Even the needs of the shaggy and unshorn could be met in Avery at the barbershop. Located in a lean-to off the Hotel Idaho, the barbershop offered a haircut for 35 cents and a shave for 15 cents. The barbershop was then moved to the lobby of the hotel where it operated intermittently until the hotel collapsed. For the housewives, Avery's butcher shop sold varieties of fresh meat and milk from large barrels. Later, milk could be purchased from Harris Bellows who delivered it from his ranch downriver. Residents even enjoyed the luxury of fresh bread baked right in Avery at the bakery. That convenience lasted for a couple of years until a freak outbreak of rats so disgusted baker McGillis that he deserted his bakery, ovens and all. "Oh, rats!" he said—and went from baking to braking (on the railroad).

For those who felt like having ham and eggs at 4:00

a.m., the beanery in the depot was open 24 hours a day. Train crews and passengers, as well as local residents, ate many a meal at the beanery. It was opened in 1909 by the John H. Murphy Company; then the Van Noy Interstate, a restaurant chain based in Minneapolis, took it over for a period of time. Later operators included Wally Moore and Mr. and Mrs. Alex Lyons. When the beanery door was closed in 1974, a page of Avery history was also closed.

For the most current maladies, the services of a doctor were available to Avery residents for many years. Avery owed this bonus to the railroad, for the construction department had needed medical facilities to handle the illnesses and injuries of its workers as the line was being built. In the beginning, the hospital at Taft, Montana, had three doctors to care for people from Avery eastward. The St. Joe Hospital, under the supervision of Dr. Busby of Harrison, was responsible for health care to the west of Avery. When the railroad switched operation of the line from the engineering to the operating department, the Milwaukee Hospital Association became incorporated, and through that Avery got its first doctor. Dr. McNalan, a former Michigan track star, served as the first physician; then the Taft Hospital closed, and its Dr. White came over the mountain to be the second. Doctors Kading from Deer Lodge and Busey from Cottonwood, Idaho, followed. Then came Dr. Dryborough who was noted for making robin stew and serving young elderberry sprouts as asparagus. Dr. Busey returned to serve for a few years, to be replaced by Dr. Terrell, the CCC doctor. During the time when the town had no doctor, Mrs. Francis Theriault nursed everyone in the community. She kept a supply of medicine on hand and ushered many brand new Averyites into the world. Mrs. Theriault had been trained under the Milwaukee Hospital Association in St. Maries.

This view of Avery from behind the old ranger station shows the number of houses in Kelley Creek drainage. Nine or ten families resided there at the time this photo was taken about 1920. Note the Dunn Peak trail on the left and Kelley Creek trail on upper right. (U.S.D.A. Forest Service)

Avery's first doctor, Dr. McNalan, sits here with the first teacher, Miss Effie Walker in 1909. Dr. McNalan was a former track star from the University of Michigan, and Miss Walker (later Mrs. William Fountain) hailed from Lewiston. (Theriault)

During some of Avery's sad and bad times, the best efforts of the doctors were not always enough. A typhoid epidemic in 1908 during railroad construction days claimed the lives of many people along the line; so many, in fact, that a special train was required to carry out the bodies. The cause of the disease in Avery was thought to have been a slop hole with stagnant water located where the substation now sits. Barely ten years had passed before another epidemic, this time the flu, swept the nation as well as the St. Joe Valley. The flu outbreak of 1918 forced Avery residents to wear surgical masks for protection and resulted in closure of the school (to the chagrin of the children who were forced to go an extra month in the summer to make up the lost time). Dr. Busey was credited with saving many lives by administering sweat tablets, but still some lives were lost. Ruth (Larson) Lindow remembers counting the number of coffins unloaded from the train to tabulate the seriousness of the flu.

Several graves in the area tell their own story. One small girl of about three or four years old became ill on the passenger train passing through Avery. Shortly after she and her mother disembarked to see a doctor,

the child died. Resident Doris Pears gave up her cedar chest to be used as a coffin, and the small body was buried at Forty-Nine Gulch. Also buried there were an unknown man who was cut in two at the railroad yards and a man named Spores from Tekoa, Washington, who was killed in a snowslide at Adair. Packsaddle campground is the gravesite of Avery packer Arch Smith and the Schmalhorst infant.

One of the strangest deaths in Avery remains vivid in the memory of Bob Cass. Cass was a paper boy when he was growing up in Avery, meeting the morning passenger train each day to sell his papers. The morning headlines on December 8, 1941, made the day memorable enough, for Pearl Harbor had been bombed. But even more memorable to Bobby was the surly man dressed in coveralls and a foreign seaman's hat who grunted gutterally at him for a look at the headlines. He spoke no words but acknowledged that he had seen the paper by way of gestures and more grunts. The peculiar look in the man's eye alarmed the paper boy. Later that day, Cass's father John was working up the river from Avery pitching rocks out of the road when he saw a stranger in overalls who might be of help, but something about the man made him shy away. Near Bootleg Creek, he was intercepted by Red Dennis and bolted suddenly up the ridge and headed down Sisters Creek, one of the most rugged, impassable creeks in the area. Several men formed a search party to look for him, but he was not found. That is, until Bobby was down by the river in West Avery the following April and spotted some overalls bobbing in the brush. As curious boys are apt to do, he pestered the adults working nearby until they finally let him check out the object. There was the suspicious stranger, or what was left of him after a winter in the St. Joe River. No papers were found on the body, no tags for identification. Although stories circulated about the man being a German spy, Cass

This photograph pictures East Avery in the 1920's. The Grice Hotel is the large two-story building with the small building to its right being the doctor's office. The five railroad flats in the center served as housing for many of Avery's residents. Note the home in Williams Creek Canyon on the far right. (Lindow)

The building at the CCC camp in West Avery crumpled and washed downriver in the flood of 1938. The camp was damaged severely with the course of the river also being changed. (Hiigel)

figures he was probably a Russian sailor who had jumped ship and became demented and disoriented in a strange land at wartime.

Residents of Avery have endured other phenomena of nature besides death. A heavy snow once dumped 27 inches on the town in one night in 1938; then on August 4, 1964, one home thermometer recorded a blazing 121 degrees. But one of the most dramatic experiences—and also the worst flood in the history of the St. Joe—occurred in 1933. A record-breaking rain and chinook wind on top of a heavy snow caused an early thaw. The waters of the St. Joe rose high, higher, and higher, until they covered the railroad tracks. Washed away forever were the five-acre island in West Avery and a cedar flat at Roundhouse Gulch. Telephone and telegraph wires were down and portions of the railroad track were undermined. Five years later, in 1938, another flood swept through the town and carried out part of the Avery CCC camp. A foot of water washed over the rails and gushed into the depot. Ruth Lindow donned her fishing boots to wade to work in the depot, and residents of houses next to the river tied their homes down with cable in hopes of hanging on to them. Damage was high all through the valley with another CCC building washed out at Marble Creek and many cattle drowned in the lower St. Joe area. Logging roads and railroads, camps and sorting gaps throughout North Idaho were also hurt by the floods.

Bridges always suffered most in high water, and in the early years they were built and washed out consistently. Ice gorges in 1911 splintered the town's first major bridge crossing the river near the Mountain Park Hotel. That prompted Ed Theriault to build a cable bridge a few hundred feet upriver from the present bridge east of the school. It was rebuilt by the Forest Service in 1923 and replaced when the CCC installed the present concrete bridge in 1935. The first two foot bridges to Kelley Creek were put in by the Kelley brothers to provide access to their property, starting in 1908. But those bridges washed out at intervals and were rebuilt by Kelley Creek residents Bill Koehler, A.E. Blundell, and Jack Farmer until the county took over the upkeep. Always the Kelley Creek bridge has caused comment, either for the people who have crossed over it, such as an immense schoolteacher, or its condition. One man, Gunnar Bergen, drowned off the bridge and that marked its demise. A bridge also crossed the river at Williams Creek to the residences there. The roundhouse bridge, a picturesque cable bridge, was built in the late teens and destroyed by Shoshone County in 1978. The Potlatch Forest Industries installed a bridge to the log landing in 1943.

Prior to the settlement of Avery, only a foot log with a railing gave passage across the North Fork to the St. Joe Quartz trail. Pack horses going up the trail forded the stream until a log bridge was installed about 1910. The Forest Service put in a queen truss bridge across the North Fork in 1924 which fell victim to the 1938 flood. A plank bridge had to suffice for ten years, then the concrete bridge used today was installed by the U.S. Forest Service. At last three solid concrete structures join the banks of the river and link various parts of Avery together.

THOSE WERE THE DAYS

For the most part, the picture painted by those who

lived in Avery in the teens and 1920's is a happy one. Married couples met for candlelight dinners, disregarding for an evening their smelly kerosene lanterns. Couples not yet married courted under the apple tree by the fishpond. By the light of the summer moon and Japanese lanterns, a plaza off the substation became a magical spot for dancing. Or in cooler weather, Avery's own orchestra played happy tunes in the dance hall west of the ranger station on Saturday nights.

A Shriner's banquet was held in the Hotel Idaho in 1928. Standing (left to right) were: Mrs. Mary D. Theriault, Mr. Ed Theriault, Mr. Harold Craig, Mr. Jim Harben, Mr. Morley Brown, Mr. Dunn, U.S.F.S., Mr. H. E. Schmalhorst, Mr. J. E. McLain, Mr. E. White, Mr. Hallenbeck, Mr. Paul Harding; seated (left to right), Mrs. E. Shook, Mr. E. Shook, Mrs. Jean Heath, Mr. Jean Heath, Mrs. Craig, Unidentified, Mrs. E. White, Mrs. J. E. McLain, Mrs. Harben and Mrs. Paul Harding. Those absent when the photo was taken were: Mr. E. H. Walters, Mr. Henry Barclay, Mr. H. E. Theriault, Mr. Dick Boyle, Mr. Tony Boyle, Mr. Louie Bradway. (Theriault)

The town of Avery was young and new. Flowers bloomed everywhere, homes were well-kept; and civic pride was high. Such things as *two* tennis courts and a nice playground next to the substation gave the place a classy, European air. There was a brand new school in 1923 with its spacious gymnasium and stage to be proud of. The gym was ideal for big dances, and the stage—just the ticket for community plays! One group presented a minstrel show as much for their own delight as their audience's. The school board purchased a "moving pictures machine," no small investment at 280 hard-earned dollars. It more than paid for itself in the pleasure the "moving pictures" brought. Pinochle parties broke the tedium of the long winters, and a baseball field and grandstand on the lower landing provided the setting for the town team to play against teams of railroaders from other places such as Malden and Alberton.

Because there were no roads into Avery until 1930, life revolved around the trains. Two passenger trains rolled into town daily, the *Columbian* for local stops and the *Olympian,* both transcontinental runs. Both the *Columbian* and the *Olympian* had dining cars and service comparable to the finest hotels in the country;

linen, crystal and finger bowls graced every table. The *Olympian* even had a barber shop and an elaborate beauty salon! The coaches were comfortable and convenient with porters selling sandwiches and fruit from large baskets as the mountains whizzed by. Railroad workers, who comprised most of the town, had passes to travel to Spokane, so trips out of Avery were not only effortless but downright pleasurable.

The two trains into town were a social event in themselves. One resident, former packer Hugh Peyton, describes what he saw in 1917:

"There was the railroad whose gleaming streaks of steel connected us with the outside world. There were two passenger trains each day and often we would go down to town to gaze upon these golden gilded Argosies of the rails as they tarried to change engines. To relieve the tedium of travel many passengers would descend to walk about, admire the fish in the fishpond near the station, and gaze upon us with the same curiosity in their eyes that we in turn looked at them. These travelers, in their crisp and fashionable attire, seemed to us to be aliens from another world. With hissing sounds of airbrakes being released these trains moved out of our world as the locomotive's whistle sent a farewell sound that echoed from canyon wall to canyon wall. After this brief encounter we would then turn to the everyday world of toil and the business of living. Meeting the train was a traditional pastime that pervaded all of the West in those 'Then' days."

Some firsts occurred during this time, too. Two Avery houses were the first in the upper St. Joe to get electricity, for in 1917 the two houses closest to the substation tapped onto the electrical source. Naturally a celebration was in order when the rest of the town hooked up to the power in 1928; people as well as houses got lit that night! And then there was the exciting day in 1927 when the automobile came to town. (Actually, it was not the first car in Avery, for two Stanley Steamers had made it in over the tote road from Montana before the 1910 fire.) This shiny black Hudson Essex belonged to Harold Theriault who cut the back out to make a pickup. No one realized just how much of a change that car signaled as it sputtered on the short stretch of road in Avery. Within a few years, the isolation and total dependence on the railroad would end with a network of roads, and things would never be quite the same again.

Life in Avery, no matter when, has had some similarities for its residents. For recreation people have always enjoyed the beauty of the St. Joe River. Nothing on a hot summer day is quite as refreshing as a dip into the river. Early residents swam off a gentle beach on a seven-acre island in West Avery until the entire island washed away in the flood of 1938. Others dipped into the spot known as "Fishhole" by the mouth of Storm Creek, but the force of the river has eliminated that, also. Today swimmers go to a deeper spot by the Potlatch Bridge, to Hoyt Flat, or to the Allen Ridge bridge upriver. "Roughing it" in the early days meant a camping trip at Bottle Creek, 16 miles upriver, where a campground along the trail was

Avery residents take a dive in the river in 1916. The St. Joe has always been a source of recreation for people who have lived in Avery. The swimming hole and the nearby island in West Avery were washed out by the 1933 and 1938 floods. (Theriault)

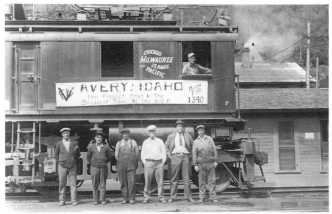

A proud banner bears this inscription for the Veterans of Foreign Wars in Avery: "Avery, Idaho. The Biggest Post in the Smallest Town in the U.S.A. North Fork 1390." Left to right are C. C. Hiigel, Curly Terrian, Ralph Jahnke, George Sterling, Frank Schmalhorst, and Bill Craig. The engineer is J. A. "Hooter" Drake in one of the old G. E. boxcabs. (Hiigel)

complete with tables, bunks, benches, tent poles and good water. Now, of course, several Forest Forest Service campgrounds provide such facilities.

Each changing season offers residents and visitors a chance to be outdoors: mushrooming in the spring and fall, huckleberry picking in the late summer (Lady Korb, once a resident of Camp 44, recalls picking 40 gallons of huckleberries one summer). Some people like Sam Salla have cultivated lovely gardens. During the winter, people once enjoyed sledding parties which have now been replaced by cross-country skiing and snowmobiling. Sometimes when the river freezes over, the brave and adventurous few have found good spots for ice-skating.

Plenty of other activities have made life interesting in Avery throughout the years. It is hard to believe that such a small place has had some sort of meeting nearly every night. But then look at the organizations mentioned in the school paper, the *Avery Hi' Gra' Booster,* for March 29, 1940; Young Married Women's Club (who gave their husbands a special dinner on St. Patrick's Day), Betty Co-Ed Club, Shadowy St. Joe Service Club, Baseball Club, VFW and its Ladies Auxililary, and Milwaukee Women's Club.

Avery was justifiably proud of its Veterans of Foreign Wars, North Fork Post, for it had the distinction of having the largest membership in the smallest town in the United States! This large number could be attributed to railroaders up and down the line who had no local chapter to join, and to the veteran's CCC work camp at Bathtub. The North Fork Post later combined with the St. Maries Post. The social function which has functioned longest, the Milwaukee Women's Club, was founded in 1922 with Mrs. Earl Huseby, Mrs. Dave Saunders, and Mrs. Harold Theriault among its charter members. Its members have been

responsible for a variety of charitable projects such as paying doctor bills for the needy and giving Christmas presents to residents of nursing homes. According to the St. Maries *Gazette Record,* the Milwaukee Women's Club membership totaled 94 in 1962. Although its rolls have declined radically since then, the group is still semi-active.

During the 1950's and '60's, the Avery Sportsmen's Club was a prominent organization in the St. Joe Valley. It became active politically to protest proposals to dam and dredge the St. Joe River, so active that it put out its own small newspaper. The annual dinner attracted 250 members and residents, but its biggest event socially was a fish fry which it sponsored for three years at the mouth of Fishhook Creek. Advertised nationally in the *Field and Stream* magazine, the fish fry drew as many as a thousand people, many from faraway states. The group offered

The Milwaukee Women's Club is Avery's oldest social organization. Shown here at a rummage sale in its clubrooms are members of the organization which has always been involved with charitable projects. Pictured from the left are: Mrs. Sam Griffith, Mrs. Eric Johnson, Mrs. Emil McKinnon, Mrs. Jimmie Peterson, Mrs. Herb Uttley, and Mrs. Emmett Peterson. (Lindow)

Avery's residents have always found plenty of things to keep them occupied. Here is an art class, taught by Ruth Lindow in 1948. Seated are: Ruth Lindow, Mrs. Mahoney and Mrs. Ficke; second row: Doris Boyer, Mrs. Hattie Mace, Mrs. R. F. O'Laughlin, Mrs. H. L. Ensign, Mrs. R. C. Christianson, and Mrs. Roy Peterson; in rear are: Ernie Dunlap, Mrs. Scott A. Lamb, and K. R. Estes. (Lindow)

its guests fish, barbequed buffalo, many types of salads, the chance to win firearms or a buffalo (wrapped and ready to cook). Free beer appeared to be the biggest selling card, however, and the crowd got so exuberant that the club decided to discontinue the event.

The spiritual guidance of the community has been an important part of its history. The townspeople of Avery turned out in full force to hear sermons given by the lumberjack preacher, Dick Ferrell, whose parish covered the woods of Oregon, eastern Washington, a slice of western Montana, and the whole Idaho Panhandle. In spite of traveling more than 19,000 miles in one year, Ferrell still had time to baptize Avery's babies, preach to its youth, administer to the sick, and usher out its folks after death. An accomplished actor, Ferrell delighted Avery's school-children with magic shows. The force with which he presented his sermons and the common language he used never let people forget exactly where they stood in God's scheme of things. Ferrell gave such a stirring sermon on the 23rd Psalm to Avery's CCC camp in 1939 that the editor of the CCC newspaper commented, "Rev. Ferrell is one of the few true preachers who knows and loves the Bible from cover to cover."

Visiting ministers came monthly on the morning train from Spokane to give services in Avery for many years, and a regular Sunday school met for worship. Catholic priests as well held mass in different homes. Then the leadership of Mr. and Mrs. Emmett Peterson brought Avery its first pastor, Reverend Eric Johnson, in the fall of 1955. Reverend Jim Howell came on occasion to help out until 1962 when the community church became affiliated with Village Missions. Since

then that organization has helped Avery retain its own pastor, and church activities have been very much a part of the community calendar.

In **1967** Avery residents Ruth Lindow and Thelma Cramp recognized the need for a joint voice within the community and formed the Avery Citizens' Committee. That group has since been active in handling civic issues, sponsoring a television cable and an ambulance. When the railroad closed the beanery in the depot in 1974, the Avery Citizens' Committee purchased the building and raised funds to renovate it as a community building. Other civic and social

These young ladies are dressed up to sell poppies on Veteran's Day in 1934. Audrey Curry, Kay Schmalhorst, and Carol Hiigel were appealing salesgirls. (Hiigel)

organizations continue to thrive in the little isolated community, including P.T.A., Bridge Club, and Water and Sewer Board, Ladies Bible Study, Boy Scouts and Girl Scouts, and a group of Emergency Medical Technicians.

Of course, in small towns like Avery everyone knows the comings and goings of everyone else. "Folks is folks," observes one Avery resident; and all the folks' faults and foibles soon surface for the rest of the canyon's residents to see. It isn't long before someone is sure to spread the word about other people's activities. What the *Avery Hi' Gra' Booster* observed in 1940 still holds true today: "There isn't much to see in Avery, but what you hear makes up for it."

NAME-DROPPING

As the years rolled by, so did the trains and the people. The narrow corridor in which Avery sits bore the footprints of all kinds—poor and unknown as well as rich and famous. In seventy-plus years of history, a share of Very Important Persons has passed through. A month before his death in San Francisco in 1923, *President Warren Harding,* his *Secretary of State Work,* and railroad dignitaries stopped in Avery on the train. Harding, the handsome, dignified man who "looked like a President," walked around town and became so interested in the pack string at the ranger station that the train was delayed 45 minutes as he visited with packer Arch Smith. Secretary of State

Work, meanwhile, carried two local babies, Fritz Theriault and Bernice Maxwell, during the entire visit.

In a different era another political figure visited with Avery residents on the platform. It was 1944 and a little-known candidate for Vice-President on the Democratic ticket stopped to campaign while the engines were being switched. One avid young Republican from Thelma Bellows' (Cramp) class raised his flag and yelled, ''Yay, Dewey!'' That didn't daunt ''Ol' Give 'Em Hell'' *Harry Truman,* though. He told the group about his daughter named Margaret, that he played the piano and that his favorite song was the Missouri Waltz. His neighborly visit won friends, and the Republican students unobtrusively slipped their campaign buttons in their pockets. Many years later in his biography *Plain Speaking* by Merle Miller, Truman was to recall that one stop he made on his tours. He said: ''I had every kind of audience there was from those big auditoriums in places like Boston and Madison Square Gardens to. . .one time in a little town in Idaho there were just three people (and some kids) showed up, three schoolteachers as I recall it.''

Harry Truman

The train brought several other famous people through Avery. *Gertrude Ederly,* a beautiful girl who swam the English Channel in the 1930's, chatted pleasantly with residents. One admirer brought her a box of candy—which she promptly opened and fed to some hungry dogs milling around the depot! *Dolores Del Rio,* a Spanish movie star, didn't seem to mind the twenty or thirty kids that followed her as she walked down the platform. And once *Clark Gable* was seen stretching his long legs on that same platform while the engines switched.

The St. Joe River's reputation for good fishing attracted two of Spokane's celebrities to the upper St. Joe. One was Boston Red Sox baseball hero *Ed Brandt* who vacationed here for several years. The other was that beloved crooner *Bing Crosby* who fished around Red Ives for several summers. Imagine the stir he must have created when he casually dropped into Mahoney's pub for a beer! That is especially amazing in view of the fact that he allegedly took a cab all the way from St. Maries to get there, not just once but twice! When Marble Creek resident Red Powell stopped in a St. Maries bar once for a beer, owner Bud Spiesman said, ''It's on Bing Crosby. He just bought drinks for the house.'' Red asked where Bing Crosby was. Bud replied, ''Sitting right next to you!'' And there he was.

If a person looks closely on Skookum Creek Hill, he might find the name *Clyde Pangborn* pounded into rock. The young man who left his mark later made a bigger mark—on aviation history. The year after

Lindberg flew the Atlantic, Clyde Pangborn flew solo across the Pacific. He had been a clerk for the Forest Service commissary here for two summers, and later gave youngsters in the area their first airplane rides for free.

The rails brought through a different sort of person—famous hobo *Hood River Blackie.* In one of his many articles about his life traveling the country, Blackie talks about staying in the Avery hobo jungle on the St. Joe and catching trout for his breakfast.

For a charity project, the St. Maries Elks Lodge once gave the founder of Boys Town in Nebraska a paid vacation and fishing trip on the St. Joe. The good priest *Father Flanagan* came accompanied by his brother, also a priest named Father Flanagan. At their cabin at Red Ives that month, they held mass daily attended by the only Catholic in the area, the cook at Red Ives Ranger Station. When Father Flanagan saw the Theriault cabin at Bird Creek, he announced that this was the place where he wanted to write his memoirs. He made arrangements to rent the cabin the following year of 1948, but he died, never fulfilling his plans to retire on the beautiful St. Joe.

FAMILY PORTRAITS AND VERBAL SNAPSHOTS

A family portrait of the Saunders family would have to have trains for a background. *David Saunders* settled in Avery with his wife and three sons when he was an engineer on the *Columbian* between Avery and Deer Lodge, Montana. Before his railroading career had ended, he was number one in seniority of all engineers in the Rocky Mountain Division. *Mrs. Saunders* was responsible for founding the Milwaukee Women's Club, maintaining several of the town's civic organizations, and chairing the school board.

Their son *Nile* followed his father's career on the rails, first on the Milwaukee Road out of Avery and then on Great Northern for 20 years. His wife, Leitha, was a clerk for the Forest Service under Ranger Ashley Roche. After working as a brakeman and switchman for the big lines, Nile retired to an apple orchard in Peshastin, Washington. But trains were not out of Nile's life for long. In 1960 he bought his own railroad—only it was one-sixth the size of the ones he and his father had worked on. ''The Peshastin Great Western'' as he has named it, stands hip-high and chugs by steam on 12-inch tracks. The cream of the crop in Saunders' orchard railroad is an engine he constructed himself, Steam Engine #6615, the exact replica of the famous Columbian his father engineered out of Avery.

Unlike her father and grandfather, Nile Saunders' daughter has not chosen trains as a way to ascend mountains. *Frances Randall* earned her distinction as one of the first women to scale Alaska's Mt. McKinley.

Having the largest number of children born while the family lived in Avery must have made *Mr. and Mrs. Tom Wurth* interested in schools. Tom Wurth worked as an employee of both the Forest Service and railroad but for his community project, he chose the

Two United States Presidents have passed through Avery and other towns along the line. Here President Warren Harding (center in the hat) stands next to Milwaukee's electric locomotive draped in stars and stripes at Falcon on July 2, 1923. Also pictured (left to right) are J.A. Phephlan, Superintendent of the Missoula Division; H.R. Earling, Vice-President of the Milwaukee, the President, and an unknown lady. Behind her is Frank McAvery, the traveling engineer, and two men thought to be Secret Service men. A month to the day later Harding died in San Francisco. (Theriault)

school board, serving as clerk for several years. Mrs. Mary Wurth (founder of Campfire Girls here) developed her interest in school later after the family moved to Spokane where she chaired the school board. In fact, she cast the declining vote in favor of that city's Shadle Park High School. She writes that her children were taught to "keep their ears open and their mouths shut" when their parents were on the school board. That advice must have taken; three out of five Wurth children have been cleared for security on military bases in Colorado, Ohio, and California. Mrs. Wurth was honored as Washington Woman of the Year in 1954.

Her brother, *H. Wilson Smith,* left Avery to become an artist of such prominence that his drawings made the cover of Saturday Evening Post. He now lives in San Diego and gives one-man art shows in the prestigious Balboa Park.

The *Pears family* originally came to Avery to help the construction of the Grice Hotel in 1911. Long a part of Avery, the Pears name appears often throughout the town's history. "*Dad*" and his son *Al* were the carpenters who helped build the hotel. Two other sons, *Ed* and *Hardy,* were locomotive engineers whose families made Avery their home. Ed's children were *Emma, Doris,* and *Lee.* Emma married the local druggist, Earl George, partner in the Avery Drug until 1920. The name of *Lee Pears* reached far around the world from Avery. Lee was a jazz singer and pianist with a style similar to Liberace. He toured the world as an accompanist for singer Eva Tangway. Pears' fascination with Japan led him to spend a great deal of time in Tokyo, from where he corresponded with several Avery friends.

Hardy's children—*Virgil, Charles (Bud),* and *Milton*—all were well-known Forest Service employees. Bud and his wife Marg in later years operated the Avery Merchantile and the Avery Trading Post until moving to Wallace in the early 1960's.

For an Avery family, mining is an unlikely field in which to excel, but that is just what the *Boyle family* did. Two brothers, *Dick* and *Tony,* both chose to

Tony Boyle is pictured here next to the railroad switch in the early 1920's. Boyle who was raised in Avery, worked several years for the railroad before moving to the Montana mines. Handpicked by the union's founder John L. Lewis, Boyle became the second president of the important United Mine Workers Union and a natural labor figure. (Boyle)

become electricians at the roundhouse after growing up here. The family moved to Red Lodge, Montana, where both brothers got jobs as electricians in the mines and joined the miners' union. Their father and uncle were leaders in the mining industry in Montana, and another brother, Jack, was superintendent of Baer Collins Mining Company out of Missoula. With that kind of backing, it was no surprise when Tony and Dick rose quickly in their union ranks. *Tony Boyle* was elected head of the United Mine Workers when John L. Lewis retired; his former job as leader of the state union was filled by his brother Dick. A later promotion earned Dick the top slot for all the Northwest including Alaska. And who was the union attorney for all that area?. . . Tony's daughter, *Antoinette,* who has since served as legal counsel for her father in his murder trial.

Avery has had its portion of residents to earn verbal snapshots in our album of interesting people. One example was *Bonnie LaFevre,* who completed her

schooling in Avery. She went on to become a manuscript editor in Seattle. She was the recipient of numerous press awards and was writing a book before her death.

Avery residents recall a tall, handsome ranger who danced beautifully. *Franklin "Judge" Girard* waltzed out of Avery and into politics. In 1933-1936 he was Idaho's Secretary of State. He ran for governor in 1936 as a "trained water, forest and soil conservationist, of ten years experience," according to his advertisement in the *Idaho Statesman.* "Judge" Girard was one of eight candidates for the governorship, and when he placed fourth in the race, his name faded from the spotlight.

Two men who worked in Avery prospered and became millionaires. *Joe C. Parker* worked as a ranger in Avery before becoming interested in raising peas in the Moscow area. From that successful venture, he entered real estate in Spokane and made a name for himself as a realtor in Washington.

About the same time that Parker was here, a young man named *Harold Van Poel* hired on as packer for the Pole Mountain Ranger District (Red Ives). He returned to his piece of property on the Snake River and worked to expand that property into a major sheep and cattle ranch, so large, in fact, that he herded his stock by plane. Van Poel, the prosperous rancher, still returns to St. Joe country to hunt and fish.

Within the town of Avery, our spotlight should pause on women who have settled and stabilized the community. Although the isolation of the narrow canyon has bothered some women at times, those same ones and others have devoted their time to making the town function. It would be impossible to mention every woman who has given something of herself to the community and left it a better place; nor is there any way to name those who've lived, loved, learned, given birth, helped others or left here better people for having done so. Two names definitely stand out, however. *Mrs. Mary Theriault,* one of the first settlers, had an impact that can be seen to this day. She was responsible for forming the first school in Avery, for hiring its first teacher, and for serving on the school board as chairperson for ten years. A person who loved flowers, Mrs. Theriault did much to beautify the young town with flower boxes. The Hotel Idaho, which she managed for 21 years until her death in 1944, was always surrounded by a mass of color. Cherry and apple trees throughout the town still bloom as a memory of Mrs. Theriault, someone who really cared.

And of course, Avery would not be the same place to a great many people without *Mrs. Ruth Lindow.* Coming here as a second-grader in 1917, Ruth attended school here through the tenth grade. She returned after finishing high school to work for many years as Avery postmistress. Besides that and raising her daughter Betty, she spent 26 years as clerk of the school board and another 16 years as a member of the board. She helped to found both the Avery Citizens'

Franklin "Judge" Girard was ranger at Roundtop in the 1920's when this picture was taken with Avery postmistress Doris Pears. Girard later became Secretary of State in Idaho and unsuccessfully ran for governor. (Theriault)

Joe Coddington was a lawyer from Colfax, Washington, who spent his life in a small cabin east of Avery. "Disappointed in love" Coddington moved to the mountains of Idaho where he led a reclusive life, raising strawberries and living off the land. He is shown outside his home with Marietta Hiigel, left, and Floss Pears. A small tributary of the St. Joe is named for him. (Hiigel)

Committee and the Avery Water and Sewer Board. As an artist in her spare time (if she had any!), Ruth taught painting classes for several years. She has always given her support to Avery's church and Sunday school.

Her achievements have received more than local appreciation, for in 1972 Mrs. Lindow was awarded a place in that year's edition of *Community Leaders of America.* In 1976 she was chosen to be a participant in the Rural Women's Oral History Project with a taped interview on file at the University of Idaho. Along with that honor came a certificate of appreciation from the Idaho Commission on Women's programs. Certainly the letters she has written to former residents number in the thousands, and her continuing devotion to the community will not be forgotten.

Lots of people have loved Avery, some have hated it, but all have been touched by it. The little place has always been unique, that's for sure. And it has managed to survive, come hell, high water, fire, floods or epidemics. It was undaunted by World War I; women and children folded bandages for the Red Cross. Although services to the community were cut by nationalized train service, the population grew and the spurt of growth made up for the loss. Avery survived the Depression too, probably better than most places. Here there were no suicides, no bread lines, no broken lives. Instead, people raised gardens and hunted for food, aware of many unlucky travelers on boxcars who spent the night at the hobo camp in East Avery. In fact, the economy of the area actually rose with all the CCC camps and the activity they generated. Although there was a void when the CCC left, it was filled by wartime activity and the advent of modern logging. Black soldiers guarded the portals and trestles during the second war, and thousands of troops passed through on the trains; still, Avery was not touched. Later, another void was created when Potlatch's Camp 44 moved out of the area, but still Avery hung on, its countryside now opened by a network of roads.

Businesses throughout the years have flourished, then floundered as the shopping areas of St. Maries and Wallace became more accessible and as the population declined. The last store, which had been owned by Wally Moore, put a lock on its door in 1970, and then one sad winter day in 1972, the handsome old Hotel Idaho gave up the ghost and crumbled wearily into the street.

The worst blows to Avery have come from the institution that created the town, the Milwaukee Railroad. Increased mechanization brought about many changes that affected the town. After 1917 and the completion of the substation, the population began to shrink. Then the car shop gradually shriveled from 80 employees in 1917 until it closed in 1959. That was the first blow of many. Discontinuation of passenger service on May 21, 1961, cut off many benefits for the town's residents; the end of electrification changed its image. Avery even lost out as a division point when that responsibility went to St. Maries in 1974. The beanery was no longer needed. In 1979 the proud old roundhouse was destroyed for salvage. Now as the

One of Avery's outstanding women, Mrs. Mary D. Theriault, did much to establish the community. She was responsible for starting the school and for planting flowers and trees throughout town. As a businesswoman, she operated the Hotel Idaho for many years, from which balcony this snapshot was taken in 1928. (Theriault)

One of the last businesses to operate was the Avery Mercantile, which closed its doors in the early 1960's. Bud Pears was the last manager of the store which specialized in groceries, hardware, clothing and practically everything a person would need. This photo taken in the 1940's shows two young Avery women posing outside the store on the first floor of the Hotel Idaho. (Hiigel)

Ruth Lindow came to Avery as a small child and has devoted her life to Avery's civic affairs. She served as postmistress and clerk of the school board; through her efforts the Avery Citizens' Committee and Avery Water and Sewer Board were formed. She displays her painting of the snow service at East Portal in 1948. (Lindow)

status of the railroad continues to be cloudy, fewer and fewer railroad families reside in Avery.

More than ever, the town's livelihood lies in the woods. Loggers throughout the general area rely on timber near Avery. They live either in camp trailers near their sales or commute through Avery. The majority of the residents are now Forest Service personnel. Within the community, civic pride runs high, and its residents work hard to provide services. Volunteers maintain the television cable system, the town's water and sewer system, and the quick response ambulance unit. Through hundreds of hours of work, and financial backing of former residents, the old depot has now become the Avery Community Center. It has a volunteer library and a museum, named in honor of David "Norgy" Asleson in 1979. Asleson's determination and leadership made the renovation of the building a reality. A dedication of the building and a reunion for former residents was another occasion when the first Avery Day was held in July of 1978. The event has become an annual occurrence.

5 Rails Through the Bitterroots

LAYING THE TRACK

Picture the hogger (engineer) old and gray
Manning his compound on her way;
Picture the tallow (fireman) bowing his back
Over the diamonds (coals) he has to crack;
Picture the head screw (brakeman) taking a snooze;
Picture the captain (conductor) licking up booze
Instead of buying his baby a new pair of shoes;
It's a picture no artist can paint.

(Old-time railroad song)

When the United States recovered from the Civil War, a fever seized the states; the Union must expand West! An outburst of railroad construction opened up land to settlers that hitherto had been virtually useless for homesteading. Massive land grants and subsidies encouraged not only the building of the track but also the exploration and surveys that might have been delayed indefinitely without the urgency of expansion by railroad. Frontier villages fought for the lines, for the magic of trains that would change their towns into flourishing cities. If the villages were ignored, they withered away and became ghost towns. The great railroad fever was not to touch the St. Joe valley until the first part of the twentieth century, but when the sixth transcontinental railroad made its path, the impact was immense.

In the early 1900's, the Milwaukee Road was a prosperous operation with more than six thousand miles of track through five states and the Dakota Territory. Its terminus was in what poet Carl Sandburg described as the "City of big shoulders. . .player with railroads and the nation's freight handler"—Chicago. Despite the bustle and promise of that city, the future of the Chicago, Milwaukee and St. Paul Railway was not bright in its present state. The tightening network of track in the Midwest would soon slice its business into mere feeder lines for the major routes. The rich West Coast market and the Oriental trade would be tied up by other lines. And already the Road had to rely on its competitors for freight and passenger connections west of Minneapolis at a time when manufacturing and agriculture were booming. The Milwaukee Road decided it must expand west, and the extension to Seattle-Tacoma was formally approved November 28, 1905, by the board of directors. It was not, however, granted land by the government as its competitors had been.

Earlier, in 1853 Congress had authorized government surveys for all principal routes across the continent. Isaac I. Stevens, the new governor of the Washington Territory, was chosen to explore the country between the 47th and 49th parallel and from the Great Lakes to Puget Sound. One of the goals of his expedition was to explore the northern flank of the Bitterroot Mountains. A member of the party wrote about that part of the expedition in 1854: ". . . A road might be built over the tip of the Himalaya Mountains— but no reasonable man would undertake (it). . .Tunnels of two miles in length are not our only obstacles; gullies, steep grades and deep cuts are bad enough, but the almost innumerable heavy and strong bridges required and the large number of short and sudden curves, frequently of less than one thousand foot radius, are very serious obstacles." While the observations were accurate to the letter, the forecast that no reasonable man would undertake to conquer them was not. Fifty years after this was written another set of explorations began for a suitable railroad route through the Northwest.

Before official plans for the construction of the new line had even been announced, the first explorers had already set out. In fact, the exploration and surveys were to take longer than the construction itself. In Montana and Idaho the reconnaissance covered over two thousand miles. The country was wild and uninhabited; there were few trails and virtually no maps. Time was a big factor, so the explorations could not stop for winter weather. The reconnaissance crews had to carry provisions a great distance by pack train, sled, raft, or on men's backs just to ensure survival. Of course, once a party set out, there was no communication with it. President Albert Earling of the railroad admitted in January of 1906 that surveyors were searching for a route through the Bitterroots, "but we haven't heard from them since last winter."

Choosing the route was no simple matter, and several possibilities over a wide area were explored and surveyed thoroughly. The reconnaissance in Montana started west of Butte, November 1, 1904, and went on to Anaconda, continuing the following spring up Ross Fork into the Bitterroot Valley. Another party started at Missoula in October of 1905 to explore Lolo Pass but the heavy snow turned them back. The next January still another group succeeded in exploring all important streams flowing easterly to the Bitterroot and Clark Fork Rivers. Their success was amazing in view of the fact that they plowed through fifteen to thirty feet of snow. In the summer of 1906 more parties searched for possible routes through the

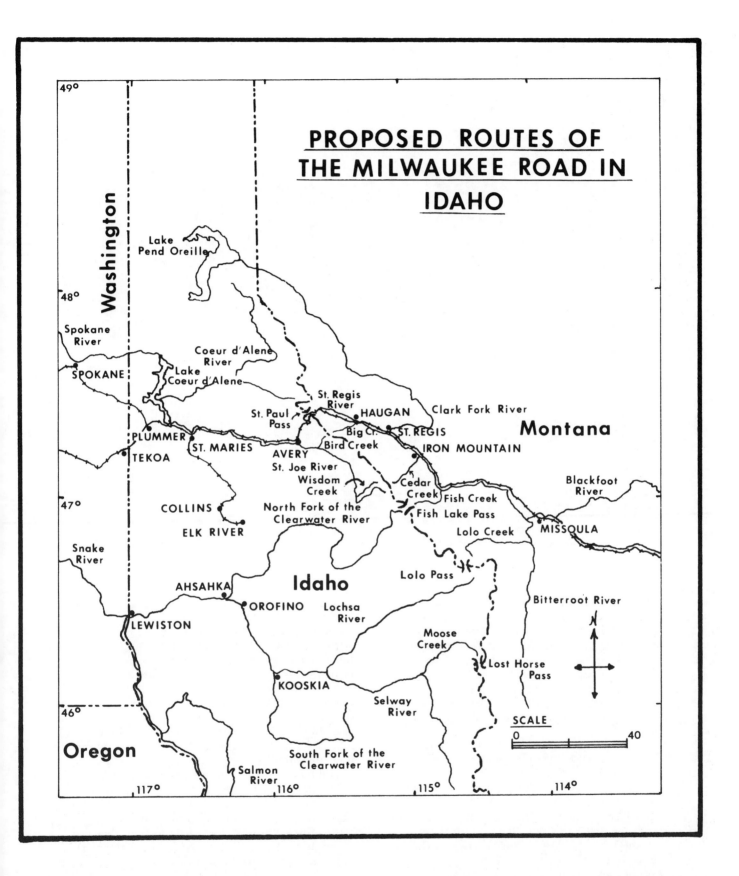

PROPOSED ROUTES OF THE MILWAUKEE ROAD IN IDAHO

Washington

49°

48°

Lake Pend Oreille

Spokane River

47°

Spokane River

SPOKANE

Coeur d'Alene River

Lake Coeur d'Alene

St. Regis River

St. Paul Pass

HAUGAN

Clark Fork River

Montana

PLUMMER

TEKOA

ST. MARIES

AVERY

St. Joe River

Wisdom Creek

Big Cr.

Bird Creek

ST. REGIS

IRON MOUNTAIN

Cedar Creek

Fish Creek

Blackfoot River

COLLINS

North Fork of the Clearwater River

Fish Lake Pass

Lolo Creek

MISSOULA

ELK RIVER

Snake River

AHSAHKA

Idaho

Lolo Pass

Bitterroot River

OROFINO

Lochsa River

N

LEWISTON

Moose Creek

Lost Horse Pass

46°

KOOSKIA

Selway River

SCALE

Oregon

South Fork of the Clearwater River

0   40

Salmon River

117°

116°

115°

114°

53

Construction of the Milwaukee line in 1907 through the Bitterroots was a difficult, expensive project. Here a crew by Roland, Idaho, is constructing a skeleton track, using horse-drawn dumpcars to do necessary fill work. Note the right-of-way clearing just in advance of the skeleton track. (Petroff)

Rockies up the St. Regis River to Saltese as well as up the Deer Lodge, Hellgate and Missoula Canyons. With roads already existing and the Northern Pacific railroad nearby, these routes were simple to explore—but surveying up the rugged Bitterroots with almost no trails to follow became a struggle indeed. Just to survive, the crews had to rely on pack horses and toboggans to carry in three or four weeks' supply of food.

On the Idaho side the exploration started at the most southerly route thought to be practical, the Nez Perce Trail. In May of 1905, explorers went from Magruder Creek to the Selway Fork of the Clearwater River then east up Moose Creek to Lost Horse Pass into Montana. That country is so remote, it is still accessible only by plane or trail. The next proposed route was from Fish Lake Pass in the Bitterroots, down the North Fork of the Clearwater to Ashahka near Orofino. Another group set out from Lewiston and headed west to Garfield, Washington; yet another started at Collins, Idaho going north to St. Maries. In

May of 1906 an exploration started east of Avery and went up to the headwaters of the St. Joe to connect with the Cedar Creek explorations on the east side of the Bitterroots. The choices were beginning to be narrowed down, for the most significant search was carried on extensively from the St. Paul—St. Joe River area northward to Watts summit in the Coeur d'Alene Mountains and westward to Tekoa, Washington. The parties trudged over three hundred miles of territory in that expedition, blazing most of their own trails.

The reconnaissance surveys were just the beginning; next came the engineering surveys. Starting in Montana from Missoula, surveyors headed to Lolo Pass, one group searching to the northwest for routes through the Bitterroots and the other group going down Lolo Creek to Lolo Hot Springs. Then came the survey to the headwaters of Cedar Creek over the hump from the St. Joe into Montana, a project requiring seven months' time and a crew of nineteen. From Cedar Creek to the headwaters of the St. Joe, three separate parties of sixteen men each spent five months working on the Montana slope. It must have been a relief in August of 1906, when they were able to pinpoint their activity to the St. Paul Pass area.

Some of the surveyors had a bad time of it. One Idaho group began at Kooskia in December of 1905, and headed up the Clearwater and Lochsa Rivers with a large crew that included boatmen, trail makers, and extra ax-men. This fifty miles of survey in the Black Canyon were not only difficult and hazardous (one boatman drowned), but it was also extremely expensive. The group was scheduled to meet the Lolo Pass-Lolo Hot Springs group out of Missoula, but the Montana surveyors were beset by bad luck. They had hauled two or three months' worth of provisions by team and sleds from Missoula to the divide for storage; when snows closed the trail behind them, they were forced to carry everything along on sleds rather than store it. During the spring as the snow melted, the party built rafts to transport the supplies. By May they had successfully surveyed 45 miles of the rugged box canyon, but then a raft capsized and their entire outfit was lost. Although the Idaho crew was only twenty miles away, the Montana crew had to blaze a trail just to get out. They had no food and the prospects of getting any were uncertain. After meeting with the Idaho crew, the weary group faced a fifty-mile walk to Greer, Idaho, before they could later disband in Spokane. The survey was completed by the Idaho group who then went back to Kooskia and surveyed west. At long last, the Lolo Pass-Lewiston preliminary work was done, 150 miles having been covered in eleven months' time.

Two surveying parties had scheduled a rendezvous in the upper St. Joe Valley in the summer of 1906. One came down the headwaters of the St. Joe from Wisdom Gulch and were met by a group going east from what later became Avery. The upper group's supplies were hauled in to Iron Mountain from Missoula, and the other had its supplies packed in from St. Joe City over newly built trails. Work for both of these parties was dampened considerably by ice jams and high water. The groups considered one possible route up Bird Creek, but they abandoned the idea because it entailed contruction of a tunnel longer than the Taft Tunnel which exited at Big Creek between Haugen and DeBorgia. Between July of 1906 and March of 1907, twelve separate parties surveyed the 25-mile stretch between St. Paul Pass and Avery. The survey establishing a 1.7 percent gradient to the proposed tunnel was difficult and costly. Fortunately, the work downriver from Avery was merely a choice of which side of the river to follow.

It was at this time that a recommendation was made: "it might be well to make a division in the general description at North Fork (Avery), the foot of the mountain grade." That recommendation was to mean a great deal to the future of Avery.

The surveying job was finally complete. In its wake were some admirable statistics: it had employed eight hundred men in Montana and Idaho for a total of 76 non-consecutive months, and for every mile that actually became a part of the adopted line, eight miles had been surveyed.

A main topic of conversation throughout North Idaho in 1905 and 1906 was speculation about which route the new transcontinental railroad would take. Maybe it would go over Lolo Pass to Lewiston; but then Lewis and Clark hadn't found that route exactly a breeze a century before. Chief engineers predicted that the Milwaukee would never box itself into a steep river canyon of such length that it couldn't branch out to small industries and fields, so that eliminated the Snake and Clearwater Rivers. Even so, the final choice for the route was a real surprise for most people: the road would follow the path of the Northern Pacific on the Clark Fork and St. Regis Rivers nearly to Lookout Pass. Then it would turn south to St. Paul Pass and head down the St. Joe River to Avery and St. Maries. A branch line would go to Spokane and another from St. Maries to Elk River and its timber resources.

The news must have buzzed, and the skeptics no doubt had their heyday gossiping about the treacherous country the train would cross. To the rest of the world, the new line was to be a noted engineering feat—and for Milwaukee's board of directors, one expensive project.

With its financial future in danger, the Chicago, Milwaukee and St. Paul Railway had to connect the new line as soon as possible. Every day of delay meant dollars lost to its competitors. So the first step in the construction process was the organization of labor into sections that could be completed simultaneously. The engineering department divided into three sections: Mobridge, South Dakota, to Butte; Butte to Avery; Avery to Seattle-Tacoma. Then the areas were subdivided. Avery to St. Paul Pass fell under the Montana Division (this incidentally has never changed and that is why Avery railroaders have gone by Montana time to this day). The work contract for this section was let to Winton Brothers Company who in turn sublet the work to six other contractors. The portion from Avery to the Washington-Idaho state line fell under the jurisdiction of the Idaho Division Engineer H.C. Henry; the work westward from Avery to St. Maries was contracted by the Grant, Smith, Henry, and McPhee Company who chose to subcontract to nearly one hundred parties. Winship and Henderson were the subcontractors for the work from St. Regis west to Avery, including the tunnels.

Clearing, grading, bridge, and culvert work may sound like a minor matter today, for modern contractors have easy access, heavy equipment, modern technology, and ready labor. None of these things helped the contractors of the Milwaukee Road in 1907. There were basically no roads in the entire area except from St. Regis to the Saltese mining area. Heavy equipment consisting of cranes on work trains did some of the work, and the rest was done with plain old human muscle and sweat. Finding and keeping laborers was also a big problem. In their earlier western expansion, other railroads had exploited Chinese and other foreign labor.

The Milwaukee, however, was forced to compete for any experienced American workers they could get, at a time when a great deal of railroad construction was going on elsewhere. The labor force was made up of a variety of nationalities, but wages were not cheap.

Often the Road was forced to pay travel expense for laborers on a competing line just to attract workers; and the work itself was back-breaking. The heavy timber, so appealing to homesteaders, meant more work for those clearing the path for the railroad. The clearing process was also slowed down by deep cuts, tunnels, high embankments, and streams.

Construction of the 8,771 foot-long St. Paul Tunnel required the labor of many nationalities. Shown here at Roland on the Idaho side are workers from Eastern Europe. A vigorous contest went on between the Montana and Idaho crews to see who would reach the halfway point first. Idaho won. (Petroff)

Transporting the supplies was a project in itself, for the railroad had to build its own wagon roads. From Taft, Montana, all the way to the St. Joe, the railroad wagon road was reputed to be one of the best maintained roads in the area. It should have been, in view of the fact that it cost $335,000 to build! The original wagon road on the North Fork-Loop Creek coincides with the present one in some spots. At Avery, however, the road passed some fifty feet above the track and continued downriver on the north side. Traces of it are still visible, especially when snow outlines the edge of it.

From Marble Creek to Calder the road built by the railroad is still used and maintained as the North Side Road. A rugged but scenic trip, the road comes out at Calder on a very steep hill. During the construction era, extra teams were kept at the base of the hill to provide needed horsepower for boosting heavy wagons to the top. Various distribution points were set up to make transporting things simpler. For example, at Burton Creek near Hoyt Flat, subcontractors Chindall and Anderson had a commissary and blacksmith shop.

During the construction period, stage runs were started to provide daily services. One named the Goat Rock Line was operated by Frank Theriault of Marble Creek and delivered supplies from St. Joe City to Goat Rock (Spring Creek). Another stage made a daily run from Taft, a major distribution point, to Avery with

mail and fresh foods. Both stages were discontinued with the completion of the tracks.

The construction camps occupied nearly every spot wide enough on the river. In fact, seeing now where they were, one finds it is hard to imagine how sixty or seventy men could possibly have camped in some of the places. But that they did, and in rough-hewn bunkhouses built of logs taken from the right-of-way. To accommodate so many men in such small areas, the bunks were sometimes three deep; and there certainly was no room for luxuries like chairs. To keep laborers, the camps had to feed well. Indians from the Palouse country herded cattle by horseback to Slaughterhouse Gulch east of St. Joe City (which is how it got its name), and to Goat Rock for butchering, so that the camps always had fresh meat. Weathered skulls and skeletons of the cattle from those days can still be seen in these places. Each camp made its own ovens out of big flat stones and baked loaves and loaves of bread daily on big wooden paddles. The large camp at Squaw Creek had two huge ovens built so well they remained intact for many years.

Another benefit the Milwaukee offered its employees was health care. Hospitals were built at Taft and St. Joe City to take care of the many typhoid cases and injuries. Branch hospitals opened at Grand Forks and Marble Creek, where a doctor and a nurse were on hand. The building which housed the hospital stood on the flat across the river from the mouth of Marble Creek.

Construction camps were scattered along the tracks. Most were temporary camps as this one pictured near Roland, Idaho, in 1907. (Petroff)

The doctor and nurse at Marble Creek relax on the steps of their hospital. The hospital operated in 1907-08 when hundreds of men were laying track up the St. Joe River. (Theriault)

The actual construction of the track through the Bitterroots was no easier than the surveying or clearing had been. In order that track could be laid as soon as possible, numerous temporary trestles were built, 21 of them on the west slope alone, for a total length of 9,800 feet. Eight million board feet of lumber was shipped from the Coast by competing rail to Taft, then hauled by team and tramway to the sites. Some eighty tons of iron necessary for the bridges and trestles came from the East, much of it prefabricated.

In fact, the 22-mile stretch from the St. Paul Tunnel to Avery was not only the most difficult, but the most costly part of the whole Milwaukee line. Numerous fills, 16 tunnels, and 21 bridges made the cost soar to $75,000 a mile! In order to make the 1.7 percent grade up to the big tunnel, the track had to be high on the mountainside. It was built in a ten-mile semicircle over a long, deep fill, through a tunnel, over another fill, through a curving tunnel and out onto a bridge. Loop Creek drainage derives its name from this semicircle. Near the site of Adair, a tunnel had to be constructed to divert Loop Creek.

Just to see what was involved in that construction project, let's zero in on the activity at Kelly Creek and Clear Creek, both tributaries of Loop Creek. The railway company chose Clear Creek as the spot to set up a portable sawmill to cut small dimension lumber. The machinery hauled in by teams of horses from Taft turned out lumber for bridges, tunnel-lining, culverts, and flumes. (The major part of the lumber still came from the Coast via other railroads, perhaps because the Milwaukee Land Company owned timber there.)

Because some of the fills were to be sluiced in, the railroad had to buy the damaged timberland from where the topsoil would be sluiced (washed). Today's consciousness of environmental damage probably would never have permitted this practice.

The next step was the construction of a V-shaped flume, extending over two miles up Clear Creek and close to Shefoot Mountain. The flume flared out seven feet wide on each side with a blocked-in bottom and provided enough water pressure for a nozzle system to swish soil down to form the base of the bridge. Five bridges in the Loop Creek area were built in this manner; the bases for the others were filled in with muck from the cuts and tunnels. The sluicing method, despite its disadvantages, was still the preferred and cheaper process. The flume at Clear Creek was later used to transport lumber from the portable sawmill to be used for construction of the line.

In order that the track could go through on schedule, the concrete foundations for the Clear Creek and Kelly Creek viaducts had to be built early in the construction period. While the cement came from Taft, the steel work was shipped to Plummer and then taken to the bridge sites by work train. A traveling block with ropes attached to trees or rock cliffs lowered the lumber into place. And this was all done in dead of winter. The final product was worth it, though—the Kelly Creek bridge towers 208 feet above the ground, the Clear Creek bridge 246 feet. The track between the Clear Creek viaduct and the St. Paul Pass Tunnel was then laid by hand in the fall of 1908 with ties cut locally and gravel hauled in from Haugan, Montana.

And then there were the tunnels: sixteen between Avery and the St. Paul Pass Tunnel for a total length of 8464 feet, lined with two million board feet of lumber. From Avery west, three more tunnels at Herrick, Ramsdale, and Plummer Hill varied in length from 341 feet to 2550 feet. Some required concrete; others were sustained by their own rock, and still others were lined with timber from the Clear Creek sawmill.

The granddaddy of them all, of course, was the impressive St. Paul Pass Tunnel. Considered to.be the most difficult of all the tunnels on the main line, it stretched through the mountain for 8,771 feet. A special power house was built at Taft to furnish electricity for the construction of the tunnel. Air shovels were used to load the material on electric cars, the air was cleared by electric fans, and electric lights enabled workers to see. Three shifts of men kept the steam-operated power plant in full gear. Transmission lines running from the East Portal substation and over the summit to the west end provided the small settlement of Roland with electricity in its section houses. Considering that even cities like New York and Chicago were not fully electrified at that time, it was amazing that Roland, in the middle of nowhere, had such lighting.

Although the modern innovation was appealing, the work on the tunnel was not. Several large veins of water and deep snow made the struggle of building the tunnel most unpleasant for a thousand laborers, so the Milwaukee had to offer a bonus system of pay just to keep them on the job. The bore pushed on through at an average of twenty feet a day though, and six months later the tunnel was complete. It was only a fraction of an inch off its mark when both sides met in the middle.

With the labor of nearly nine thousand men and a two-year construction period behind it, the Chicago, Milwaukee, and Puget Sound Railway Company finally went west. The original estimate in 1902 of a line similar to the Northern Pacific was $45 million; President Earling upped the estimate to $60 million. The actual cost exceeded $234 million. Nevertheless, the workers joyously drove the last spike at Garrison, west of Deer Lodge, on May 14, 1909. Freight service began July 4, 1909 and local passenger service followed six days afterwards. The Milwaukee made connections with Tacoma's lumber mills, and in August they drew a contract with Japanese shippers for five hundred tons of freight to go east.

The Milwaukee had met its goal!

"Million-dollar Silk Train at Avery, Idaho about 1912," reads this Milwaukee Railroad postcard. When the line was completed in 1909, Milwaukee carried the Japanese silk from Puget Sound to the East Coast. The railroad's western expansion required this business to compete with other lines. (Theriault)

The St. Paul tunnel, shown in its early stages here, took months to complete. Right-of-way clearing has just been completed to the summit in this 1907 photo. The east entrance to the tunnel shaft would be in the lower center of the photo. (Petroff)

A ten-mile loop wound its way up to make the grade into the St. Paul Tunnel, giving the Loop Creek drainage, shown here, its name. A flume in the clearing in the upper right transported water from Clear Creek to sluice in the fills for five different bridges. Note the crew in the foreground sluicing in this bridge, using water from Cliff Creek. Wood for the flumes came from a mill on Clear Creek. The buildings on far left were storage sheds and quarters for the construction crew. (Saunders)

SIDINGS AND SETTLEMENTS

As the railroad line nosed its way through the mountains, construction camps and settlements sprouted in all sorts of unlikely places. Though few people today bother to drive the narrow roads to these places, at one time hundreds of people lived there. Just imagine—nine thousand people along the right-of-way and another thousand working on the tunnel! Suddenly people of every description, nationality, and moral code inhabited the rough terrain. On the Montana side of the tunnel the town of Taft sprouted five miles from Lookout Pass. On the Idaho side people occupied at least a half dozen other sites for varying amounts of time. Some of the places were riotous construction camps; others served briefly as railroad stations and sidings. Post offices existed in some of them but none had schools, for most of their residents were not family men or women. And some of the places have stories to tell that come straight out of the Old West.

When the railroad surveyors chose places for sidings and stations, their decision depended upon practical matters. The spot had to be wide enough for two trains to pass each other and still be a convenient location for water tanks. Consequently, as the line crossed the Bitterroots, the plan to locate the sidings about five miles apart was subject to a good deal of

Many of the sidings along the Milwaukee line consisted only of a section house and a sidetrack. This picture taken at Stetson in the early 1920's shows Dave Saunders, one of the first engineers on the Milwaukee Lines West, and fireman Jack Boyle. The boxcab No. 10224 built by General Electric was one of the first electric locomotives. (Boyle)

variation. The stations and their distances ran about like this: Taft to East Portal, three miles; East Portal through the tunnel to Roland, two miles; Roland to Adair, four miles; Adair to Falcon, five miles; Falcon to Kyle, six miles; Kyle to Stetson, three miles; Stetson to Avery, four miles. From the division point at Avery,

the next siding was at Ethelton (east of Hoyt Flat), five miles; then Ethelton to Pocono west of Marble Creek, nine; Pocono to Elk Prairie (Calder), eight; Elk Prairie to Zane, five; Zane to St. Joe City, five; St. Joe City to Omega, six; Omega to St. Maries, six. A siding was put in at Bogle Spur, nine miles from Avery, for loading logs, and a depot was built at Herrick at Big Creek where an operator worked, but no siding was built there. Names for the sidings such as Stetson, Kyle, and possibly others came from the civil engineers who planned the track. Sometimes names were chosen from the Milwaukee board of directors' families, as were Avery and Ethelton. The name Pocono is the same as a mountain range in Pennsylvania.

(Another railroad siding was important to early mines on the St. Joe long before the Milwaukee came into the country. Located at Borax along the Northern Pacific line one-half mile east of Lookout Pass, this siding was used to load ore, including some from the Bullion Mine on the St. Joe side of the mountain. The Sildex mine and mill and the Borax mine relied entirely on it. Nearby was a settlement of some size at the Borax mine, an operation still in business through the 1920's.)

The sidings along the Milwaukee served as loading sites, but mainly they were planned for the trains to

Jack Boyle and Margaret Germaine enjoy cake at Kyle in 1917. In the background is the crane for the staff system, a method ensuring the safety of trains passing in mountainous areas. Trains which had the right-of-way picked up a steel rod (staff) from this crane, depositing it at the next station. (Theriault)

pass each other safely in the high mountain areas. Any mistakes at the sidings could result in a fatal collision. To ensure the safety of each train in the Bitterroots, a foolproof method known as the staff system was used. It involved the exchange of a steel rod about the length of a brick with an individually corrugated side like a key. This corrugation fit only one machine. When operators at adjoining stations were aware of a locomotive coming, they agreed by telephone to push the machine's automatic release simultaneously to eject the staff. The engineer passing into Stetson, for example, hooked his arm through a bag holding the staff and that was his go-ahead. It was also his guarantee that the line was his alone between Stetson and Avery. Three people were therefore responsible for the staff: the two operators and the engineer. If the staff was not released to the engineer, he waited at the siding for another train to pass and the track to be clear. Passage through the long St. Paul Tunnel posed a problem, so a divided staff system was used—a half staff for the engine and another half for the caboose. In this way, the operators could be sure that all the train was out of the tunnel before another train could enter. As the trains passed through each station, they threw the staff off onto the platform indicating that the line was clear. They also threw mailbags off at the stations. The person working on the platform was not only kept hopping but ducking as well when the hefty bags sailed through the air. Today a system similar to the staff system is used for orders, utilizing a hoop of string which the engineers hook as they pass each station.

In the early days when trains entered the sidings and stations, another signal awaited them. A paddle sticking up meant the go-ahead for the westbound train; the paddle dropping down automatically meant a *stop* for the eastbound train. When the line was electrified, the battery-operated paddle system was changed to modern electric light signals.

The sidings during construction days had rough log bunkhouses used both as housing for workers and as depots. Certainly a winter night spent in the unhewn

and uncaulked bunkhouses was a drafty ordeal for the shivering workers as they hurried to finish the line. Soon the log depots were replaced by ones prefabricated at the Milwaukee's carpenter shops in Tomah, Wisconsin, and transported to the location. Carpenters put up the buildings on site at Roland and Avery.

The sidings at Stetson, Kyle, Ethelton, and Zane had nothing but rooms for an operator, but several of the settlements along the Milwaukee line achieved enough permanence to last for awhile. Falcon, for example, managed to get its name on several maps. This station is in a spot above the valley floor in the Loop Creek drainage from the mouth of Cliff Creek; even by Avery standards it is isolated. But for a period of years Falcon had a jewelry store! The owner had apparently been a jeweler elsewhere and simply chose Falcon as a place to relocate his business. When the jeweler died, his wife remarried a moonshiner who operated his business from the former jewelry store.

A post office was established at Falcon in October of 1911 and remained active until the 1930's. The small store and post office were their busiest during the teen years when railroad logging was going on in the North Fork drainage. A mile and a half west of Falcon was the site of the St. Joe Ranger Station, built in 1905 or 1906. It burned in the 1910 fire, was rebuilt on the same spot, then was dismantled in 1918. A patrol station was then built at the Falcon siding which functioned into the 20's. Its mahogany door was originally part of the St. Joe Ranger Station. All that is left of the St. Joe Ranger Station is a water pipe sticking out of the ground. As for Falcon, it provided a home for a section man who remained there until the 1960's but that also is gone.

The town of Adair, high on the railroad loop above Loop Creek, was the campsite for three or four hundred people during construction days. It served as a loading site for ore from the Idaho-Montana Mine, the Richmond, and the Monitor. A specially built tramway carried ore down the mountain to the siding. When C.H. Gregory salvage-logged near Adair during the teens, he constructed an unusually long log flume over the tunnel to unload his logs at the siding. Adair once had several sporting houses (houses of prostitution), saloons, and a small store that sold clothing and general merchandise. The Adair section man built a small fishpond between the depot and section house that entertained passengers on the train for many years.

Perhaps the most dreary description of Adair came from Ed Thenon, a crew boss for a group of firefighters in 1910. When Thenon's crew disembarked from the train at two o'clock in the morning, he couldn't figure out why the place even had a name. "Nothing met the eye," states writer Betty Goodwin Spencer, "just blackness, a deep excavation in the hillside, and then a flicker of a lantern far up the track." When Thenon asked where his men could sleep, he was told, "Just anywhere, the country's all vacant."

The Avery depot, completed in 1909, offered the 24-hour service of a beanery and a telegraph office. The left end held the beanery and kitchen while the right end was a waiting room. Note the oil lamp on the outside of the building in this 1915 photo. (Theriault)

Falcon, Idaho, and its nearby neighbor, Grand Forks, were exciting towns during construction days of the railroad. Note advertisements for the various businesses. (Oregon Historical Society)

That winter following the 1910 fires, the hillsides everywhere were devoid of trees. There was nothing to stop snowslides as they gained momentum and roared down the hills, knocking everything out of their way. Seven people were sitting in the section house at Adair one winter evening when a slide rolled off the mountain. The impact of the snow smashed the section house and killed three or four people. One victim named Spores was buried near Avery at Forty-Nine Gulch.

The history of Adair's post office leaves some unanswered questions. It had been opened in March of 1910 for only fifteen months and operated by three different men before it was discontinued and the mail was sent to Avery. Then on November 21, 1917, it was reopened, not as Adair, but as *Delage.* That name stayed with it for seven years, but oddly no local person has ever heard of the name "Delage." Perhaps that has something to do with why the name Adair was restored in 1924, less than two years before the post office was discontinued again. This time the mail went to Falcon.

The settlement of Roland on the Idaho side of the

St. Paul Tunnel once boasted a population of three hundred men as the electrification project was being completed in 1915-18. A turntable enabled locomotives to turn around at Roland and make the run back down the hill to the division point at Avery. Its handsome two-story depot housed the depot and agent's office on the first floor while the upstairs provided housing for one family as well as several single rooms. Several large bunkhouses and single-family dwellings provided homes for the construction workers.

Picture this scene in a little mountainous settlement in the late 1930's: a train pulls into the depot as usual on a snowy February day. A number of passengers, well-bundled and laughing, carry their ski equipment from the train. They are obviously enjoying the chance for an outing. The Alps? Hardly. This was Roland, Idaho. Through a cooperative agreement with the Forest Service and the railroad, a ski course was set up nearby. Special trains carried groups from Spokane, Coeur d'Alene, Missoula, and Avery to the slopes for several winters. The Roland ski course was closed in the mid-1940's, and now trees have grown up and obliterated the run.

Situated near the Montana-Idaho border, Roland, Idaho, was an important railroad community in the early years of the Milwaukee Road. This photo was taken in the teens when Roland was a community of 150 souls composed mainly of workers cementing the St. Paul tunnel. The two-story depot survived the 1910 fire and was a familiar landmark to railway passengers. The entrance to the tunnel is in the center of the photo. (Theriault)

The last people moved from Roland in the early 1960's, and the buildings were moved to East Portal, its sister siding on the east side of the tunnel. East Portal remained one of the more important sidetracks in the Bitterroots with room for 120 cars. It also had two industry tracks to accommodate ten cars apiece for camps and work crews, and its substation like the one in Avery transformed power for the electrification project. Since the deepest snows along the line fall near East Portal, a section crew always was needed there during the winter and during storms to man the heavy doors to the tunnel. It is one of the last sidings within the area that housed a section crew. Of course, its real heyday was during the construction era. As in all the sidings and settlements, people were everywhere then.

And they were every sort of people. They spoke a variety of languages, they ate their own kinds of foods whenever possible, they played their own kinds of music over campfires at night. There were Italians, Irishmen, Swedes, Norwegians, Austrians, Belgians. From Eastern Europe came Hungarians, Bulgarians, Serbs, and Montenegrins. Spaniards came to work,

too—dressed in black velvet garb with red sashes and headgear. On their shoulders they carried small trunks filled with white homespun linen underwear which they washed religiously each day. On their Sabbath the Spanish twang of guitars and castanets floated out of their bunkhouses.

Nearly a thousand railroad workers scattered from Taft to St. Joe were Montenegrins, a moderately dark-skinned Balkan people from the tiny kingdom of Montenegro, now a part of southern Yugoslavia. In Avery the group of workers settled at Hogshead Gulch. Nicknamed derogatorily "Mountain Niggers," these people wore their national dress and honored one man as their natural leader above all. This man known as their "King" wrote their letters home, handled their finances, and translated English into their native tongue. No American foreman had clout over him. When the "King" was shot in 1908 near Taft by a construction foreman named Reddy, hundreds of Montenegrins from St. Regis to St. Joe City threw down their tools, stopped work, and growled in anger. Tension grew as the men went to Taft to form a funeral procession. Aggrieved pairs of men tramped

Skiers ready themselves for a day on the slopes at Roland in the late 1930's. Special trains brought the skiers from Missoula, Spokane, Coeur d'Alene, and Avery. A big bonfire near Roland warmed them throughout the day. (Hiigel)

behind the homemade casket, holding white streamers in one hand and huge lighted candles in the other. Each vowed vengeance on the man who had killed their brother; then they danced and sang warlike songs. Edith M. Schussler, a Taft doctor's wife, recounted later that the doctors, staff, and patients watched fearfully as the grieving mob decided to bomb the hospital. They were eventually dissuaded because hospitalized Montenegrins would also be killed, and the angry group finally dispersed. The next day most of the workers were gone from the line, never to return. As the group from Avery packed their belongings, they passed out excess things and gave eleven-year-old Harold Theriault their blue dishes.

The story about the dead king was not over, however. Reddy, the foreman, was acquitted on the murder charge and returned calmly to work, assured that the Montenegrins were long gone. It was only a few minutes, Mrs. Schussler remembered, before the shots rang out. Reddy and three Montenegrins lay dead, and in the spring two more bodies were found dressed in the native clothing. All were buried in a hospital graveyard above Taft, along with countless victims of typhoid—and murder.

For murder was common in Taft, Montana, one of the most notorious towns along the line. Though thousands of workers squeezed into the town at times, its permanent population reached 3200 during the peak. Taft got its name when President William Howard Taft journeyed through on the Northern Pacific Railway. Hearing of the town's reputation, President Taft ordered his special train to a stop. From the back of the train, he lectured the inhabitants on their evil ways. Their town was a dirty smudge on these fair United States, he said, and he sternly demanded that they do something about it. They did. With wild cheers, they named the town in his honor!

Certainly Taft was the nearest thing to the wild western towns painted by the pulp magazines. It roared through the night with gambling, dance halls,

and prostitution. Sleep for the saner folks was nearly impossible in the canvas-walled rooms above the dance halls. But there were others who got more sleep then they bargained for. When the heavy snows from the winter of '06 and '07 melted in the spring, six or seven men were dug out of the drifts, says one account. A reprint from an old letter found in the Taft Hotel, complete with its own spelling and capitalization, gives this description:

"Built for the Benefit of the N.P.R., the Boom Days was when the C.M. & St. P. Ry. hand drilled the big tunnel threw the Bitterroot range, 1000 men was employed. A hospital with 3 doctors and other staff of help was here.

"The story goes that there was 17 men killed over this bar. . .In the spring of '07 there was supposed to have been 18 men done away with by foul means. When the snow melted down in the spring there was a mass burial.

"At one time there was 23 saloons and 10 cafes in Taft. 300 women and only one decent one in town. Wages run around $2.00 per day. a quart of whiskey is $1.25, 2 shots for 25¢, ham sold for 16 c., beef sold for 9 c, coffee for 25 c."

As fires blasted through Montana and Idaho in August of 1910, the people of Taft could see their town was doomed. Obviously, it would be a terrible waste for all that good booze to be burned up, so they took it upon themselves to consume as much of it as possible before the fire did. When it was time to evacuate, they had done an amazing job on the whiskey. The fire destroyed Taft, leaving only the old Taft Hotel whose bar was once noted for being the longest in western Montana. Now that too is gone, removed for the path of Interstate 90.

Taft was not alone in its wild behavior. "It is universally admitted that the town of Taft was the toughest town in the country until Grand Forks came into being. This town quickly went into first place for the honor," reminisced William W. Morris of the U.S.

Heavy snows over St. Paul Pass required regular snow service to clear the tracks. "The Rotary" is the title of this 1914 photo, copyrighted in Falcon. The steam-operated rotary is shown here plummeting snow high over the turntable at Roland. (Theriault)

Forest Service. Grand Forks was located at the mouth of Cliff Creek, a tributary of Loop Creek, across the valley from Falcon. Its buildings literally overflowed with illegal whiskey (sold without a permit on the National Forest) and with ''sports,'' as prostitutes were then called.

Joseph Halm, also of the Forest Service, wrote this colorful description of Grand Forks: ''Grand Forks was a wild mushroom construction town. The main section of town had no streets. It was built in the form of a hollow rectangle around a sort of court. Both sides and ends of this court were almost solid with rough-lumber and log buildings. During the mornings the court was deserted except for a few sobering stragglers sitting on empty beer kegs piled in front of the twelve or fifteen saloons. Some of these saloons also served as eating places and one or two had store annexes. Behind the saloons, scattered all around through the woods were nondescript assortments of tents and shacks which served as dwellings for all the town's population.

''Toward evening the town would begin to show signs of life and as night came on and as oil lamps began to glow, player pianos began their tinny din, an orchestra here and there began to tune up. Women daubed with rouge came from the cribs upstairs and sat at lunch counters or mingled with the ever-increasing throng of gamblers and rough laborers from the camps. As the hours wore on, the little town became a roaring, seething, riotous brawl of drinking, dancing, gambling and fighting humanity.''

Even delivering the mail to the place had its hazards. One time the mailman was carrying railroad workers' checks between Roland and Grand Forks. He was found with an ice pick in the back of his head. The body was buried on the spot but the gravesite was lost after the 1910 fire.

Besides a post office established in 1908, Grand Forks had the Bitterroot Mercantile, owned by the Kelley brothers of Avery. It also had a small emergency hospital as an offshoot of the Taft hospital. One patient in the hospital was a gambler who had the misfortune to have a bullet lodged in his tongue. It seems that the gambler had cheated a tunnel worker at

Grand Forks, a mushroom construction town, was located on Cliff Creek, a tributary of Loop Creek. The Bitterroot Mercantile, owned by the Kelley Brothers of Avery, is on the left. Anheuser-Busch Beer is advertised on the Anheuser Hotel, while a ''girl'' advertises her wares by hanging out the window of the North Pole Bar and Restaurant. Note the railroad right-of-way clearing in the background as well as the wealth of empty beer barrels and stumps lining the street. (Oregon Historical Society)

cards. As the man grew ugly about his loss, the gambler drew his pistol and fired two fast shots. The second shot killed the man but as he fell over backwards, he blasted a shot off in retaliation. It went right through the chin of the gambler and buried itself in his tongue. That was one deal that left him speechless!

On another occasion in July of 1910, a prostitute robbed and poisoned one of her customers. Then she calmly set the building on fire to destroy the evidence. The entire town burned, though no one was hurt except the hapless victim of the crime who was already dead. When the prostitute disappeared, no one bothered to follow her. But it was necessary to hold an inquest. The townspeople set the body with blackened irons from the bed bent around it in the center of town. Spectators hauled out beer barrels and put planks on them for seats to witness the evidence as it was presented. Apparently they reached a consensus; the man was indeed dead.

But how he got that way was as much their hard luck as his, for because of his death the town had burned. It didn't take long before tents and tent frames had replaced the wooden buildings, and liquor started flowing again. Two enterprising women of the night perched themselves in a treehouse, and business went on as usual!

Not more than a month later, the tent town of Grand Forks was burned up as the fires of 1910 ravaged the countryside. This time most of its shady residents fled for good. But a persistent saloon-keeper, Basil Rizzonelli, reopened his saloon, and Forest Service officials were plagued with enforcing liquor laws in the Grand Forks area through 1911. Finally the saloon-keepers were issued stiff fines and forced to leave the area. Grand Forks had lived a fiery, violent life, but it was a short one of a little more than two years. Nary a marker nor an old scrap of lumber marks its place today on Cliff Creek.

In looking at places like Taft and Grand Forks (and even St. Joe City), one finds it is impossible not to ponder their death. Was it Nature's own brand of justice that destroyed them? Would they have survived if the devastating fire of 1910 had not wiped them out? Would travelers on their way over Lookout Pass stop at Taft, maybe for a night's rest at a plush Ramada Inn? Would a few hardened old-timers peer out of dilapidated buildings at Grand Forks, curious about stray passers-by? Or would the main drag by Loop Creek perhaps be covered with shiny new Burger Kings and Seven-Eleven stores?

Only a few ghosts lingering in the new crop of trees know the answers to those questions, and they aren't saying.

THE PROUD ERA

The track was laid, the trains went through, but the story of railroading in St. Joe country was by no means over. In fact, for railroad buffs the best was yet to come; the proud era of the Milwaukee Road's

electrification was still ahead.

Steam engines puffed their way through the Bitterroots and three other mountain ranges when the line was completed in 1909. The same year an additional line opened up the Elk River country. More advanced technology was available to the builders of this last transcontinental railroad, and as early as 1905 farsighted railroad officials had plans to change the mode of power to electricity. In anticipation of that, land purchasing agents bought the right-of-way and timber lands in the name of the Milwaukee Land Company. Over 450,000 acres in Washington and

Electric locomotive E50 (originally No. 10200) is engineered here by Harold Theriault at East Portal in 1944. When this engine came to the Rocky Mountain Division in 1916, it was hailed as the largest electric locomotive in the world. (Hiigel)

Idaho were purchased for the express purpose of electrical development, with plans to include substations and generating plants. Most interesting was the fact that the Milwaukee bought the flow rights to the St. Joe River, and made plans for eleven dams and generating plants to produce 180,000 horsepower. The track was constructed high above the river at Ethelton (near Hoyt Flat) to allow for a dam there. Skookum Canyon and the Big Hole at Spring Creek also were sites. Where the other dams were planned is conjecture now. How different the swiftwater of the St. Joe would have been with eleven dams!

The railroad had several considerations in mind when the board of directors ordered a feasibility study in 1912 for electrification of the line from Avery to Harlowton, Montana. For one thing, the difficult terrain out of Avery posed problems for the steam locomotives. Big steam mallets (double engines) were required to tug the trains up the grade to St. Paul Tunnel, and the many tunnels were filled with ashes and cindery smoke. In winter the engines were often frozen with thick ice, making it difficult and time-consuming for them to get up the mountain. Hauling coal for the engines on the entire route involved not only long distances, but it also meant tying up fourteen percent of the railroad's cars that could be used for paying freight. Besides, Forest officials had banned the use of coal-burning engines on the National

Forest Reserve out of Avery after the disastrous fire of 1910. The engines had to use crude oil instead, and that was expensive. The area would be ideal for electrification because its water resources could provide power easily.

Electrifying the engines had drawbacks, though. There was no way of knowing ahead of time if electric locomotives would work because they simply had not been used for any distance. Then the Butte, Anaconda and Pacific Railroad converted its seventy miles of line to electric power, proving that electricity did indeed work. An electric train also ran successfully between Coeur d'Alene and Spokane about 1905. But there was the problem of power availability. What would happen when seasons were dry and the rivers were low? Was electricity reliable? Was there a readily available power source to be tapped in Montana? Certainly building and maintaining power plants would be costly, especially when they would be used only ten percent of the time.

This photograph of Kyle was taken in 1911. As with the other railroad sidings from Avery into Montana, Kyle was destroyed in the 1910 fire and was quickly rebuilt in the following months. Workers are constructing a new siding as a passenger train heads west out of the Kyle tunnel. (Dewald)

The power problems were partially solved when the Milwaukee board of directors added John D. Ryan as a board member. Ryan, the president of Anaconda Mining Company and a major stockholder in what was to become the Montana Power Company, encouraged the railroad to use commercial power instead of building its own power plants. When the first contract for power supply was signed with Montana Power in 1912, Ryan's expertise and influence made the changeover more efficient. Things began to roll quickly after that. The Milwaukee formed the electrification department in March of 1914, and a year or so later the Montana Power built the Avery substation and other substations along the line. By 1917, it had gradually extended electrical operations from Harlowton to Avery, a distance of 440 miles. The eyes of a good many people everywhere watched the experiment.

The results were astounding. By eliminating coal,

numerous complications such as the coaling docks, water plugs, and ash pits went too. The Harlowton to Avery run had once had four divisions in steam; now electricity made it two. Maintenance was cut by 75 percent, crews cut by two-thirds, and the system immediately began to pay for itself in increased

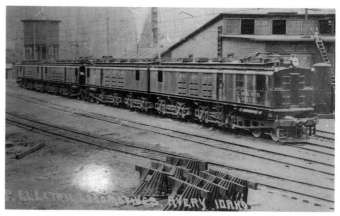

Engine 10222, one of Milwaukee's proud boxcabs, was first in Avery in 1916 and used until the end of the electrification project. In the background is the sandhouse, water tank, and pumphouse. Notice the cow-catcher on the front of the locomotive. (Theriault)

efficiency and cheaper operating costs. In five years, the electric line running out of Avery was paid for, and a new line was planned from Othello, Washington, to Seattle-Tacoma through the Cascades. A company spokesman said this about the project: "Our electrification has been tested by the worst winter in the memory of modern railroaders. There were times when every steam locomotive in the Rocky Mountain district was frozen, but the electric locomotive went right along. Electrification has in every way exceeded our expectations. This is so, not only as respects tonnage handled and mileage made, but also the regularity of operations."

The original plans called for electrification of the entire line from Harlowton to Seattle-Tacoma. Instead, the electrification stopped at Avery with a 210-mile stretch known as "the gap." The numbering of the substations to this day reflects the original plans; the numbers started with number one at Two Dot, Montana, to fourteen at Avery, and began with twenty-one west of Taunton, Washington. Numbers fifteen to twenty were never constructed because the board dropped plans to electrify in 1921 with a downturn in the economy. "The gap" was to be the thorn in Milwaukee's "siding" though, for the use of steam in that one section hampered efficiency and versatility. During those active railroading years, Avery was never quiet, with the daily switching of the locomotives from steam to electric and back again.

Meanwhile, railroaders from all over the world came to view the electric line, labeled as the "most widely known section of railroad track in the world." It was the first long distance electrification in America and the longest of its kind in the world (six times the length of any other). Seventeen countries eventually adopted similar lines after studying the Milwaukee.

Here's how it all worked. The existing Montana Power Company plants on the Missouri River provided power for the Harlowton area; the Avery area to the west was supplied by a new 35,000 kilowatt plant at Thompson Falls on the Clark Fork River. The power was a 100,000 volt, three-phase alternating current zapped to fourteen substations. There it was reduced by transformers to 2300 volts and converted by motor generators to a 3000-volt direct current. Idaho cedar poles held the twin copper feeder wires over the track.

The interior of the Avery substation was a well-maintained, impressive setting for the huge transformers pictured here. Transformers cut the voltage, and converted it to direct current for the trolley in the days when electricity provided power for locomotives in the Bitterroots. (Scribner)

Each substation was responsible for energizing a certain section of catenary (the wire that carried the trolley), and the distance between substations, normally about 32 miles, was determined by the amount of power required for that section of track. Inside the motor, the electricity operated a magnetic field, causing the armature to revolve and propel the locomotive through the gears.

Saving energy may seem like a contemporary issue, but in 1915 the Milwaukee Road developed a unique braking system that reused its energy. The regenerative braking held trains back on grades, at the same time building resistance which the motors (turned to generators) fed back into the catenary. Some forty to sixty percent of the power used going up the grade was returned while the train was going down. The braking

created its own form of energy instead of absorbing it. This was an engineering marvel, so successful that every electric locomotive built thereafter adopted it.

Indeed, the Chicago, Milwaukee and Puget Sound (later to be the Chicago, Milwaukee, St. Paul and Pacific) was a proud railroad. Although the nickname for the CMPS was "Cheap Men and Poor Service," that was not necessarily the case. Especially when the luxurious trains, the *Olympian* and the *Columbian,* began in 1911, service was not only the fastest across the country, but among the best. With its glamorous bi-polar locomotives, the *Olympian* pulled an observation car so that its passengers could admire the rugged Bitterroots in comfort. Barber and valet service,

The Milwaukee carried many sophisticated passengers on its tracks during its proud era. Here Miss Laura Kroll, an attractive Avery resident, poses thoughtfully on Engine 10301, in the 1920's. Watching the trains was a popular American pasttime in those days. (Boyle)

baths, radio, and a library were also available; for fifty cents a hot meal could be purchased in the dining car. A typical menu offered such luxuries as Fricassee of Lamb, Olympian; Potage Florentine; Broiled Fresh Fish, Hoteliere; Potatoes, Rissolees; Clam juice cocktail and a maple nut sundae.

President Warren Harding made this statement after he piloted the electric engine across the mountains: "We rode today over many miles of electrified railway, and our train slipped along with the greatest comfort and steadiness. . .I drank in an inspiration from the thought that as we were coasting downgrade for twenty miles, having our train steadied by the process of driving the motors in the opposite direction, that we were storing up energy sufficient to pull another train up-grade. This is an era of great possibilities. . .It was the most delightful ride I have ever known in my life."

The Milwaukee was proud of its various locomotives, too. General Electric built No. 10200 with eight motors and a total of 228 tons with its

"The day of the christening" states this photograph showing the new diesel engine, Engine No. 40, in Avery. Mr. James, Engineer, and Frank Gustafson, railroad official, pose for the occasion. As division point, Avery was the switching station between diesel and electric locomotives. The lines for the older electric engines hang above the newcomer. (Hiigel)

112 feet of length, making it the "Largest Electric Locomotive in the World" in 1916. The Milwaukee's five bi-polar locomotives were gearless motors, built

for passenger service and capable of pulling 1120 tons over any grade. They were unique in their day and pictured in various railroad advertisements. Later in 1950, the Little Joes joined the Milwaukee fleet. Built for the Soviet Union and named for Joseph Stalin, the 5500 horsepower locomotives were never delivered to Russia because of the Cold War embargo. They had been built for the five-foot gauge used in Russia and had to be modified for the 4.85-foot standard gauge in the United States. The dozen Little Joes added versatility to the line with their capacity to haul either large loads or reach speeds up to eighty miles per hour. Besides that, they gave a new boost to the electrification project that might have been scrapped after World War II.

These glory days for the railroad were reflected in Avery, the thriving division point. The Avery roundhouse employed 150 workers on three shifts, for the road needed machinists, boilermakers, fire-

Avery, the division point on the Milwaukee Lines West, had a modern roundhouse and turntable, built in 1909. During World War I 100 men were employed at the Roundhouse and another 80 were employed as car men at the riptrack. (Theriault)

builders, and laborers to keep the two types of engines rolling east and west. Eighty-eight men manned a rip track at its peak to repair cars. West Avery (site of the

The night force at the Avery roundhouse is shown here. At one time, the roundhouse itself employed 150 men on three shifts. Standing: (left to right) David Saunders, next 3 unknown, Harold Theriault, Tom Eagan, Bill Moriaty, Tim O'Leary, and Ed Gronwald. Sitting: —— Malone, unknown, —— Malone, Shorty Carpenter, and Pat Curran. (Theriault)

present Potlatch landing) alone grew to a population larger than all of Avery now. Even into the 1960's, the Avery depot maintained an icehouse to provide ice for passenger service and refrigeration. Crews from Montana or Lake Chatcolet shipped the large blocks to be stored in sawdust until they were lugged to bunkers on ice cars. They used salt to melt the ice for refrigerating carloads of vegetables and earlier raw silk from the Orient. When the salt dripped down onto the tracks, it attracted so many deer that at times they were a real hazard! It has been only in recent years that electric refrigerator cars have replaced the ice cars.

In spite of its accomplishments, the Milwaukee Road had more than its share of hardships from the beginning. The original estimate for the Pacific Extension of $60 million was far lower than its cost of nearly $257 million (including $23 million for electrification), an overrun simply not justified by the amount of freight. With the opening of the Panama Canal in 1914, foreign business on the new transcontinental line, including the lucrative silk trade, did not begin to meet expectations. Competition with Union Pacific, Great Northern and Northern Pacific

was formidable too. The government took over the track during World War I and did not maintain it adequately. Then a slowdown in the economy and a strike in the early 20's were crippling blows. The board of directors had no choice—the Milwaukee Road was forced to go into receivership March 18, 1925, its first bankruptcy. A year and a half later, however, things were back to normal with the reorganized (and

"Who wants to be the ice man?" is the title of the 1910 photo. Ice was an important commodity in railroading until refrigerated cars became common. Here an iceman wheels his load down Avery's boardwalk in 1910. The Bitterroot Mercantile and Grice Hotel are pictured on the left. (Turner)

Running was not always smooth for Milwaukee's electrics, as this tipped-over General Electric boxcab testifies. This train wreck at Motor Creek in 1919 gave that stream its name. Derailments in recent years have been costly and destructive to the Milwaukee. (Theriault)

renamed) Chicago, Milwaukee, St. Paul and Pacific Railroad Company.

In the years between 1921 and 1940, only three years ended in the black for the Milwaukee accounts. The road declared another bankruptcy on June 29, 1935. This time it regained its foothold with the speedy one hundred mile-per-hour *Hiawatha* in the Midwest and the *Olympian Hiawatha* from Chicago to Seattle. A degree of prosperity followed World War II, but that was short-lived too, and some services had to be dropped.

The first to go was the *Columbian* in the mid-50's, after a long career of whistle stops across the country. The steam locomotives puffed their last breath in 1957, and the last passenger train, the *Olympian* Hiawatha, passed through the Bitterroots in May of 1961 after various incentive fares failed to boost business. Electrified locomotives were also doomed—after 57 years of service, the railroad announced on February 20, 1973, that the wires would be torn down and that fall the era of electrification ended.

The orange and black diesel engines pulled carloads of Montana grain, lumber from the Northwest, and new automobiles from Detroit through the Bitterroots in the 1970's. In fact, more freight passed through then than the line ever handled. But the future of the railroad and the future of Avery as a railroad town are still the subject of rumors galore. The economics of the line have continued to be grim, unfortunately. The big roundhouse once bustling with activity is gone. Property such as the substation may be for sale, as Milwaukee is unable to pay its bills. Frequent derailments in the area have been costly and discouraging.

The final chapter for the Milwaukee Road is no longer rumor. Its third bankruptcy, filed in December, 1977, cited the cause as reduced shipments of grain, bad weather, and other reasons. The expensive crossings of three mountain ranges in areas that produced little or no revenue could be abandoned. While forty percent of the line lies west of Butte, only six percent of the Road's revenue came from that section. The final ruling on Milwaukee's plan to abandon its line west of Butte awaited ruling by the Interstate Commerce Commission but the last train passed through on March 17, 1980.

The end of the Milwaukee Road through Avery will be more than the end of an era. It will mean closing the door on the chapter of history that made Avery and opened the St. Joe to thousands of travelers. The line's pride and the achievements will be no more than memories, and the sixth transcontinental railroad will join other relics of the past in the annals of history.

Since the time the first surveyors recommended it as a division point, Avery has been a railroad town. A Little Joe stops in front of the depot in this 1969 photo. A few years later, the electrics ceased operating, and the existence of the line became questionable. (Steinheimer)

6 Barrooms, Bootleggers, and Bad Guys

If there was anything the railroad workers wanted most, it was probably beer and whiskey. Soon saloons popped up like spring mushrooms in every nook and cranny of the upper St. Joe. The budding town of "North Fork" (Avery) had the "49" Saloon and Sporting House, as houses of prostitution were called in those days, located near the mouth of the North Fork on Sam "49" Williams' homestead. Another saloon stood at the mouth of Miller Creek, about three miles up the North Fork. Grand Forks, Adair, and other towns in between all had spots to quench one's thirst. The Loop at the mouth of Loop Creek was downright notorious for such operations.

In 1911 the '49' Saloon and sporting house stood in East Avery next to the tracks and below the present road. The '49' was the subject of such controversy that saloonkeepers Reid and Danke were jailed as a result of a 1912 court case. Note the barberpole above the left door. (U.S.D.A., Forest Service)

With a license such saloons were not illegal until 1911, but as early as 1908 saloonkeepers were raising the ire of officials for operating without a permit. Two saloonkeepers named Culhane and Hanson from Grand Forks applied for a roadhouse permit in the spring of 1908 and were closed down two months later for not conducting business in "an orderly and legal manner." Even a hearing before the U.S. Commissioner did not deter them, and they reopened immediately. In Adair two more men ousted the belongings of a third man from his cabin on a mining claim and set up saloon operations. And in "North Fork" Tom Martin was ordered to close the 49 Saloon on or before July 15, 1909.

These joy-juice problems were brewing when the cork popped on the issue. United States statutes went into effect in the beginning of 1911 restricting the sale of alcohol on National Forest land. This put the Forest Service in the predicament of enforcing a most unpopular law in a rugged area inhabited by a few miners, lumberjacks, and hundreds of railroad workers.

The saloons were to close January 1. The proprietors of the 49 Saloon told their Avery friends to bring bottles, jars, and jugs to empty the stock. The forest officials were optimistic when the saloons appeared to be closed. But within three weeks official correspondence on the subject began to flow as freely as the booze still was. Stores were being opened as a cloak for more lucrative trade, and whiskey was being dispensed all along the CMPS line. The 49 Saloon explained that since it hadn't been able to get rid of all its stock, of course it had to continue sales. At Grand Forks, Basil Rizzonelli hoped to get a patent to a mining claim which would permit him to open a saloon semi-legally. In the meantime, he was receiving strange barrels of freight with the shipper's name obliterated.

Officials were particularly perturbed by the 49 Saloon business going on right under their noses, and some local residents even complained. Lee Setzer and Billy Lynch had already left the country for Eureka, Montana, because of trouble over the 49. Then a popular pair took over. George "Fuzzy" Reid had decided to stay in the upper St. Joe after finishing the steel work on the railroad. He enjoyed singing opera and had been well-educated. He had only one ear; he'd lost the other after a particularly wild party when he rode a rotary to Saltese, jumped off, and fell under it. Today Fuzzy Peak bears his name, but in 1911 he and his partner, Fred "Dutch" Danke, were best known for keeping the firewater flowing in Avery.

No one from the Forest Service knew exactly how to handle the offenders. W.C. Weigle, the Forest Supervisor at the time, felt that the Forest Service should either proceed with vengeance or "leave the saloons have full sway and leave the country when their business ceases to be profitable." Besides that, the 49 Saloon posed a special problem, for the land of Sam "49" Williams' estate was in question. It was as yet unclaimed by Williams' heirs—so the question was did it revert to National Forest land and fall under Forest Service jurisdiction? What about land not owned by the government? Could the alternate sections of land belonging to Northern Pacific operate saloons?

If the Forest Service was going to proceed with vengeance, then how were they going to catch Reid and Danke? Ranger Henry Kottkey was continually frustrated in his attempts to catch the saloons in operation. The railroaders not only supported the places; they unloaded the whiskey at the yards and brought it on the front of the switch engine to the 49 to avoid the agent and his records. Then the Forest Service rangers devised a plan to catch the offenders. The rangers from another area would allow their beards to grow, disguise themselves in raggedy clothes, and walk to Avery down the tracks from Falcon. They would cash a check at the saloon and buy some drinks. Then the jaws of the trap would snap shut. Clever, right? Wrong. Someone alerted Reid and Danke, and the only response the rangers got was the sound of a bolt locking the door in their faces. Through the window they saw men playing dice.

Eventually, though, the officials drummed up witnesses, and in May of 1912, a year and a half after the law went into effect, George alias Fuzzy Reid and Fred Danke stood trial in St. Maries. Danke pleaded guilty and was fined $150 and sentenced to sixty days in jail. Reid pleaded not guilty and a trial proceeded. Some of the witnesses were Avery rangers W.H. Daugs and W.H. Rock, Forest Guard T.C. Wurth, and Gene and Jess Turner, the unwilling witnesses. The jury found Reid guilty and he was sentenced to three and a half months in jail.

So that ended the 49 Saloon. However, it did not end illegal liquor in Avery. In 1919 prohibition of alcohol became an amendment to the United States Constitution, and nationwide the effect was an actual stimulant to the forbidden fruits of drinking. Bootleg Creek, flowing into the 'Joe, got its name for obvious reasons, and bootlegging thrived all over. Packer Bobby Stauffer, who supplemented his income with the sale of booze, especially worked in the vicinity of the old St. Joe Quartz Mine and in Bird Creek. His sugar and corn came in on the train and he packed it by horseback to his hideout which he moved from time to time. Bootleggers with their "blind pig" (illegal liquor) operations distilled moonshine at Marble Creek and Hoyt Flat; at Kelley Creek the steam from Arch Smith's still could be seen by local residents. In the '20's the restaurant now known as the Log Cabin Inn was owned by A.B. "Blackie" Beales who sold his bootleg whiskey and the services of shady ladies. This form of advertisement for his establishment was written on the hewed wall on the cabin at Bootleg Creek:

A.B. Beals—
Square deals
Squawks and squeals
Shoes, booze and screws.

The reputation of that place improved when the Stanley family bought it—but its name didn't. Because the family had a baby the business was nicknamed "The Dirty Diaper."

"A still huddled furtively in every draw along the St. Joe River in 1927," writes Thelma Cramp. "Every time

James Peterson, a friend of the Setzers of Setzer Creek, poses with a "blind pig" (illegal liquor operation) near Bird Creek in 1914. Harold Theriault is on the left, Bobby Stauffer playing "revenooer" on the right. "Blind pigs" flourished on the St. Joe after liquor sales were banned in the National Forest in 1911 and during Prohibition. (Theriault)

a batch was run off, you should have heard the yipping and yelling and whooping and the cracking of pistols. 'Yippee! Yahoo! Crack, crack!' We had just moved onto the Jim Montgomery place (near Bellows Hill) and the Benton boys had a still in the place that Dad later called the Cattle Chute Draw. I must admit that Dad (Harris Bellows) didn't object too much at first to this state of affairs because he wasn't adverse to accepting a shot of mash. One day he was working on the field hauling stumps while the Benton boys ran off a batch. Dad was probably anticipating a cup of brew when the yahooing started and the pistols started cracking. Suddenly a bullet whizzed past his ear—and that ended *that*. He removed the still, and later on when the CCC built the road, they put in the cattle chute."

The Twenty-first Amendment in 1933 brought beer back at a time when business everywhere needed a boost. The legal sale of beer stimulated business in Avery. At one time seven different bars served Averyites, among them the Antlers Bar in Kelley Creek. Though no drugstore, hotel, or grocery store exists now, many of the community's laughs go on over a beer.

Now called the Log Cabin Inn, the Riverside Gardens was once owned by Blackie Beales, a well-known bootlegger. At the time this picture was taken in 1934, the establishment owned by the Stanleys, was nicknamed "the Dirty Diaper." The Log Cabin is now owned and managed by the Dick Parker family. (Lindow)

The Avery Trading Post, pictured here in the 1950's, has been a popular hangout for Avery people for many years. It has been owned by Bud Pears, Wally Moore, Sam Salla, Frances Spiesman, and Barbara Abramson. (Lindow)

BAD GUYS

Sometimes there have been people in the valley who did not make anyone laugh. Take Harry Orchard, for instance. A name that sent chills down the spines of Idahoans, the name of the calm, cold-blooded murderer who nonchalantly took the lives of 27 people. The man who dynamited the ex-governor of Idaho, Frank Steunenberg, in half; the man whose trial involved the issues of claim-jumping, and the nation's labor movement. The man whose trial commanded the efforts of none other than the famous criminal lawyer, Clarence Darrow.

What possible connection could this man have with the history of the St. Joe? On the other side of the mountains in 1898 in the Coeur d'Alene mines, labor problems were brewing. Into the scene came one milkman, alias wife-deserter and petty thief, as a new miner—Harry Orchard. When miners wanted to make a point about poor working conditions and set off the dynamite that destroyed the Bunker Hill and Sullivan concentrator at Wardner, Idaho, it was Harry Orchard who set off some of the charges. Idaho Governor Steunenberg, although backed by labor, called in federal troops to restore order and was thereafter branded a traitor by the Western Federation of Miners. Some of the miners involved fled over the mountains to avoid arrest. Out of Wallace they followed the Slate Creek trail, to Charlie Hoyt's homestead, then went high into Fishhook country. They hid away in a small cabin on an unnamed creek and had their supplies discretely packed in. The creek today bears the name *Outlaw Creek*.

Harry Orchard, an ubiquitous man, was active in areas other than Idaho. He left the St. Joe for the mines of Cripple Creek, Colorado, and casually set off a bomb at the railroad depot there which killed 13 miners and mangled 24 others. With the backing of the Western Federation of Miners, he plotted vengefully to kill judges and the ex-governors of both Colorado and Idaho. Failing with both of these plots, in Colorado, he came to Idaho, set his plans for Gov. Steunenberg in Caldwell, and later had a week's hunting trip with Jack Simpkins at Marble Creek. (Simpkins and Steve Adams were later accused of killing Marble Creek claim-jumpers Boule and Tyler.) Orchard's plot against Steunenberg was successful on December 20, 1905, in Caldwell, and he was arrested several days later.

Clarence Darrow, labeled as America's greatest criminal lawyer, came to Boise and later to Wallace and Hayden Lake in the complicated trials that followed. He defended the president of the Western Federation of Miners, Big Bill Haywood, who was accused of plotting the murders. Then he defended Steve Adams in the murder trial involving the claim-jumpers at Marble Creek. Orchard spent the rest of his life in prison and died in 1954 as the oldest prisoner in the United States. While his part in the history of the St. Joe was minor, certainly Outlaw Creek carries a bit of the Old West in its heritage. To add to the intrigue, legend says that Orchard and his cronies stored their guns in a hollow cedar tree. They have never been found. . .

The Coeur d'Alene mining district drew all sorts of fortune-seekers, not all exactly desirable. Wyatt Earp and his two brothers opened up the White Elephant Saloon out of a tent in Eagle City in 1884. That spring they engaged in a gunfight over a town lot in Eagle City with another notorious character, William Buzzard, who later found his way down to Pierce. In the south end of the Avery District, there is a spot known as Buzzard's Roost. Since no buzzards have ever been known to be in that area with the exception of William Buzzard, possibly that is how the place got its name. And the neighboring point? "Getaway Point."

Another "bad guy" hid out in the back country of the St. Joe in the 1930's. A Forest Service employee, Guy Lovely, left a blister rust camp and came to Avery for a break. For some reading material he picked up a detective magazine at Theriault's drugstore. Inside the magazine was a picture of Baby Face Nelson, who bore a striking resemblance to the man working as a dishwasher at the blister rust camp. The dishwasher mysteriously left soon after, fading out as inconspicuously as he had come.

To quench the thirst of hundreds of construction workers during the building of the railroad, rough shacks and tent saloons like the Summit Bar, located on the Idaho–Montana divide near the wagon road connecting Taft, Montana, and Grand Forks, Idaho, were built. (Clark)

The town of Taft, Montana, established in 1907 as a railroad supply town, attracted adventurers from all parts of the country and soon became one of the most notorious places in the West. Women of the underworld, gamblers, and other shady types flocked there. Taft was almost entirely destroyed by fire on August 13, 1908. As the town burned, the liquor stock in the saloons was carried into the streets and broken open, and when daylight broke the place was seething with drunken men and women, who reeled cursing and shrieking around the flames, reported the Wallace Times. *Taft was quickly rebuilt, only to be destroyed again by the Big Blow-up of 1910. (Clark)*

7 The Devil's Broom: Fire in 1910

The St. Joe Valley in 1910 was rich with promise. Prospectors and miners had staked claims here and there, while homesteaders had staked their high hopes on the lush stands of white pine. The country had been opened up by the new transcontinental railroad; the potential was there. But one circumstance led to another, and the very presence of man in the Bitterroots set the stage for a tragedy. To say that a great many dreams went up in smoke is an understatement, for when the Great Idaho Fire of 1910 struck, it wiped out more than dreams. With demonic fury, the fire destroyed timber, property, and human lives. The face and fate of the St. Joe were altered irreparably after August 20, 1910, the day of the big blow-up.

Many stories have been written about the fire of 1910, and several of these have grown into legends or even myths. It is not our intent to dispute any of these stories, but instead we hope to add to the general knowledge of that disaster. We have relied on Forest Service reports, firsthand accounts, and written articles of the day for primary sources, rather than previously published works. Our focus is on the fire in the Avery area, not on its effects in other sections of Idaho and Montana. Although the basic story has been repeated several times, no history of the swiftwater country would be complete without it. The deaths, the impact, the intense drama are part of Avery's story.

What came to be known as the Big Blow-up was the culmination of many separate fires burning in the whole area of the northern Rocky Mountains that summer. The winter of 1909-10 had not been unusually dry, but little rain fell to green up the hillsides in the spring. Instead, scorching winds swept out of the Columbia Basin, through the Palouse country and up into the canyons. They burned up crops, dried up creeks and rivers, and whipped the forests into a tinderbox. The record-breaking heat of May and June seared what was left, and lightning storms with little or no rain struck with regularity throughout June and July. A bad storm on July 15 ignited more than three thousand fires, making 1910 officially one of the worst fire seasons on record and one of the driest summers known to the Forest Service in northern Idaho.

The weather tindered the fuel for the impending disaster, but it took man to light the match. Records indicate the vast majority of the fires were man-caused: over 80 percent of the 219 reported fires on the Coeur d'Alene Forest, of which the St. Joe was a part then,

were traced to careless logging, homesteaders, recreationalists and even arsonists. The biggest cause by far, however, was the railroad. The newly constructed Chicago, Milwaukee, and Puget Sound Railway, which was completing bridge and fill work through the summer of 1910, was responsible for a large number of fires in Montana as well as along the St. Joe, North Fork and Loop Creek drainages. A 1911 report by Roscoe Haines, acting Forest Supervisor of the Coeur d'Alene, stated that over one hundred fires started along the Milwaukee Road's right-of-way in that forest alone. The right-of-way clearing built up the fuels, and the coal-powered locomotives set them off. To combat the problem, the railroad hired spotters to walk the tracks and extinguish flare-ups. Most of the time they were successful in curbing the small fires under ten acres. As the summer grew hotter and drier, the number and intensity of fires resulted in a shift of manpower from the bridge and fill construction to containing fires.

The railroad and settlers were not the only new additions to the valley; the Forest Service was an infant itself. It was only five years old and burdened with a tremendous task. The Northern Rocky Mountain Region stretched over Idaho, Montana, Washington and North Dakota. It included 22 national forests and forty million acres, an area as big as a few New England states and New York combined. This meant that each man hired by the Forest Service was responsible for 250,000 to 400,000 acres! In no conceivable way could the fledgling operation be geared up to fight a massive fire; thus many fires were ignored for weeks. Even if the manpower had been available, there was no bank of previous experience on which to rely. No lookouts existed and only intermittent patrols reported new outbreaks. Maps were not drawn of some parts of the St. Joe until 1914. No reserve fire equipment was on hand, so hardware stores in the area were soon cleaned out of shovels, axes, and camp supplies. Locally, Cliff Theriault recalls that the Avery district had forty hand shovels, ten axes, five cross-cut saws, ten grubhoes, four horses, bedding for four men, and no supplies. Pack horses were so scarce that Ranger Ralph Debitt hired Bobbie Stauffer and fifteen-year-old Theriault to haul supplies to the fire camp on Skookum Creek by canoe.

Although hundreds had been recruited, the average was only one man per fire; still the men on the ground did what they could. These were by no means professional firefighters. They had come from everywhere. Many were European immigrants. One victim at the Bullion mine was from Persia; some had come from the mines in Butte; others were straight off Spokane's skid row. Some were local men who had volunteered or been forced to duty in the emergency. In some instances brothers fought side by side, but no family was as involved as the Theriault family. All four brothers and three uncles had supporting roles in the drama that nearly destroyed the family property.

The Forest Service fire-fighters were paid 25 cents an hour, plus room and board that was at best basic. The standard bed was one shoddy blanket or cheap soogan (a feather-filled quilt). The basic board was sourdough: for breakfast, sourdough pancakes; for

Fresh from the night train, these firefighters were getting ready to face the Setzer Creek fire burning northwest of Avery. Picked off the streets of Spokane or Butte, they came ill-dressed and poorly equipped to fight fire. (U.S.D.A., Forest Service)

lunch, sourdough pancakes with a chunk of ham or bacon, for dinner, sourdough pancakes or potatoes and lots of canned tomatoes. There was always coffee and occasionally canned peaches. The first men to be hired were the ones with decent shoes and their own bedrolls, but after awhile that didn't matter. Men of every description were put on the firelines.

Not everyone who fought the fire had been hired by the Forest Service, however. To protect their property, the railroads, the mining and timber companies, and the timber protection associations had hired their own men that summer. Various homesteaders and loggers also joined the ranks. The efforts of all these men, scattered in several main crews throughout the valley, had paid off even after August 10 when a new batch of fires sprouted. On August 19, most of them were under control.

Then the winds came. A gale from the southwest whipped little fires into bigger ones, all the way from the Salmon River to the Canadian border. For two days the wind howled and the flames spread. A threatening haze hung low in the valley; the sky turned dull and yellow. Crews setting up camp at four

o'clock on Saturday, August 20, worked in the dark, and conductors on the passenger trains lit their lanterns hours earlier than usual. Some observers saw a great white pillar of a cloud, much like the steam cloud of a volcano. The air felt electric, tense, and suddenly ominously still. The red sun glared from behind a black wall of smoke.

That was when the tornado wind hit. Within seconds the many fires were one giant monster, thirty to fifty miles wide, gobbling up the land in seventy-mile per hour strides. The winds in front of it jerked up trees by the roots and hurled them like toothpicks, while the massive fireball leapt from ridge to ridge. Indeed, "all hell broke loose."

With the scarcity of horses, firefighters hiked long distances by foot. This crew was led by Ernie Bell who is holding the horses. On the right with the white shirt is Ranger Ralph Debitt, the only other identified individual. (Theriault)

MONUMENTAL BUTTES—FORTY-NINE MEADOWS

The fire gained its momentum on the Nez Perce National Forest, grew east of St. Maries, and surged to the northeast. At that time, the Monumental Buttes—Forty-Nine Meadows area was on the Clearwater Forest under the jurisdiction of Ranger Ashley Roche. Roche, whose career had only begun July 1, was responsible for a district which included parts of the St. Maries River and Marble Creek plus the entire drainage of the Little North Fork of the Clearwater River—some 500,000 acres. His first project on the job had been fighting the fire in the southern part of his district in cooperation with the Clearwater Association, a timber protection group. On July 15 he headed for the Monumental Buttes in the central part of his district where he found fourteen or fifteen large fires. He went to the Forty-Nine Meadows fire next. His only access was the Old Montana Trail, and that didn't even reach the timber stands where the fires were.

A young single woman from Moscow, Idaho, Miss Iona Adair, had staked a homestead at Forty-Nine Meadows. She was staying with a neighbor, Mrs. Taylor, in July of 1910. "During the daytime," she recalled, "it was quite cloudy, hazy. Of course, we'd never been in the woods and never been near the fire, had no idea, really, what to expect in that section of the country." The women were leaving to ask the other homesteaders what they thought of the mysterious haze when a knock came on their cabin door. It was Ashley Roche, wanting to know if there were any trails going further east.

"And he said, 'We have a crew of fourteen men out here and they haven't had breakfast yet. . .Will you get something for these men to eat while we pack on in to the fire.' So we went over with them. And that was our first experience with the fire: going with the packhorses and going with these men and packing across the river and getting a campfire set up, and cooking potatoes for fourteen men. Do you have any idea how many potatoes fourteen men eat?"

Essentially, Roche commandeered the women to cook for the crew of fourteen men and sixty prisoners released from short-term sentences in Missoula to fight fire. For the next few weeks, Mrs. Taylor and Iona would be confined to firecamp, unable to return to their homesteads or notify their families of their whereabouts. All trails into the area were closed so that Miss Adair's father was not allowed in to get her. For an entire month he knew nothing of the fate of his daughter.

As for Ashley Roche, he had experienced quite an initiation to the Forest Service. He was forced to build miles of trail to reach the Forty-Nine Meadows fire. A crew was sent by Ranger Debitt from Avery to help, and another crew was en route from Spokane. Without communication and instructions, the Spokane crew could not find Roche in the wilderness, so hc was forced to leave the fireline and meet the group in St. Maries. Transportation was another problem—how was he to get the men to the woods? It took an additional day or more to hire pack strings out of Fernwood and Moscow.

What must have been extreme pressure for Ranger Roche was excitement for Iona Adair.

"A great deal of excitement because you never knew when you got up in the morning whether the wind was bringing the fire your way or taking it some other way. And you always had guards out. In case the wind changed, they'd come back into camp and notify us, and we'd cross the river and go on the other side and stay until the wind had changed its position so they felt we could go back to the other side. . .It was exciting, very exciting. You never knew whether you were going to be in your own bed that night or a grass bed or sleeping next to the horses. . ."

At this time black men joined the fire-fighting battle on the Little North Fork. Some had come as a part of the Twenty-Fifth Infantry of Fort Wright, others were from Butte, and a few were short-term prisoners out of Missoula. Not only were blacks rare to the North Idaho area, but there was an undercurrent of distrust about their presence. Typical of black history, the following headline echoed that prejudice: *(Daily Idaho Press,* Aug. 29, 1910) WHITE MEN BREAK NEGRO FIREFIGHTERS AT CRAPS. Under prospector-crew leader Con Faircloth were fifty men, fourteen of whom were black. Faircloth told reporters:

"There were no better fire-fighters picked up anywhere than the Negroes. They worked willingly during the day and at night they made the mountain echo with their songs. . .They began shooting craps around the camp fires in the evening but some white man won all their money and the Negroes spent the rest of time shooting craps for matches. . .The papers said that these men were a bad lot, but I did not find them so. Of the fifteen Negroes who were sent out on the fire line only one was a dope fiend, and he did not leave Avery."

Faircloth also recalled a black man named Sunny Jim. Thirteen-year-old Harold Theriault was working as a messenger boy under Ranger Debitt when Sunny Jim, a freed slave, came to sign for his pay. Theriault recalled that he had no last name and laboriously put his X on the line.

Iona Adair was a bit more nervous about the black short-term prisoners for whom she cooked. One man came back to the fire camp during the day instead of working. He asked if she could really fire the pistol she always wore strapped to her side. He put up a tomato can to see if she could hit the tomato.

"So I got Betsy all ready and I said to Betsy, 'Good Lord if you ever helped me, help me now,' and I shot and hit the tomato on that can. And he looked at me and he said, 'You can use that thing.' And I said, 'Yes, I can use that thing.' I said goodbye and that was the last time he ever came into camp."

Another blaze broke out east of Clarkia at Gold Center and spread to join the one at Forty-Nine Meadows just as Roche's crew thought it was under control. Then the situation became hopeless. The growing fire had raced across the Clearwater Forest; the flames and wind surged ahead and pulled other fires into its vacuum. The Monumental Buttes, Forty-

These two forest guards played important roles during the 1910 fire. Harvey Fern, on the right, was in charge of the 49 Meadows fire. On the left stands Lee Hollingshead who lost several men from his crew on Big Creek. Many of the men in charge of large crews were in their early twenties. (U.S.D.A., Forest Service)

Nine Meadows, and Camp de Miserie fires had joined up with the dragon. The big conflagration had also run into the Little North Fork, and the fiery thing was beyond the control of mankind. Realizing the danger, Ranger Debitt sent word with Eddie Theriault to Roche's crew to evacuate. As the inferno passed through, the Theriault family was convinced that 18-year-old Eddie was gone forever, especially when his uncle Frank Theriault searched over the smoldering Dago Creek trail and burned his horse's feet. Nearly a week later Eddie returned with the troops under the command of Ranger Fern. At midnight they walked triumphantly up the tracks from Hoyt's Flat to Avery, safe and singing. Eddie's role in evacuating the troops was as much an act of heroism as any in the fire.

Meanwhile, Iona Adair had still not notified her father that she was alive and well. She walked 28 miles to Avery and safety, accompanied by a man also planning to catch a train out of the fire-swept country. Her hair and eye brows were singed, and the riding skirts she had worn for days were greasy and smoky.

Con Faircloth and his crew of blacks had thought the fire was under control too, "especially when it snowed one night." But then the terrific winds had come, forcing them to evacuate before any lives or property were lost. Ranger Roche's big district was badly burned, but the blow-up had not logged any fatalities there.

BIG CREEK

Ranger Edward Pulaski of Wallace was in charge of about 150 men spread out over the divide between Big Creek of the Coeur d'Alene River and Big Creek of the St. Joe River. Fleeing from the St. Joe Big Creek burn, his immediate crew was at Placer Creek a short distance south of Wallace. An old Texas ranger and Indian Scout on the crew, S.W. Stockton, remembers: "Saturday evening a regular hurricane sprung up and in a moment the fire had broken over the branches and was in every direction about us. . .One cannot imagine what a roar of wind there was in those small canyons. The mountainsides were aflame and trees were falling in all directions about us, faster than one could count. The noise of falling trees only added to the din. It was terrible. In this frightful confusion we tore along single file with Pulaski at the head. At times it would seem that the canyon in front of us was blocked with flame. Then Pulaski would order us to halt. He would take a gunnysack, soak it with water, place it over his head, dash through the smoke down the trail to see if the coast was clear."

Pulaski's heroism and knowledge of the area led the crew to a mine tunnel on Placer Creek just before the fire reached them. One man was too slow and was burned beyond recognition before he could reach the tunnel, but 41 others and two horses made it. As the air was replaced by smoke in the tunnel, the men lost consciousness. They were there for five hours.

"Two men died under me," Stockton told reporters, "and when I regained consciousness I was lying on their bodies. One of the horses fell dead in front of us; his dead body backed up the water so that there was nearly a foot of it where we lay. The two men had their faces in the water and were drowned while they were unconscious. My face was buried in their bodies and it was by this means that I did not lose my life."

When the men regained consciousness, most were dazed and bewildered. "We were all paralyzed and couldn't use our limbs so we floundered along on the ground," survivor Vic Grantham explained. "Someone helped me into the water of the creek. I remember there was a big snag just above me that was burning and threatening to fall onto me. I didn't care at the time whether it fell or not. I just sat and looked at it." Stockton pleaded with other people on the crew to give him a drink of water, offering them a dollar for a drink until he realized they were as bad off as he was.

After a while the crew regained their wits and straggled toward Wallace. They took a toll of the damages. The smoke had partially blinded Pulaski and damaged the lungs of many of the men. It was here that the list of dead began: five had died from suffocation and one burned to death. But Ranger Pulaski was credited with saving 36 lives.

Under Pulaski's leadership was John Bell and his crew of fifty working at the head of the Middle Fork of Big Creek (St. Joe drainage). The terrific wind struck them at four o'clock that afternoon with such intensity that it overturned and snapped off practically every tree around them. Barely a minute later the huge fire was devouring the rest of the forest. Bell's crew raced for safety—a two-acre clearing by the homestead cabin of Joseph Beauchamp which would normally have been a safe enough place. Most of the men dove face down into the small stream flowing through the clearing. Seven others fled to a small dug-out about five feet deep that Beauchamp had used as a vegetable cache.

The flames raged at the men, sweeping over them from both sides, roaring with a vengeance they'd never forget. It was a night of horror; first the furnace-like heat, then unusual cold. One of the firefighters, David Bailey, later recalled:

"It was while holding a covering over my head that I burned my hands. We were in the creek for about two hours, I believe, and we were all shaking from the cold as though we were suffering from the fever when we piled out. It was pretty tough up on the summit without any covers and soaked to the skin. One of the boys contacted pneumonia. . ."

All were burned on their faces, their hair was burned off, the skin scorched on their necks. Three men also had broken legs caused by falling trees. Bailey and most of his fellow workers in the stream at least lived to tell about it. Not so the crew members who tried to escape the jaws of fire in Beauchamp's little cellar. All seven were, in Bailey's words, "cooked alive. All of them tried to get at the very end of the small hole and they were piled up in an awful heap. It was impossible to take out their bodies, for they would fall to pieces." The rest of the crew had endured the screams of the dying men.

The death count mounted still higher here; three more men were killed in the stream by a huge falling tree. The first two died instantly but one lingered in agony for several hours. Among the ten who died were two Italians, one Austrian, one Canadian, and homesteaders Joseph Beauchamp and Roderick Ames. Ames had come from Kellogg the day before to bury his household articles on his homestead claim on Ames Creek. He had decided to stay and lend a hand to the crew, hoping to save his own timber. He lost much more than the timber . . . All but two were buried on the spot in a Christian service conducted by Reverend Carter, a Congregational minister from Wallace who came in with the rescue party the next day.

Another crew had come to Big Creek on the orders of Ranger Ralph Debitt. On August 12, the group had been pulled off the Skookum Creek fire and placed under the supervision of Lee Hollingshead, age 22, with Clifford Theriault as timekeeper. After a train ride from Avery to the Big Creek station, they walked nine miles up Big Creek to the West Fork and Grace Early's homestead. "Let me tell you, it wasn't all down hill either," says Theriault. They set up tents for the kitchen and bunkhouses but used the cabin as an office and prepared to confront the flames creeping in from Trout Creek to the northwest. The fire was about a mile away, and they too thought it had been controlled. But on the twentieth of August everything changed. All hell broke loose.

A homestead cabin served as headquarters for the West Fork of Big Creek (St. Joe drainage) fire crew. The sixty-man crew, headed by Lee Hollingshead, would tally eighteen dead. (Theriault)

"The pack train came in at noon with supplies," Theriault explains, "and then is when things began looking bad around our camp, the fire was burning on three sides of us. They quickly unpacked the horses and started for town. As a precaution we put the canned goods in the spring, filled buckets, tubs, tin cans, or anything around to put water on top of the cabin and barn. Before we got finished the wind started to blow, tearing six-inch limbs off the cedars, uprooting others, and twisting others in two."

How is it possible to imagine the emotions of people in a situation like that? Enclosed on three sides by fire whose roar could be heard for miles, trees thrust in the air, the pieces bursting and exploding all around—it had to be terrifying. Men all over the St. Joe reacted in different ways. Nineteen men on Lee Hollingshead's crew panicked. Instead of trying to reach Big Creek as Theriault's group did, they tore out ahead of the fire to Henry Dittman's homestead and into the cabin where five pack horses were stationed. When fire turned the roof of the cabin into a crematorium, the men tried to claw their way out through the wall of flames. It was too late. Eighteen of them died within a few feet of the cabin.

By a quirk of fate, the nineteenth man plunged through and survived. With the skin burned off his face and hands and his clothing nearly gone, he stumbled into St. Joe City two days later. Rescue crews returning to the Dittman homestead found the eighteen bodies in addition to five dead horses and a large black bear. Among the dead men were twin brothers Joe and James Denton. The site of these deaths now bears the name Deadman Gulch.

The rest of Hollingshead's crew headed for the fork of the creeks. As Clifford Theriault remembers it:

"There was a real timber-beast (lumberjack) in our crew, who was the one who decided when we would leave and where we would go. On the trail someone would holler and say, 'Let's go down to the creek as I think there's a falls,' and another would say, 'Let's go this way!' Finally the timber-beast said, 'We all came in here together, we are all going out together or we will all die together, and the next Son of a B. that wants to do something foolish, I'll plug him on the spot.' That settled it—we stayed together.

"When we got to the fork of the creeks we all began looking for some kind of a place for shelter. . .We also started a backfire but before it was as big as a bonfire the tops of the trees were burning.

"Lucky for us one of the packers who left camp ahead of us met the fire and let his pack train go and found a cave. How he ever saw or heard us I'll never know but he did and we twelve people crowded into a space about four by six by three. When eleven men and a boy crowd into a space that small, you might say they were like sardines in a can. (I was the boy; the day before was my fifteenth birthday.)

"We spent twelve hours in the cave, the first two very bad. I'm at a loss to explain how a human being could live in such terrible heat and smoke. It seemed every breath would be the last.

"An old fellow and I were on the open upstream side of the cave and every once in awhile the wind would change and a volley of flame and sparks would hit us. On the other side was loose shale rock. A burning tree came sliding down the hill and loosened the shale and the flame was coming in the cave and hitting the 'timber-beast' in the back.

"One fellow on the edge of the cave about two feet from the creek would dip his derby hat in the water every chance he could get and throw water on the rest of us. We held wet rags to our mouths and noses and you would be surprised how quickly they would dry out. Without my saying a word they would hand a fresh rag to the men in front of me and say, 'here is one for the kid.' I didn't dare take it away until I got a fresh one.

"After two hours of hellish heat we were able to breathe a little easier and say a few words. The old fellow next to me kept repeating, 'I wonder where Charley is.' Charley was his twin brother who was one of the packers that had left camp ahead of us.

"The next morning after much talk as to what we should do and what a hard time we were going to have getting out of there as the ground would still be burning and the creek bed would be impassable on account of fallen trees. We started for the St. Joe River and my friend of the night before met his twin. They rushed to each other, hugged and kissed. The walking was not as bad as expected. The ground was not burning and the trees were not piled up in the creek. However, it wasn't like strolling on a bridle path in Golden Gate Park either."

The Milwaukee Lumber Company was building a railroad into a large timber stand it had just purchased from the Forest Service on Big Creek when the fires hit. Nearly all of its large labor force had been trying to protect the tract of white pine all summer. On August 25 headlines in the *Daily Idaho Press* read, "FIVE HUNDRED MEN ESCAPE FROM THE BIG **CREEK FIRE—WERE ENGAGED IN FIGHTING** BLAZE FOR LUMBER COMPANY AND ALL FLEE AND SAVE LIVES." Out of ten camps seven were destroyed, and the 100 million board feet purchase was severely damaged. So was the pocketbook of the new Milwaukee Lumber Company—to the tune of a million dollars in marketing loss.

The group of survivors from the Big Creek burn trudged to one of the Milwaukee camps. In Theriault's words:

"Next we came upon a Milwaukee Lumber camp burned to the ground. They had put the canned goods in the creek before they left so we found something to eat, but were not able to keep it in our stomachs. We opened cans of tomatoes, peaches, pears—not one of us could keep from throwing up. It was due to the water we had been drinking the night before. It was a dirty brown color and very bad tasting due to the ashes.

"The lumber company had been using horses for logging and we passed many of them dead and bloated. Believe it or not, when we were within a mile of the St. Joe River there was a patch of green timber that hadn't burned the day before and it started to burn as we got near it. We didn't lose any time there and it really was going very strong before we got through."

But the group did get through to the railroad station at Big Creek. What they left behind was devastation. "Where before was one of the most magnificent forests in the United States there is now nothing but a blackened wilderness. Not even a bird hovers over the fire-swept hills of that district. . .The great trees have been uprooted by the wind and cast down by the fires, making it a most dreary-looking scene." *Daily Idaho Press,* August 27, 1910.

AND ON UPRIVER. . .

The fire acted like a tornado. It swooped without mercy on one stand of timber, then by-passed the next one. It sometimes traveled a mile with one leap and bounded from one ridge to the next without touching the bottom of the valley. For some reason it snubbed the Marble Creek area. Homesteads were left intact, their owners leaving without any problem. Many returned later to fight small fires and even brought in election supplies for the primary election that Tuesday. (It is no wonder that election results were reportedly "light," however. With the world around them aflame, there was a good excuse for voter apathy!)

The firefighters on Slate Creek had no time for frivolous elections, for by six o'clock on Saturday they had been chased out. S.A. Lienlokker, the timekeeper for one crew, reported to the paper, "We were not able to stop until we had gone ten miles or so. Sunday morning we tried to return to Slate Creek and couldn't." Instead they walked out to Hoyt's Flat, on to Avery, and out on the train. Homesteader Fritz Uhlman and three other men spent the night in the creek to save their lives. All that was left to mark Uhlman's efforts in the Slate Creek area are two creeks that bear his name, Fritz Creek and Uhlman Creek. Homesteads such as his burned with such intense heat that even the kitchen range melted.

The big burn did not single out only homesteaders and timber owners for its abuse; mine owners and prospectors suffered as well. A group of prospectors at the Silica mine properties in the Loop Creek area escaped with their lives not just once but twice. They had gone peacefully to bed that Saturday night ". . .when the fire came on us. It was traveling then at a rate of not less than forty miles an hour. It was about ten o'clock that I awoke and got up, going to the door to see how things looked. I saw the fire right at hand. I yelled to the men, 'For God's sake, get out of here!' We grabbed a few of our clothes and ran.

"We went to Avery that night and stayed all night. Sunday the wind seemed quiet and we returned to the Silica. We found things in horrible shape there. All the timber had been burned off the claims, causing a damage of about $40,000. There are not a dozen trees in fifteen square miles that will live. There is not enough live timber left on the Silica to furnish two sets of timber for the tunnel."

Then came their second escape. Because two of the prospectors were relatives of Falcon Ranger Henry Kottkey, they went to his ranger cabin for the noon meal. As they were eating, the darkness closed in so that they had to light a lamp to see their food.

"Soon we saw the fire coming right through there and we all lit out up the track. About a half-mile up the track we came to this water tunnel. We went in there.

The smoke became so bad that we nearly suffocated from the gas and we lay two hours on our faces in the mud," said Kottkey. Small wonder that the prospectors sang on their way to Wallace on Tuesday. "I want to be congratulated on getting out of that alive," William Sites, one of the fortunate Silica employees, exclaimed.

The Bird Creek fire camp was manned out of Avery. Ranger Ralph Debitt is pictured in the right foreground. Local homesteaders including Jesse Turner, on the far left, and Eugene Turner, far right, assisted in the fire-fighting effort. (Theriault)

All of Ranger Kottkey's belongings, his newly built St. Joe Ranger Station, and his home at Falcon, were destroyed. He was not at home at the time; he was at Bird Creek—lying in a creek with eighteen men. (His crew included Eugene and Jesse Turner, homesteaders of Turner Flat.) According to the *Spokesman-Review*, August 22, "Two of the fighters (from a camp of two hundred) took a horse and, riding the animal to death, reached another camp and organized a rescue party, which penetrated the fire to Bird Creek." On August 24, Kottkey's crew straggled out to Saltese. Their loss was sixteen pack horses. All two hundred men reportedly under his jurisdiction were safe.

Young Ranger James Danielson, age 22, had his share of problems near Stevens Peak, a part of the Avery District but geographically closer to Mullan. Realizing that he and his crew of eighteen were surrounded on four sides by fire, Danielson headed for an open area near timber line that was covered by beargrass. In a flash they burned off the beargrass, assuming that the burned-off area would protect them. Under normal circumstances that would have been the case, but this holocaust was hardly normal. It reburned the same place. The only protection each man had was a blanket as the fire seethed and raged over them. One man accidentally inhaled the flames and died immediately; another man leaped over a 35-foot cliff and sustained bad injuries.

Early Sunday morning Danielson, himself badly injured, stumbled with his crew into Mullan, a five-mile hike. The *Daily Idaho Press,* August 27, reported: "The most pitiful sight ever witnessed in Mullan

occurred Sunday morning when the fifteen survivors of the Boulder Creek (Stevens Peak) fire limped into town. All were staggering and all carried their arms in the air. They were badly burned and the only relief that could be obtained was by holding their arms up. Some of the men were blind from the flames that had burned them, and they held on to the men in front of them. They walked in single file and made a most distressing spectacle. They were so overcome they could not at first give a coherent account of what had happened. . .J.G. Danielson, the forestry official in charge of the crew, is deserving of the highest honors . . .he kept the men together and it is due to him that all but one escaped."

Meanwhile, the firefighters at Bullion Mine were startled by a two- or three-foot burning brand falling from the sky at 9:30 that Saturday night. By midnight the roar of the fire could be heard and there was just enough time to reach the mine tunnel. Fortunately, one crew member carried his blankets which he stretched across one small crosscut shaft stemming off the main tunnel. All but eight men huddled in this drift, and those eight died instantly. One man cried pathetically for help when he became wedged underneath a car in the tunnel, but the smoke was so stifling no one could help him. The sixteen survivors and their leader, S.M. Taylor, a prospector, made it out four hours later. They had been fighting the Bullion fire for two weeks on the Idaho side while Roy Phillips' crew of 25 tackled it from the Montana side.

It was Sunday night, August 21, when another group acted out their drama near the headwaters of the St. Joe. Mr. and Mrs. Pattison and six others were driven from their mining claims on Sherlock Creek by the fevered winds. As they fled, they had to lie flat on the ground every ten minutes in order to breathe because of the oppressive smoke. When their clothes began to smolder, they would hurry on down the trail. It was a night of extremes: the terrific heat was replaced by a dramatic drop of temperature that reached an unseasonable low. It was also a night of tragedy for one member of their party. Con Roberts, a wooden-legged prospector with the group, veered off the path to a clearing and was not seen again. Ironically, his cabin was not touched by the flames. Frank Heller, a prospector from Heller Creek in the same vicinity, lost everything but a badly singed, crippled setter dog that he carried out with him to Wallace.

A group of Forest Service firefighters were trapped on a tributary of Bean Creek near the headwaters of the St. Joe (the tributary was later named Halm Creek), and the question of their fate occupied front page headlines for a week. Ranger Joseph Halm had been a star college football player; his failure to report with his crew after the big blow-up made the story spicy reading. No one knew for sure if the extra crew of 65 had joined his initial crew of sixteen as had been planned; it was possible that eighty men had been roasted. On August 26, the papers erroneously reported that "Head Ranger Debitt Concedes the Death of Ranger Halm and His Party of 70 on the Headwaters of the St. Joe.''

What really happened to Halm was nearly as dramatic as the newspaper accounts. His crew of sixteen had been on the large Bean Creek fire since late July. On Sunday the ridges to the northwest were suddenly a mass of rolling flames. Three men frantically gathered their belongings to leave but Halm's order to stay was reinforced by his revolver. A sandbar in Halm Creek was their only refuge for the night as burning brands crashed over them. A large pine fell on the sandbar with such force that its blast of air knocked one man over. When they finally had a chance to leave, a freak wind forced the exhausted men to take shelter under a hollow bank. More trees crashed and toppled around them. Halm's two packers escaped by racing the fire out over the Bitterroot Divide, covering a phenomenal distance of forty miles over mountain peaks in less than six hours. Their pack string was destroyed but not one life was lost. It was impractical, if not impossible, to reach Halm from Avery so on August 27, Deputy Supervisor Roscoe Haines went into the Bean Creek area from Iron Mountain out of Missoula. He returned with the reassurance that the crew of sixteen (not seventy or eighty) and Halm were alive.

SETZER CREEK

In Avery action was building that would make a Hollywood disaster movie look tame. Ranger Ralph Debitt had two crews of seventy men each fending off the fire near the headwaters of the Setzer Creek area, three miles northwest of Avery. One had its camp on Storm Creek, three miles up on Section 29, to work on the west side of the fire; the second crew, headed by Assistant Ranger, William H. Rock, was settled on a ridge close to Cedar Mountain. The Storm Creek crew was left under the supervision of James Shehee while Debitt attended to the vast amount of fire business at the North Fork Ranger Station. Debitt found Avery buzzing with rumors about the fire racing upriver, and when severe winds blasted the town at about four o'clock Saturday afternoon, he realized things looked bad. He sent Ed Bessett and Henry Dittman, brother of Mrs. Mary Theriault, to bring the Setzer-Storm Creek crew out immediately.

Most of the seventy men, including Byron ''Doc'' Theriault who was the timekeeper, were relieved to go. One group of Butte copper miners and tough skid row characters growled with displeasure at Shehee's orders to evacuate. The big burly cook, Pat Grogan, flatly refused to go, and 27 of his followers also would not budge from a clearing they felt was safe. Avery's Deputy Sheriff Sullivan later remarked, ''The men were warned of the danger. Through a mistaken sense of bravery, they refused to leave.'' The main part of the large crew headed for Avery around 6:30 that evening, the flames traveling so fast after them that at times trees above their heads were on fire. They were singed and burned, and one man's shoes had burned through when they arrived at Avery.

These fire-fighters, fresh from the Butte mines and Spokane, were being served breakfast. The man in the cook's apron is Pat Grogan, leader of the men who burned on Storm Creek. The hazy outline of the Avery Ranger Station is in the background. (Theriault)

They were the lucky ones. Pat Grogan and his followers were cremated within seconds after the fire struck them. Grogan and his dog stood their ground at the camp site and died; his watch stopped at 7:27. The remains of the others dotted the canyon for half a mile. The one the longest distance from camp had added seven minutes to his life by running. His watch stopped at 7:34. Some had attempted to climb the canyon wall in their helpless flight. Burned flesh, skulls and skeletons were all that were left of most of the men. A few were found with their faces turned grotesquely backward toward the oncoming fire. Even the silver found in their pockets was melted, along with their watches and pocketknives.

It was a gruesome task that faced Ranger Debitt and Deputy Sheriff Sullivan when they later checked on the crew. Identity of many of the men was impossible, and only by timekeepers' records could any reckoning at all be taken. Many were Bulgarian and Austrian in nationality which posed additional problems for

Little remained of the Setzer Creek crew but charred flesh and a few personal possessions. These items were found on the bodies of the victims, and later they were displayed at the Avery and Missoula Forest Service offices. The coins were warped from the heat, and the glass melted from the pocketwatches. Note the time changes on the watches: one says 7:27 and the other, 7:33. (U.S.D.A., Forest Service)

The Devil's Broom: Fire in 1910

notifying next of kin. Burying the bodies was such an odious job that a young man eaten with sores from a chronic illness was hired for $25 a day. Twenty-four of the casualties were buried on Storm Creek and later removed to the St. Maries cemetery.

Debitt's second crew headed by William H. Rock was in danger too. Although a motley crew of green firefighters had arrived in Avery the night before, Debitt chose Harold Theriault to deliver the message to get out. "You're the only man I've got," Debitt told him. The local boy was proud to be chosen and knew the area well; he ran up the Cedar Mountain (Dunn Peak) trail and back so quickly that Debitt thought he had not even gone. The fire was just as fast—for before Rock's crew was able to reach Avery, the trail was cut off.

Assistant Ranger for the Avery District, William H. Rock, was in command of seventy men fighting the head of the Setzer Creek fire; their camp was located near Cedar Mountain at the origin of Hammond Creek. Rock's crew suffered one casualty, a suicide, en route to safety. Rock is shown cruising salvageable fire-killed timber that following year. (U.S.D.A., Forest Service)

This picture postcard, showing the ruins of the Storm Creek fire camp, was sent to Mrs. Mary Turner in Chicago. Ranger Debitt was in charge of this seventy-man camp, located near the headwaters of Storm Creek. Conflicting reports show that either twenty-eight or twenty-nine men died at this location. (Turner)

Rock was a 25-year-old man with responsibility for the lives of seventy men on his shoulders. Fortunately he knew the country well enough to lead the men to a burned-over area in a flat meadow just north of Avery. Here they were safe for the night with blankets over them. All night huge columns of smoke seething with fire brands passed over them and burst into flames that shot thousands of feet in the sky. Trees around the men exploded into fire, a sight frightening and awesome enough to shake the endurance of the heartiest of men. Oscar Weigert was so terrified he left the group, and the sound of two shots rang out. His body was discovered the next morning a couple miles from Avery on the east side of Setzer Creek. His death, thought to be suicide, was the only death among Rock's crew.

"The body of Weigert," stated the *Daily Idaho Press*, "the man who, while in a panic, shot himself, was brought into Avery. It was placed in a canvas tarp which was sewed (sic) together. The body was then lashed onto two poles which were attached to a horse and dragged Indian fashion behind. His trousers were burned on one leg but he was not burned. His face,

though, was badly blackened. . ." The five apartment buildings in East Avery were under construction at the time, and the one with the work bench was hastily transformed into a morgue. A wooden casket was built and Weigert was buried at the mouth of Forty-Nine Creek. His parents later moved his body to Missoula.

A RIDE THROUGH HELL

There were three major rescue runs on the railroad that Saturday night of August 20 in the Loop Creek area. At the risk of being overly descriptive, one must say that those train rides were daring, ridden with terror, and little short of miraculous. With the railroad construction still in progress, there were hundreds of people, perhaps even a thousand, between Haugan, Montana, and Avery. Workers were completing the bridge work and living in construction camps or with their families. Work trains, fire trains, and helper engines were scattered up and down the tracks, and Avery's roundhouse had several engines on hand. Few trails or roads provided a way out for the little railroad settlements of Stetson, Kyle, Falcon, Grand Forks, Adair, and Roland. The trains represented the only means of escape from the impending disaster.

All day Saturday the fires burned, but then that was nothing new. Grand Forks had already burned to the ground in July. Its notorious residents were undaunted by that fire and soon resumed the business of their shady night life from tents. They may have felt a little closer to the breath of Hell as the flames crept closer that August afternoon, though it was still nothing to worry about, no reason to evacuate. Then suddenly the hurricane winds moving at seventy miles per hour at times blasted the entire area into fire. The people

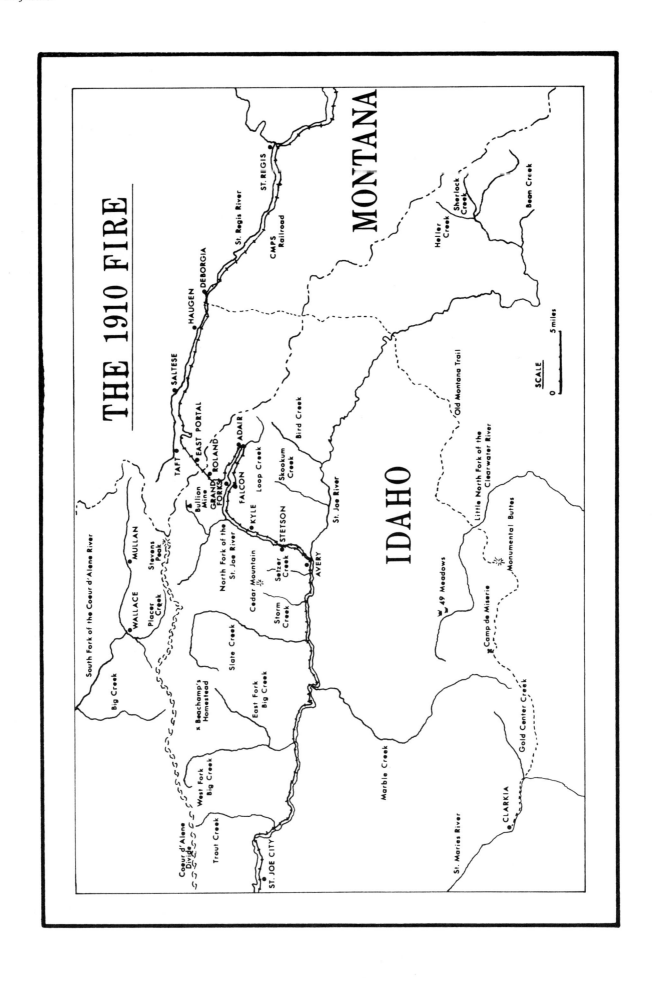

were instantly caught in a fiery deathtrap. The railroad that had brought them into the area had to get them out immediately. The prostitutes, gamblers, camp followers, and saloonkeepers wasted no time watching the fire brands ignite their tents. They hurried to the Falcon railway station nearby where the families of Falcon were already collecting.

There is conflicting information about the events of that evening. Several trains were shuttling back and forth, dodging burning trestles, and shooting blindly into tunnels for safety. The exact relationship of one happening to another is a matter of interpretation, but the happenings themselves are factual.

Nothing was terribly unusual about the jobs two different men were tackling that August afternoon. Division Superintendent C. H. Marshall was on a fire train putting out hot spots on bridges east of Falcon, and Engineer John Mackedon and his assistant Lew Bradway had taken a helper engine from Avery to boost the passenger train over St. Paul Pass. They were on their way back to the roundhouse at Avery when the operator at Kyle, Maud Martin, flagged them down. The operators at the Falcon station had sent an SOS: Grand Forks had already burned and the Falcon station was sure to go soon! Mackedon attached a boxcar to his engine and backed the six miles to Falcon to bring the people to Avery and safety. What had started as a routine run was to be the ride of their lives.

Mackedon pulled into the Falcon station to find dozens of panic-stricken people knotted on the platform. "The moment he stopped, his engine was besieged by people who climbed aboard or clung to it wherever they could find a place to take hold. . .(He) left Falcon with the car and engine packed with most of the survivors of the flaming town," stated Mackedon's obituary in the Deer Lodge, Montana, newspaper many years later.

The fire literally pounced on its victims. It was only a short time later that Maud Martin at Kyle found herself surrounded. She telephoned a message to Superintendent Marshall: "A big fire is sweeping down on us; what shall we do?" As if to verify her words, the wires went down before her question could be answered. Marshall did not know Mackedon had back-tracked to make a mercy run. Marshall would have to get the families out of Kyle; if his train were caught in that direction, at least the tunnels were longer and safer. Two trains were headed toward Avery: Mackedon's made it through but Marshall's did not.

Mackedon's run was far from a pleasure trip. Trees barred the path of the engine on its way to safety. The heat was so overpowering that he and Bradway stayed on their knees. Twice the engine was forced to stop at burning bridges which the men doused with water. When they had gone the seven miles to Kyle, they stopped to pick up Maud Martin and her family. On to Stetson. Was the high trestle between Kyle and Stetson still standing? It was; things were looking better. The engine whistled to a stop to rescue the section crew at Stetson who squeezed gratefully into whatever spot they could find on the crowded boxcar and engine.

They raced through the fire and smoke, timber blazing all around them in the narrow canyon of the North Fork. Avery was ahead; they ended the thirteen-mile run for their lives at two o'clock in the morning!

Superintendent Marshall was not so sure about his train. He had gone only a short distance west of Falcon when the tracks were cut off by fire. He ordered the engineer to pick up everyone along the tracks as the train turned to make a run for Tunnel 27, less than a quarter mile from Falcon. Several people along the right-of-way and the remaining residents of Falcon and Grand Forks jumped aboard. Everyone lay flat to escape the terrible heat.

"When Tunnel 27 was reached the cars were smoking and would probably have caught fire in a short time. Tunnel 27 is a short one, being but 365 feet in length, but it is located on a ten-degree curve and this is what undoubtedly saved the 167 people that were on the train with Mr. Marshall. It was impossible to stand outside the tunnel and observe the flames, as they were whipping past both entrances of the tunnel and rendered all passage suicidal. Mr. Marshall said: 'I will never forget that ride. Six or seven trees would fall at a time and every minute I expected one to roll across the track and cut off our avenue of escape. The scene beggars description. The roar of the fire was deafening and the heat terrible. We stayed in the tunnel until next morning and the way different nationalities and different classes of people mingled and fraternized shows that a leveler is danger,' " commented a newspaper account of the incident. Miraculously, the 167 people missed the jaws of fire.

The third rescue mission started from Taft in the late afternoon. Earlier in the day Chief Carpenter W.E. Lanning had left Haugan on a work train going west toward East Portal, doing bridge work. In a flash the mountain glowed with fire, and Lanning quickly organized a mercy run for the big St. Paul Tunnel. Along the way the work train picked up dozens of people and emptied the Bates and Rogers' construction camp of 100 men below East Portal. The sea of flames raged outside as nearly 400 people, including residents of East Portal and Roland, hovered inside the two-mile tunnel. But Chief Carpenter Lanning was worried about Marshall and the others. Engineer Blundell and Conductor Harry Vandercook volunteered to run an engine down to pull them out.

There were still people along the tracks, paralyzed with fear. Railroad men and their families (Hungarians and Montenegrins), homesteaders, and refugees from Roland and Adair had probably been counting their last moments on earth when the engine and boxcar came churning down the tracks through the flames. Forty-seven in all clung to Lanning's train. Bridges behind them were cracking with fire; way ahead another one burst into flames. There was no way they would make it back to the St. Paul Tunnel or Falcon and Marshall. Tunnel 22 was closest, a short bore but their only hope. They opened the throttle wide—it was now or never! High over a burning trestle they raced, the three men forced flat on the deck by the heat. The tension was so great, the experience so terrible, that one passenger on the flatcar was seized with panic. He dove off the flatcar to his death on the rocks below. To the others a tunnel had never been such a welcome sight. Tunnel 22 may not be anyone's idea of home, but to nearly fifty people that hot August night the tunnel meant their lives.

This grave at Adair contains one unaccounted death of the 1910 fire—a suicide victim who jumped off the train not far from this location. The gravesite was maintained for many years by George Murray, Milwaukee signal maintainer from Avery. (Theriault)

The next morning Lanning and the others walked out into a blackened world. They found that the only death in the Loop Creek drainage was the crumbled body at the bottom of the burned out trestle near

Adair. The man was never identified; he was probably Hungarian and had worked as a gandy-dancer (a railroad laborer). His death was the direct result of the fire, but it has never been officially recorded or listed in the fire statistics. Newspaper accounts do mention a body found at the Loop, and his grave at Adair is obvious proof of his death.

As for the railroad employees who made the heroic rescues, their pay was well-earned that day. At least six hundred people had lived to see dawn on August 21, thanks to their efforts. And those big holes in the mountain, the tunnels on the Loop, were credited with saving hundreds of lives.

AVERY

Avery was one of the last places on the Coeur d'Alene Forest to be reached by the fires. Except for the parties on the headwaters of the St. Joe, people had staked their battles against the Devil's Broom the night of Saturday, August 20. One-third of Wallace burned that night. Setzer Creek, the Cedar Mountain area, and parts of the Loop Creek drainage were ablaze— Avery was surrounded by fire. It was not hit that night, however, and people still came to the little town for shelter. When the morning of August 21 dawned murky and gray, nervousness hung in the air as thick as the smoke. The strong winds were marching in front of a twenty-mile wide beast determined to eat the town. The tempo of fear increased.

The devastation following the 1910 fire is clearly shown in this 1918 picture of the Columbian heading eastward over the Turkey Creek trestle near Loop Creek. The Milwaukee Railroad is credited with saving hundreds of lives along its tracks through the Bitterroots. The country at that time was populated by railroad employees, homesteaders, prospectors, and others who followed the construction of the line. (Theriault)

President Taft had ordered troops to the scene of the fires, and the Twenty-fifth Infantry, an all-black regiment from Fort George Wright in Spokane, arrived

Black troops of the 25th Infantry out of Fort Wright in Spokane were detailed to Avery to fight fire and to maintain order through the hectic days of the 1910 fire. As fires raged around the town, the soldiers patrolled to protect the residents and property in Avery. Ranger Debitt is on the far left. (U.S.D.A., Forest Service)

in Avery on August 17. This regiment had participated in the Indian wars, on strike in 1892 in the Coeur d'Alene mines, in the capture of the Spanish position at El Caney, and in conquest of the Phillipine Islands.

The tents of Company G of the 25th Infantry were situated just east of Avery Creek. The tents and latrine, pictured on the far right, were the same type as the troops had used in the Philippine Islands. Note the Pearson Mercantile situated on the hillside. (Theriault)

Although fire fighting was new to them, they took to the trenches on the railroad right-of-way four miles east of Avery. As the fires became unmanageable and as refugees crowded the town, Ranger Debitt requested the troops in Avery to preserve order.

That morning of the 21st Ranger Debitt and Shoshone County Sheriff H.D. McMullan went west on a special train to check out the fire zone. They telephoned Lieutenant E.E. Lewis of the Infantry: Get the women and children out!

Two special trains were made up, one for the women and children to head west to Tekoa, Washington, and the other to head east toward Montana with the men aboard. Stationed on the platform were privates Chester Gerrard, William Hogue, Roy Green, and G.W. Bright. Other troops loaded water cans onto the cars of the train and fastened windows down. Those maintaining order aboard the trains were given instructions—if the cars were cut off on all sides, the soldiers were to take the women and children into the river. The group was to be kept together as much as possible but a stampede must be avoided. In a little more than half an hour, the train headed west. Its passengers had no time to gather possessions. The fate of the town looked so gloomy that when the black soldiers asked Harold Theriault if they could take his pet bear Teddy, he figured it would be all right. His uncle Ed Theriault was not so positive the place was doomed and ordered that the bear be returned.

The train chugged its way down the smoky valley. At the Big Creek Station Hollingshead's crew had straggled out of the woods. Cliff Theriault started to board the train to join his family, but a black soldier stopped him with a fixed bayonet. Fortunately, Harold Theriault explained that Cliff was his brother, and Cliff climbed aboard. Mrs. Theriault and her two sons got off the train at St. Joe City. Harold had been ordered by Ranger Debitt to get pack strings at St. Joe, but none were to be found.

Meanwhile, in Avery it was obvious the town was soon to be struck by the two huge waves of fire pulsating closer all the time. Those men remaining in Avery met at the depot to decide what to do. For two long hours they wavered in indecision. An old mining tunnel on the east end of town had been stocked with provisions; that would do for the old and lame men, but no more people would fit in. The best bet, advised Ranger Debitt and Deputy Sheriff McMullan, would be a march upriver. A half-mile trek out of town proved to be a foolhardy move, for the fire was thick there. By then it was evening and one trainload of men chose to go east to an old burn five miles away at Stetson where they might be safe. For the rest Debitt recommended taking blankets into the forks of the river, but Lieutenant E.E. Lewis and McMullan disagreed. Besides being too deep in places, the river could easily be dammed by falling trees and many men might drown.

Instead, McMullan, his deputy, Charles Sullivan, the soldiers of Company G, and nearly everyone left in town boarded a train to go west in the falling dusk. The train pushed through the first wave of fire, the varnish on the coach blistering in the intense heat. Would they be able to make it through the second wave? They were blocked—the fire was too thick! They had to turn back. The first furnace had expanded, and now the train could not get through it, either. They were caught between fires!

Lieutenant Lewis in his report noted: "The scenes of the fires, the dense smoke, the intense, blinding heat and the crackling of the flames were indescribable. The flames seemed to be over a mile and a half high. We traveled back and forth, attempting to get through at one end or another, but it was impossible. Progress was constantly impeded by landslides or rocks, burned logs, etc. . .'' It was another night of horror on the St. Joe, the train shuttling back and forth in the flames. Finally at 5:30 a.m. on the morning of Monday, August 22, the train made it back into Avery. This was their last chance.

Avery, the town that had been teeming with people and excitement the night before was totally empty Sunday night. That is, empty except for a few men either courageous or crazy enough to try to save the valuable property in the town. R.W. Anderson was foreman of the roundhouse; he chose to stay and save that structure. He was joined by F.D. Putnam, Emil Engelholm, and Ed Theriault, part-owner of the Mountain Park Hotel. They decided their only recourse to protect Avery was to set backfires at night when the wind was down. This was not something Ranger Debitt agreed with; various stories say that guns were drawn to prove a point in the ensuing argument. At any rate, the fires were lit at midnight.

The backfire destroyed only one building, by far the most expensive building on the St. Joe. It was lovely log mansion owned by A.B. Kelley in Kelley Creek, valued at $10,000 and full of exquisite antiques. As the backfires edged out from the town, the men slept for a couple of hours in the shelter of a rock across the river from the Mountain Park Hotel.

The wind came up at dawn and with it the furnace boomed back to life, even worse than before. The trainload of men, black and white alike, had returned to stand siege against it. They organized their battleground: they dug pools and filled them with water, they filled barrels and placed them near buildings, and they planned bucket brigades and stationed men all over town to watch for sparks that might ignite the buildings. There was nothing to do but wait for the attack.

It was three o'clock in the afternoon. The second fire was gaining fast. It was sure to join the first wave. They appeared to unite as they slammed into the backfire. This was it!

Then, quietly and quickly, the wind died. Somehow the breath of fate snuffed it out at the last minute. If it hadn't stopped right then and if there had been no backfires, Avery and its defenders would have been victims of the battle. The men watched in amazement as the flames died rapidly and passed them by within an hour.

Avery was intact.

Joy, relief, jubilation. . .exhaustion. In spite of all their feelings, there was work to be done. By 5:30 the fallen dispatch wires were back up and messages were again transmitted. The first relief train was on its way in, loaded with supplies. Captain George J. Holden, 25th Infantry, assumed command of the U.S. troops in Avery at 6:30 p.m. with the news that four hospital corpsmen were to arrive the next morning.

"TOWN IN IDAHO IS SAVED FROM A FOREST FIRE,'' read the headlines. "The 200 residents of Avery, Idaho, resumed their normal life today as more than 600 firefighters assured them the forest fires which threatened to destroy the town definitely were checked.''

The ordeal of 1910 was over; the Devil's Broom was stilled.

AFTERMATH

Or was it really over? For the survivors the work was just beginning. The burning stopped at the end of August that year when intermittent light rain squelched most of the fires, but the damages and aftereffects are being assessed even yet. Nothing changed the St. Joe valley as much as the Great Fire of 1910. Those who lived through it barely scratched the surface when they took a toll of their demolished world.

The first project, of course, was to rescue anyone else who might still be out in what was left of the wilderness. "Many men are said to be lost in the river country, and four or five rescue parties of fifteen men have left Avery,'' the papers reported.

The feeling of loss and confusion can be seen in excerpts from Ranger Debitt's telegrams to Supervisor W.G. Weigle in Wallace on August 23:

"The entire country has been burned over. We are sending relief parties into the different fire camps to get all safely into Avery. We have Army surgeons with two hospital assistants to care for injured, but limited amounts of medical supplies. An indefinite number of men reported lost in the fire. Arrangements will be made to bury unidentified bodies near Avery. Injured will be cared for until shipment can be made to hospital, Spokane. . .Advise how to send checks (for labor performed on fires). . .A man stenographer is badly needed. Avery was saved by backfires. . . Kottkey's ranger section lost. . .I have not heard anything from Kottkey and men. Searching parties start for head of Clear Creek in morning. Bird Creek camp safe. All are safe in Rock's camp except one. . . Clearwater men not in yet. Food supply is short and it is necessary to ship surplus fire fighters out. . .No checks could be issued. DEBITT''

Statistics cannot accurately describe what the rescue parties found, but by a body count there were eighty-six deaths (eighty-five officially plus one more by our count.) The breakdown was like this:

Pulaski's crew, West Fork Placer Creek	6
Bell's crew, Middle Fork Big Creek	10
Hollingshead's crew, West Fork Big Creek	18
Danielson's crew, Stevens Peak	1
Taylor's crew, Bullion Mine	8
Newport, Wash., homesteaders	3
St. Joe-Cedar Ridge Divide, prospector	1
Debitt's Crew, Storm Creek	28 or 29
Rock's crew, Setzer Creek	1
Cabinet National Forest, Montana	4
Pend Oreille National Forest	2
Wallace	2
Taft	1
Adair, railroad worker	1

The statistics don't mention the others that may *not* have been found (up to this point, unrecorded). "None has been reported by the government representatives save those whose remains have been found. In addition to the list, there are 125 missing, unaccounted for," says one magazine article. While it is doubtful that as many as that were killed, most early sources do cast doubt on the official figures. There is the possibility of unknown prospectors caught in the blaze; certainly many were scouring the hills at that time without anyone's knowing their whereabouts. The official Army report of Lieutenant E.E. Lewis, 25th Infantry, states that out of Avery, "A firefighter was killed while picking rocks off the track," and his body was shipped to St. Joe City. That person was never included in the tally, nor were the three bodies supposedly found near St. Regis. And in 1911, a logging crew reportedly discovered and buried a charred skeleton in Slate Creek. With so many people unknown to each other and many of them foreign, the record-keeping was not the best. Debitt himself thought Rock had 125 men on his crew, an extra 50. At that rate it would have been easy to lose one here or there.

The true count of deaths may never be known for sure, nor can the grief be measured. In recognition of the firefighters who lost their lives, the Forest Service acquired a special plot in the St. Maries Cemetery in 1912. The bodies of 54 were exhumed from their death sites and buried there near a commemorative monument.

In addition to the dead, there were 116 injured firefighters, some with permanent disabilities. Damage to lungs, eyesight, and limbs were typical casualties which required many weeks of hospitalization. The compensation to these men was shockingly low, a mere total of $5,450. The red tape following these meager claims was exhaustive, sometimes taking two or more years to be settled.

Following similar traumatic experiences today, victims are made a part of psychological counseling sessions aimed at their emotional recovery. That was unheard of in 1910. In fact, no mention has ever been made of the psychological damage the survivors endured—damage such as nightmares, anxiety, or depression. One man on the Clearwater did end up in an asylum. Known as the "lullaby boy," he never stopped singing a lullaby after the fire passed over. Men who screamed, cried, begged for mercy, beseeched or blasphemed God, panicked, or pushed others must have experienced guilt. A common reaction was reflected in this headline: "ESCAPES PERILS: LOSES TWO BROTHERS: GOES ON DRUNK." The article continues, "Some of the survivors of the fires in various parts of the Coeur d'Alene National Forest who had suffered extreme hardships and the greatest perils in saving their lives proceeded to consume a great amount of liquor as soon as they cashed their checks.

"One man was seen intoxicated who claimed that one of his brothers had been smothered in the Placer Creek fire and that another who had been out on the Boulder Creek (Stevens Peak) fire had not been accounted for."

Even the calm, level-headed "heroes" probably had their moments of nerves or emotional exhaustion later. That, too, is another factor that can never be measured.

Immediately after the danger had passed, nothing more than rescue operations could be tackled until the pall of smoke lifted. "It is impossible to give any estimates on area burned over or probable values," Forester Silcox stated in Missoula, August 27. "The smoky condition of the atmosphere prevents our learning just where the fires have swept, and it is not till after rains have come to clear the smoke away that we can begin to make calculation as to actual damages."

Indeed, the pall of smoke was a phenomenon in itself, one of the strangest recorded in the United States or Canada. It was not just in the Northwest that daylight and sun were completely shut out. The darkness was so bad that artificial lighting had to be used for days all the way from Butte, Montana, to Watertown, New York. Passenger trains across the country required lanterns to serve lunch. During the time that is known as the "Five Dark Days," August 20-25, 1910, the cloud spread eastward to cover Montana, North Dakota, parts of Minnesota, Wisconsin and Michigan. It stretched north into Alberta, Saskatchewan, Manitoba, Ontario, and south over half of Wyoming and South Dakota. The Great Lakes region was darkened as the massive cloud passed on through the St. Lawrence waterway en route to the Atlantic. Some five hundred miles out to sea from San Francisco, a British vessel was unable to take observations for ten days because of the smoke.

The fires caused an atmospheric disturbance in Cheyenne, Wyoming, and Denver, Colorado, on August 26. "A drop in temperature of 45 degrees, 13 of which occurred in 10 minutes, was the record established here yesterday between 1 o'clock and 8:30 p.m. At 1 o'clock a 42-mile-per-hour gale swept the city and a few minutes later the town was enveloped in a pall of smoke from the Idaho-Montana forest fires 800 miles distant. From then on the temperature fell steadily until it reached 48 degrees at 8:30 . . . The sudden change in temperature was caused by atmospheric disturbances resulting from the contest between the hot air from the fire-swept districts and the snow-covered mountains of the continental divide."

When everything stopped smoldering, it was discovered that all the little settlements and construction camps from St. Joe City to Taft had been destroyed except for Marble Creek and Avery. The town of Adair was gone but for some reason a horse, two cows, and some chickens survived. Four ranger stations had been burned down. The St. Joe River and all its tributaries were clogged with ashes, soot, and thousands of dead fish apparently boiled alive. Twelve years later St. Joe ridge was still ankle deep in ashes from the fire's vicious path.

What a path it was. Two and a half million acres were burned, an area equal to 4,000 square miles. With devilish mischief it stretched over the forested area from the foothills of the Rockies on the east, over the Bitterroot divide, to the Palouse on the Idaho-Washington line to the foothills of the Rockies on the east. It swept through the forested areas of Region One, touching all 22 forests. Looking at a map was like seeing the easel of a careless painter who had thrown angry splotches of red over half the area. The Avery district was one big splotch.

The timber, the magnificent stands of white pine that homesteaders and timber barons alike had staked their dreams on—gone. It must have been sickening to see the rubble of toothpicks for miles on end. How would anyone be able to even guess how much was gone? On Forest Service land it was estimated that five and a half billion board feet had burned with a total of about nine billion counting private ownership. Homesteaders lost timber varying in value from $5,000 to $40,000 per claim, and in one county alone the assessed value of lost timber belonging to timber companies was possibly $1 million or maybe several times that. The amount of wood that had been destroyed would have lasted all the United States for the next fifteen years, built over 50,000 five-room houses, kept mills running in the Coeur d'Alenes for 25 years, or built enough homes for the largest city in the four affected states. The greatest loss of any of the forests was on the St. Joe, particularly on Big Creek, the North Fork of the St. Joe, and the Little North Fork of the Clearwater. The Milwaukee Lumber Company with its two brand-new miles of railroads into the Big Creek timber sale was badly hurt. (It did manage to salvage some of the timber, however, and its track eventually penetrated another sixteen miles into the drainage.)

In an overall estimate of the damage, the *Daily Idaho Press* estimated the following property losses: Wallace, $1 million; Coeur d'Alene Forest, $250,000; railroads, $3 million; settlers in three states, $750,000; timber lost, $15 million; for a total of $20 million. The cost of fighting the fire was an additional $800,000. The Rossi Insurance Company in Wallace carried the main burden for paying insurance claims of some $300,000. Among the clients who collected were some of the area's working mines. The Monitor Mining Company was damaged to the tune of $50,000 in addition to the loss of 1500 cords of wood; owner J.L. Bailor also suffered $15,000 in damages. The Big Elk Mining Company also filed a large claim in order to replace its compressor plant and other machinery. And remember, these figures would be multiplied manifold using today's inflationary rate.

Individuals also suffered financial losses. Insurance claims for $10,000 were paid to A.B. Kelley, Avery, for his home. Another large claim was filed by Frank C. Hopkins and W.B. Edwards for their property and saloon buildings at Falcon. Also burned out was Basil Rizzonelli at Grand Forks. His property had been burned out three times within a year, he whined to the papers. He was in the process of building a new hotel around his tent, he said, when his (illegal) establishment was again wiped out. Interestingly, his plight has been retold several times with a great deal of sympathy. That is amusing since all of his business ventures, including the painted "sports," were in flagrant violation of the law! Fire may not have daunted his spirits but Forest Service officials finally fined Rizzonelli and forced him to leave the Forest.

Other than the timber losses, the railroad suffered the most. As the work trains inched their way out of their refuge in the tunnels, they discovered that the whole line between Avery and Falcon had been ravaged by fire. Eastward to St. Regis it was not much better. Fourteen Milwaukee bridges from 120 to 775 feet in length were destroyed. Ties were burned and rails buckled from the intense heat; even pick handles that the contruction workers had thrown down were in ashes. Thirty days lapsed before the line could be open to through traffic again. Bridgemen from all over the country came in to help, and portable sawmills were set up so that the job could be completed in a hurry. The *Daily Idaho Press,* August 30, 1910, reported, "A force of 325 bridge carpenters and 200 laborers (working night and day) has been organized into a machine that is pushing its way steadily through the wreckage left by the fire and is leaving in its wake a facsimile of the Puget Sound as it was before the conflagration which crippled it so badly."

The major job of pulling everything together fell on the U.S. Forest Service, however. The immediate task as the ashes cooled was to salvage as much of the timber as possible. Salvage sales were quickly set up for the high quality, old-growth white pine, although much of it was inaccessible. The hurricane winds had created acres of blown-down timber, much of which was merchantable. Some of the sapwood had blued from fungi but was still firm, so salvage logging was a profitable endeavor. Although the logging began immediately and peaked between 1915 and 1918, some cedar burned in 1910 was still being sold in 1979.

Other jobs were clearly defined for the Forest Service in that post-fire era. William W. Morris, forest assistant on the Coeur d'Alene, explained, "One of the first things that we found it necessary to do after the fire was to clear out our old trails buried in twisted and broken tangles, often five trees high, and it was necessary to cut through all this with axe and saw. This work took much time and money."

Other problems the young Forest Service encountered had to be rectified too, especially the poor transportation and lack of communication. They had to break hundreds of miles of new trails and roads into virgin territory. Packing became quite an industry. The Forest Service and lumber companies bought their own strings and contracted the work to private packers. Horses had proven to be less sturdy in the rugged country and were edged out by mules. Communication systems were constructed to the extent that four-hundred miles of telephone wires

During the winter of 1910-11, cruisers estimated the volumes of salvageable timber. Pictured left to right are William Rock, Forest Service; Franklin "Judge" Girard, Forest Service; "Cap" Eli Laird, early St. Joe steamboat captain; C.H. Gregory, lumberman who logged fire-killed timber on Loop Creek; and Beier, Forest Service. (Rock, U.S.D.A., Forest Service)

Increased fire protection was another outgrowth of the 1910 fire. This fire display in the Avery Drugstore in the early 1930's warned residents, "This is God's country. Don't set it on fire and make it look like Hell!" (Scribner)

criss-crossed the St. Joe fifteen years later. The lines hooked into the new lookouts and backcountry ranger stations manned during fire season by a ranger and small crew. In general, administrative practices were improved and better fire protection was developed.

In the fall of 1910 the government sent the Coeur d'Alene Forest the start of another project: seeds to begin the massive planting job. White and ponderosa pine made up the bulk of the planting stock. One and a half tons of walnut seed, red oak acorn and hickory nuts were also to be part of the experiment.

Fire breeds fire, they say, and that was another tragic aftermath of the great burn. It created breeding places in fallen snags and dead timber for its destructive offspring. Probably 30 to 40 percent of the fire areas were subsequently reburned in the next two decades, the largest being in 1928 and 1934. What wasn't burned was weakened and vulnerable to a serious barkbeetle epidemic that spread to green timber in 1914 and wiped out millions of board feet of the remaining pine.

The only real benefit from the fire has been a magnificent herd of elk. The scars of the burn were soon covered with thick brush—feed and browse for elk. According to the Idaho Department of the Fish and Game, the growth of the elk population increased steadily after 1910 and peaked sometime in the early 1960's prior to the decline in available brush. Thousands of hunters can verify that St. Joe country is still the home of these majestic animals.

POSTSCRIPT ABOUT THE PRESS AND PEOPLE

The Great Idaho Fire covered the largest land area of any fire in the nation's history. Although the Peshtigo and Hinckley fires in the Midwest during the late

1800's took more lives and destroyed more towns, no fire had the press coverage nor aroused public awareness as much as the Idaho fire. (It) . . . "managed to burn its way through public indifference and to emerge as what most conservationists consider a charred and positive landmark along the road to forest protection . . . "Not ever before had a forest fire been given so big or so black headlines . . ." writes author Stewart H. Holbrook in *Burning an Empire*. Certainly the headlines were splashy, the drama was keen, and in the style of the day the details were grossly overwritten.

A magazine article published in the October 1910 edition of *Everybody's Magazine* was filled not only with flowery descriptions but a few wild exaggerations besides. ". . .The poor roasting wretches took many means to preserve from the flames letters, cards, trinkets by which they might be known. Some scraped with the last strength of their burning hands little holes in the earth, put their papers in them, then flung their shriveled bodies down upon the cache to die. . ."

Heroes were often glorified by this type of writing when actually they may have done nothing. For example, an oft told tale of "courageous" Thaddeus Roe saving the town of Avery is remarkable only in the courage he had in telling it to the Seattle newspapers. Many exaggerations did and do appear in print that are linked directly to someone's overactive imagination. Examples are headlines such as, "26 Dead at Grand Forks" or "Town of Avery Burns."

It is interesting to note the ethnic and racial slurs that appeared in the newspapers and magazines of the day. People of foreign origin were not identified by name beside the "regular folks." Thus, "John Doe, James Roe, and two Italians came to Wallace." Or how about this one: "BOHUNKS BARELY ESCAPE LYNCHING—Drank up Condensed Milk of Big Creek Survivors." The story goes on to tell that "a bohunk was crazy drunk" when he went to harass the forestry

Fire detection was also improved in the decades following the 1910 fire. The upper St. Joe country was to have over eighty lookout towers manned in the 1930's and '40's. Pictured here is Fishhook Peak which overlooked the Fishhook and Marble Creek drainages. (Lindborg)

officials in Wallace. Forest Supervisor Weigle gave him what he deserved, however, and promptly threw him down a flight of stairs.

The press was generally favorable toward the black soldiers, although their role in helping to save Avery has been largely ignored. "They stuck to their posts like men," Ranger Debitt was quoted as saying in an interview. The implication was clear: the blacks must not have been men to begin with!

Certainly the press coverage did much for furthering the cause of fire prevention and for encouraging Congress to appropriate more funds. "For the want of a nail, the shoe was cast, the rider thrown, the battle lost; for the want of trails the finest white pine forests in the United States were laid waste and scores of lives lost," chastized *Everybody's Magazine*. Gifford Pinchot, chief of the Forest Service then, blasted

members of Congress who opposed appropriations for proper equipment. In a press release, Pinchot stated, "It is all loss, dead irretrievable loss, due to the pique, the bias, the bullheadedness of a knot of men who have sulked and planted their hulks in the way of appropriations for the protection and improvement of these national reserves." He especially cited Idaho's Senator Heyburn for vetoing funds for the Forest Service. Ironically, Senator Heyburn was from Wallace or rather what was left of Wallace after the fire razed a third of the town.

As for the men whose names dominated the headlines that August, most stayed on the Forest Service roster for the rest of their careers. Ranger Edward Pulaski was eulogized as a hero and later had a fire-fighting tool, a cross between a hoe and axe, named after him. Young rangers Ashley Roche, Joseph

Large-scale planting projects have attempted to reforest lands burned in the 1910 and subsequent fires. This planting camp on the North Fork of the St. Joe in 1930 was one of several operating in the old burned area. (U.S.D.A., Forest Service)

Halm, and William R. Rock survived their rugged initiation into the Forest Service and retired many years later. Ranger Ralph Debitt, one of Avery's first settlers, ended his career with the government shortly after 1910 and became, of all things, a cult leader of a Yoga-nudist group. One can only wonder whether his exaggerated press releases, numerous and repetitious telegrams to the supervisor, and indecision in the crisis had anything to do with his resignation.

So life went on. Changes in forest protection were made; now the trees have grown up in the parts of Avery that were backfired. The scars may be healed, but always the question remains: could a fire of that magnitude happen again in the St. Joe Valley? Unfortunately, yes, given the right weather conditions. More manpower and modern technology would give tighter control, but still things could get out of hand. Looking backward all we can do now is speculate about how the St. Joe would be, its face unchanged, had it not been swept by the Devil's Broom in 1910.

This flume was built by C.H. Gregory near Adair when he salvage logged the Loop Creek drainage in the years following the 1910 fire. From here the logs were loaded from the dammed creek onto the train. Note the pole road on the left side of the photo. (Museum of North Idaho)

8 Changing Roles in the U.S. Forest

The year was 1905, the spot at Rocky Riffle was designated as one of the first ranger stations on the St. Joe. Everything was new to Ralph M. Debitt and his family: his job as ranger for the newly formed Forest Service, Mrs. Jessie Debitt's job as postmistress for a brand new Idaho settlement, their home along the St. Joe River. Located three miles downriver from the present town of Avery, the two cabins used by the Debitts sat on one of the few wide spots on the north side of the river canyon. This was Pinchot Ranger Station, its address officially Pinchot, Idaho. The U.S. Forest Service was now a permanent part of the valley. Its role has changed considerably since Debitt began his job, changes that have been reflected in the various ranger stations, types of employees, and their jobs in the woods. Often the changes have occurred because of nationwide trends, and sometimes one particular year has seen more significant action occurring than any other for several decades.

Indeed, 1905 was such a year. But before that, the history of American forestry began in the last part of the 1800's in the eastern part of the country. The forests there had been recklessly exploited, and what hadn't been taken by people was destroyed by fire. Control was needed on grazing rights, too. Justifiably concerned about safeguarding public lands, conservationists of the time exerted pressure on Congress. In August of 1876 Congress authorized a whopping $2,000 for the first federal office of forestry. (A century later the budget of the Avery District alone was 200 times that much.) Then legislative action in 1886 provided for scientific research and tree planting on the Great Plains, and in 1891 Congress set aside the first land reserve, the Yellowstone Timberland Reserve. It allocated funds in 1897 to employ caretakers for the public forests, and a year later America's first native professional forester became Chief of the Division of Forestry. Gifford Pinchot, who was later the governor of Pennsylvania, set the wheels in motion for the cause of American forestry. His name was also given to the upper St. Joe's first settlement.

The turning point in 1905 established not only ranger stations on the St. Joe, but it was the year that Congress transferred the Forest Reserves from the Department of the Interior to the Department of Agriculture. The Bureau of Forestry changed its name to Forest *Service* to imply using the timber resources, rather than holding them back. It further emphasized that concept by changing the names of the Forest Reserves to National Forests. Control of the forests

went directly to the man on the ground, and the administration was decentralized. With this action, ranger stations began to appear all over the country. In March of 1905 the main part of the St. Joe Forest was taken out of the land available for homesteading and labeled as the "Shoshone Forest Reserve;" then it was included with the Coeur d'Alene Forest on November 6, 1906. (It shifted back to the name St. Joe National Forest in 1911 when portions of the Clearwater and Coeur d'Alene were added. It combined again with the Coeur d'Alene from 1920-1923, and then until 1973 it retained the name St. Joe National Forest. Now the Idaho Panhandle National Forests encompass the St. Joe, the Coeur d'Alene, and the Kaniksu.)

The St. Joe was to become part of District One, later Region One, given its numeral because it encompassed part of that first Yellowstone Timberland Reserve. Region One, the Northern Region, stretches all over Montana and North Dakota and bites off part of northeastern Washington, northwestern South Dakota and North Idaho. It contains nearly one-fifth of all the commercial forest land in the West, including Alaska. Certainly, the 900,000 acres of the St. Joe was earmarked early for its magnificent stands of timber.

It was probably with this in mind that the Pinchot Ranger Station was built at an early date. Unfortunately, the passage of the railroad was not foreseen, and Pinchot was on the right-of-way for the Chicago, Milwaukee and Puget Sound Railway. It would have to be moved. The settlement of Avery was then known as North Fork City; when Pinchot Ranger Station moved upriver to Avery, it became North Fork Station on July 7, 1907. The two cabins at Pinchot were used as section houses by the railroad for several years, although the administrative site was returned to the public domain in 1908.

Two other ranger stations on the St. Joe were manned about this same time. The Hemlock Springs Ranger Station, located southeast of Avery between Crater Peak and Orphan Point, started out as a tent camp. The site was abandoned in a few years and moved to Roundtop where more permanent accommodations were constructed. Along with the watershed of the Little North Fork of the Clearwater, Hemlock Springs Ranger Station was originally administered by the Clearwater National Forest until 1911. The other station was the St. Joe Ranger Station, one and a half miles west of Falcon. It was one of the first to come but one of the first to be abandoned. In a sunny meadow on Loop Creek, the buildings were

The St. Joe Ranger Station, built in 1905, was one of the first ranger stations in the area. The handsome two-story structure burned to the ground during the 1910 fire, but was rebuilt in 1911 on its same site on Loop Creek. The site was one of the few fairly large natural meadows in the vicinity. (Oregon Historical Society)

nice solid pieces of construction. The 1910 fire wiped them out, but they were rebuilt. The house was made of lumber, had a brick fireplace, five or six rooms, a solid mahogany door. Quite luxurious for those times! Only two rangers, Henry Kottkey and Edward Pulaski, ever had a chance to enjoy it, for it was abandoned in 1918 and later torn down. A patrol cabin was then built in Falcon to take its place.

The introduction of the Forest Service into the upper St. Joe was not necessarily met with open arms. Lumbermen, prospectors, miners, and most importantly, homesteaders, viewed the new agency with fear and distrust. The matter was aggravated when the rangers were given the unusual task of enforcing the law prohibiting the sale of alcohol on the National Forest. Thirsty railroad workers found this offensive. In a general land survey of the Slate Creek drainage in 1909, Forest Assistant Rutledge Parker wrote, "The people generally are very antagonistic toward the policy of the Forest Service, the large majority do not take into consideration the importance of protecting the resources of the country, but take it from the standpoint that they are being barred from

certain privileges which they would have had, had the forest not been created. The intense feeling, however, **only exists among certain people who are either** grafters or who intend to use their rights as citizens regardless of the laws regulating these rights. . . It will be some years before all of these facts will be digested by the people taken as a class. As soon as the most disagreeable portion of the work has been completed, such as claims, et cetera, the feeling will be greatly reduced. The rigid policy of the Forest Service regarding claims as compared to the land office, has created a panic among the people."

Parker was right in his prediction that the antagonism would decrease as time went on. It was fortunate, because the agency's influence increased in the valley and elsewhere. President Theodore Roosevelt added 148 million acres to the National Forest system during his term of office from 1901 to 1909. Much of the land was unknown wilderness to its new keepers until major surveys were conducted in 1908 and 1909. The surveys provided a concise look at the location, topography, climate, timber, past fire damage, and possible development of the country.

At this time the rangers named many places and made older names official. Names had already been given to the most prominent places on the St. Joe Forest; often these names came from the miners, homesteaders, or incidents that happened there. But much work was still to be done. W.H. Daugs used the Chinook dictionary in deciding placenames for Wawa, Calipeen, Mowitch, and Delate Creeks. Often physical descriptions of the spot were used, such as the name of Blackdome Peak, Roundtop, Jungle Creek, Twin Creek. Occasionally, names of Forest Service personnel made the map. Dunn Peak was named for Leon M. Dunn, a Roundtop ranger. Debitt Basin honors the first Avery ranger. Crittenden Peak on stateline and Marcus Cook Point near Cedar Mountain commemorate Forest Service employees killed in World War I. In any case, the naming of each particular peak or creek has its own history.

Broken Leg Creek, for example, has a story that has to be shared. Three Forest Service men, who bore the provocative nicknames of Champagne, Siders, and "Whiskey" went to build a cabin on a creek south of Red Ives. Ranger John Siders, Al Champagne, and Frank Moore, who was known for his drinking habits, were hard at work when Siders fell from the rafters. Unfortunately, he broke his leg. Now, Broken Leg Creek is a long ways from yesterday, recounts Charley Scribner. The closest doctor was at Superior, Montana, but there were no trails in that direction. So the boys decided to fix him up right there. They tied him to a tree with a Spanish windlass (a hoist system with rope) to straighten the leg. For splints they used shakes from the cabin and carved out a crutch. No doubt Champagne and "Whiskey" underwent considerable criticism for their methods from Siders, says Charley. Siders stayed there, though, hobbling around and bullcooking for the other two as they finished the cabin. The last time Charley saw Siders his leg still pointed to the northeast, but he fared better than Champagne who got shot and "Whiskey" who burned up in a house fire in Avery.

Preliminary maps of the St. Joe had hardly been drawn when 1910 came, a year in which everything was disfigured by the terrible fires. The entire objective of the Forest Service was re-examined. If its role was to serve as caretaker of the nation's forests, something had gone wrong somewhere. It obviously had not been prepared in any way for the onslaught of fire that destroyed five and a half billion board feet of timber on Forest Service land alone. Much of the fire was beyond reach because no trails existed to get to it even if there had been manpower and equipment to fight it. Many lives had been lost because there was no way to get a message through by telephone or telegraph. The publicity generated nationwide drew the attention of the public and Congress to the problem, and soon Congress appropriated more funds to build a stronger organization.

One way of taking care of the forests was to make sure that manpower was available to contain fires in the hinterlands. With this and the idea of future

growth in mind, the Forest Service established locations for future ranger stations. These administrative sites were "withdrawn," or set aside from the public domain and eliminated from land available for mining and homesteading. Not knowing yet exactly what its needs might be, the Forest Service chose the spots for good water, good grazing for pack animals, and accessibility by trail. Some of the sites would have patrol cabins on them and their use would assure improved transportation by trail to future fires.

Jug Camp served many years as a welcome stop-over to packers, trappers and Forest Service personnel. The site was withdrawn as an administrative site in the 'teens on account of its strategic location along the Old Montana Trail near the Monumental Buttes. Jug Camp received its name from a whiskey jug left hanging in a nearby tree. (Scribner)

At least thirty sites were withdrawn on the Avery District alone. A map from the Marble lookout in the early 1920's shows these withdrawn ranger stations : Patricia Ranger Station near Wawa Creek; Ideal Ranger Station on Railroad Creek off the North Fork; Zephyr Ranger Station near Hemlock Springs south of Avery; Turner Flat Ranger Station east of Avery; and Placer Ranger Station just north of Bad Tom Mountain on the Wallace District. Also on the map is Utility Ranger Station, 165.19 acres including Roundhouse Gulch west of Avery. Mapped by Ranger W.H. Daugs (pronounced "Dawes") in 1913, this site held a fourteen by sixteen frame house worth $100, that had been built by Lee Setzer, a homesteader, and occupied by Ripley of Avery. There was also a barn worth fifty dollars and a Forest Service one-room frame house twelve by fourteen, also worth $100. The Utility site would have provided a place for sheds and corrals for stock, plus room for expansion of the North Fork (Avery) Ranger Station, "should the permanent force at Avery be increased." A similar site close to Avery was the Swiftwater site near the mouth of the Fishhook Creek, but it apparently wasn't used enough to warrant a place on the map. The Forest Service ceased consideration of most of these sites in 1952.

Throughout its history the Forest Service has changed its focus from large to small ranger districts and then back again. Administration of the forests on the St. Joe at times involved several small, locally controlled districts, which were later combined to make larger units with more centralized control. The

Ranger stations and patrols cabins were located in strategic places all over the St. Joe to improve fire protection after the 1910 fire. This 1919 picture showing Jim Uttley, alternate ranger at Avery, was taken at Turner Flat. Originally a homesteader's cabin, the site was used for several years as a patrol headquarters for one or two men. (Theriault)

trend after the 1910 fire was toward many patrol cabins and more districts so that within a decade the numbers had increased dramatically. Avery became the hub of a wheel whose spokes branched out to the various cabins and stations. By then the little town was an established population center along a major railroad, and its ranger station site was developed. When the St. Joe and Coeur d'Alene Forests were recombined into one administrative unit in the early 1920's, there were four districts on the St. Joe whose headquarters were at Avery. Stationed here was the deputy supervisor, Ashley Roche, joined in the winter by four district rangers. The districts were Avery, Ward Peak, Pole Mountain, and Roundtop. (The only other district on the St. Joe at that time was the Palouse District to the southwest, isolated by land belonging to the Clearwater and St. Joe Timber Protection Associations. Ed Haines was ranger at the Palouse District from 1907 to 1917, then W.H. Daugs left his job as Avery ranger to be his own boss there

for many years. Administration was handled in St. Maries during the teen years and after 1924).

AVERY RANGER STATION, NATIONAL HISTORIC SITE

The Avery Ranger Station, unlike some of the others on the St. Joe, has had only two moves in its history; from Pinchot three miles downriver to Avery in 1907 and from Avery to Hoyt Flat in 1967. For most of its life it has been known by one name, Avery Ranger Station, though it was first called North Fork Ranger Station. Its role in the history of the Forest Service on the St. Joe has been a significant one, starting as a tent camp set up in the summer of 1907 on the

The Avery Ranger Station donned its best decorations to celebrate the Fourth of July in 1910. Avery's first ranger, Ralph M. Debitt, his wife Jessie, and small daughter Marjorie sit on the steps of this historic ranger station. That same summer the heavy timber in the background burned in the 1910 fire. This building was entered on the National Register of Historic Places in 1971. (USDA, Forest Service)

homestead of Sam "49" Williams. On February 21, 1908, Ranger Ralph Debitt surveyed the area and recommended withdrawal which occurred the following October. He completed a cabin on the site that same year. After the devastating 1910 fire, the forest service did considerable work on the site to clear it of timber and stumps and turn it into a more level piece of ground. By 1911 the station had a two-story house, spring house, woodshed, and small barn; and in 1912 Ranger Daugs had completed a bunkhouse with two rooms. Despite these improvements, the station hardly offered classy accommodations for its employees.

C.S. Webb, a Forest Service scaler who later wrote *White Pine: King of Many Waters,* described the housing situation vividly: "Up to this time (1916) no living quarters were furnished for anyone except for the district rangers. Their quarters were pretty rough, usually of log construction without any modern conveniences. Stations such as Avery, on a road or railroad, were usually fixed up well enough for a man to keep a wife and family there if they were willing to rough it. The back country stations usually consisted of a hut and bunkhouse, both small and of logs, which would provide shelter for the ranger and a small crew. At these stations women were taboo. If a ranger was married, his family stayed behind in town during the summer. In winter he might sometimes be home but usually not for very long. . .

"If and when a ranger station dwelling was authorized, the district office would allot the forest $600, which usually was credited to the district ranger with instructions to go ahead and build a dwelling. Usually quite a lot of contributed time was provided by him, and the carpentry and other workmanship was a bit on the rough side. Even so, it was surprising how much $600 produced.

"At Avery I needed a place to live. (Deputy Supervisor) Haines sent up enough lumber to build two tent frames having four-foot walls. He provided a fourteen by sixteen tent and fly for living quarters and a ten by twelve fly for the culinary department. We had a wood-burning heating stove in the big tent and a little wood-burning cook stove in the other. The tents were set on one platform, end to end, with a breezeway between—and believe me, it was breezy—the whole thing. We carried our water from a pump about fifty yards distant, and took our baths in a galvanized washtub. A couple of gasoline lanterns provided good light. Such were the conditions that young brides put up with in the Forest Service work in 1916. . .

"We lived in a small tar-paper covered shack at Bogle Spur; in a two-room rough board shack at Adair; and then in two tents at Avery with water some distance in every instance. Our boys and girls today wouldn't do it, and I doubt if they could, since never having experienced such conditions, it seems doubtful if they would be able to manage it. . ."

Conditions improved at the Avery Ranger Station as it became the center of so much activity. It had to expand. But there was one problem that continually plagued the Forst Service. The title to the surrounding land was not clear. Complications ranged from finding the heirs of homesteader Sam "49" Williams somewhere in Arkansas, to settling mineral claims, to coping with the ire of businessman W.W. Ferrell who physically and verbally attacked the rangers.

Ferrell, who founded the town of Ferrell across from St. Joe City, was notorious for his antics. Convinced

Mrs. Mabel Scribner sits in the living room of her new home at the Avery Ranger Station in 1924. Forest Service families endured primitive living conditions before the construction of the log cabins at the station. The Carlson Brothers built the two Forest Service residences in 1922 and 1923 as well as other log homes in the community. (Scribner)

that the North Fork Ranger Station was on his claim, he waged war with the Forest Service on all fronts. In October while Ranger Daugs was out of town, Ferrell and two employees efficiently logged firewood on Forest Service land, snaked it across the ranger station, and stacked it in front of Pearson's store. Daugs and the other forest officials frowned on the logging operation on the ranger station and marked the logs "Property of the USFS." That and another trespass did not daunt our hero— he merely hauled the logs off to burn for his winter's heat.

Ferrell's own brand of heat continued well past winter. In the spring of 1913, two Forest Service employees were erecting a tent house on the ranger station. When Ferrell was told what they were doing, his famous reputation for cussing would have won him honors in Hades. He hurled logs off the frame, cursing all the while, and shouting, "I will tear it down in spite of Hell, and if you lay a hand on me, I'll put a hole through you!"

Now a hole in their bodies was not the reason why these Forest Service men had come to Avery, so they reported the whole thing to the Forest Supervisor. The next day interested spectators observed Ferrell chopping down 200 feet of government fencing and a ten by fourteen Forest Service tent, the tent house made of government logs, using—(mind you,) a government ax and sledge hammer. He did remove the logs from government land, though. He threw them over the hill onto railroad right-of-way.

It was not until 1928 that the title was finally cleared to the land for the Avery Ranger Station, two decades after the first building was put on the spot. The Theriault family sold it to the Forest Service and finally the problem was resolved.

Ranger Clyde Blake, Sr., was responsible for adding new buildings to the Avery Ranger Station. Two brothers, Charlie and Albert Carlson, were carpenters for the log structures. The cookhouse built in 1922 fed many hungry mouths before it closed down in 1960 and was torn down in 1970. Blake can also be credited with building the water system on Avery Creek and the two houses built in 1922 and 1923. With over a hundred head of mules for the pack strings, the Forest Service clearly needed a barn. So after 1926 a new two-story 40x120 foot structure dominated both the site and the job, for packing was an entity of its own in those days. When the barn burned in 1965, a time of pride for the Forest Service faded into history. The historic office building, constructed in 1908, very nearly faded away too. It was deemed excess and came within a hair of being put up for bid. Local residents raised such an outcry that the building was not only saved, it was chosen for the National Registry of Historic Places in 1971. It is an honor well-deserved, for not only is it one of the few remaining examples of the first ranger stations to be built, but its architecture is also noteworthy. Logs were dragged down from Avery Creek to be hand-hewed by Swedish broadaxes for the structure. The dove-tailing, as well as the masterly tongue and groove are testimony to the

craftsmanship of the early Forest Service men. Hans Nelson led a team of carpenters in the construction; Nelson Peak just east of Avery was later named in his honor. From the handsome building the orders were given and men dispatched to fight the awful blaze of 1910. And for the next sixty years, the Avery Ranger Station office was a hubbub of activity.

By the late 1960's it was clear that the growing Avery Ranger Station simply had no place in which to grow. Previous administrative sites were examined, and the one homesteaded by Charles Hoyt in the early

This view of Avery shows the Avery Ranger Station as it appeared in the late 1920's. The office building is in the center of the site. Located clockwise around the office are the two residences, bunkhouse, blacksmith's shop, barn, commissary building, cookhouse, a storehouse, and the alternate ranger's home. Also pictured are the Hotel Idaho (with E.F. White Merchantile on its ground floor), the substation, and the town jail. (Theriault)

days began to look appealing. Settling the issue of the land posed another problem, however. When it was first chosen as an administrative site in the early years, Hoyt had relinquished claim to 1.15 acres. However, he did not prove up on his homestead claim which made the release invalid. When Al Stanley got title to the land in 1921, no mention was made of the withdrawal as an administrative site. Somehow that matter was cleared up in 1933, but more complications resulted when Stanley sued the Forest Service in 1949, claiming that flood damage could result from the installation of a bridge crossing the St. Joe near his property.

One disgruntled forester wrote about Hoyt Flat in 1954: "We seem to be in a position of having an administrative site which we might not be able to hold legally, which we do not intend to use for a Ranger or Guard Station, which is inadequate in size, location for a log landing and loading site, but which has proved to have certain nuisance value."

Famous last words. As situations change, so do ranger stations on the St. Joe. The Avery Ranger Station moved from the North Fork Administrative site to Hoyt Flat (now with the "s" dropped) in 1967, in spite of its "nuisance value." The modern office building, warehouse and garage, and three permanent homes form the ranger station. A quadplex built in

1980 added housing for the staff which numbered about 25 full-time employees. Fifty seasonal workers now find housing in a bunkhouse built the same year at the Avery Work Center.

BUT THERE WERE OTHERS. . .

If we remember that administrative sites were chosen in far away corners of the St. Joe for fire protection, then the choice of Quarles Peak, northeast of Avery, for the Ward Peak Ranger Station made sense. The alpine area offered both water and good grazing, and it was on the way to Montana. What the place lacked was convenience. For the station was built in 1919-20 in one of the Forest's snowiest areas. Sometimes Ranger Charley Scribner had to burrow a tunnel through the snow just to get to the door of the cabin—in late spring! Still, it was needed as an intermediate station and patrol headquarters, employing a fifteen-man trail crew and seven smoke chasers. It served the Forest Service for twelve years. During that time, Blackie Kimball recalls that the bright lights of Avery were a long hike from Quarles, about

26 miles. In those days everyone got to where they were going by foot power, and Blackie would leave Quarles at 7:00 a.m. and would trot into Avery before noon.

Another spoke from the center of activity at Avery ran to a ranger district to the southeast. The Pole Mountain District, later to become the Red Ives District, had lots of name-changing and moving in its history. A trail connecting with the Old Montana Trail at Junction Peak ran south along the St. Joe-Clearwater Divide past Pole Mountain, on west to Five Lakes Buttes and south to Moose City, an old mining camp on the Clearwater. It served as a boundary for the Pole Mountain District, which started with a tent camp on Pole Mountain. An improvement was needed over the tents, so in 1920 an ex-prize fighter named Packy McFarland built a ranger station for the district at Twin Lakes, near the head of Mosquito and Fly Creeks. Whoever named those creeks had a good reason for choosing the names; probably a better reason than the Forest Service had for choosing the spot as a station. Not only was it infested with hordes of mosquitos and flies and a few hungry bears in the summer, but it was

Bearskull Cabin in 1935 was an important stop-over for packers on the Old Montana Trail between Avery and the Pole Mountain District. Charlie and Oscar Carlson built the structure in the early 1920's. It was used many years as a patrol station before being destroyed in the 1950's. (Theriault)

also completely covered over with snow in the winter. It was off the beaten path and inaccessible. Smokechasers were the only ones who could stand the place. Time for another move.

This time Pole Mountain District chose Elk Prairie, north of Pole Mountain, its first station, and south of Junction Peak, its second. Elk Prairie was along a major trail and offered the usual prerequisite of a good spring. Joe Parker built the office in 1924 for the Pole Mountain District, complete with a kitchen, warehouse-bunkhouse, and a tool house. Even though it was a better location, getting to Elk Prairie Ranger Station was still no easy matter. George L. Terrien remembers that in 1930, "The ranger station was up high, near Surveyors Ridge, a beautiful place. Walt Botts was the ranger. To get there we had to walk from Avery to Bearskull, rest overnight, then walk to Elk Prairie by way of Bathtub, etc. (A bridge was constructed across Timber Creek to provide access early in the spring.) There was no road to Roundtop then, out of Avery, just a trail. And there was no road up the main river out of Avery. From Elk Prairie, the next day we hiked to the Elbo (sic) of the St. Joe River

where we put our trail camp. . .We dropped a big pine tree across the river for a foot log and built trails up My Creek and Ruby Creek. . .''

It probably should be mentioned here that a few basic trails had existed prior to 1910; although many more were constantly being built by the Forest Service, usually patrol cabins and ranger stations were along these earlier routes. Cabins were built a day's walk out of Avery, another day's walk to the next one, and so on. Employees could count on a spot for their animals and a roof over their heads a logical distance away. When the CCC built roads, the old trails were no longer important. Suddenly neither were the cabins nor the ranger stations. The Elk Prairie Ranger Station was not on a road, but an administrative site at Red Ives Creek was. Pole Mountain Ranger District became Red Ives District (with a little more acreage thrown in) and the Elk Prairie Ranger Station ceased to exist.

Red Ives Ranger Station, built by the CCC, started off on three different foundations before it was completed. But when the job was finished, the *espirit de corps* of the district was high. That was evident in the newspaper Ern Hanson published, something

The Red Ives Ranger Station, pictured here in the 1950's, was built by the CCC in the 1930's. Named for the prospector Red Ives, who had a dugout at the location, the site continues as an active ranger district. The district was formed by a combination of the Ward Peak and Pole Mountain Districts in 1932. (Scribner)

unique for ranger districts. The paper, printed for several seasons, featured clever drawings and witty articles about life in an outback ranger station. Today, Red Ives is one of three remaining districts on the St. Joe. It employs about twenty permanent people and over fifty seasonals. The district wintered in Avery until 1969, but now the entire office, its staff, equipment, and files move en masse each winter to St. Maries.

The third station branching out from Avery was Roundtop, straight south. Although it has had "an awful hard time making up its mind," Roundtop has still been around longer than a lot of other ranger stations on the 'Joe. At first it wasn't at Roundtop at all, but a tent camp at Hemlock Springs. Then Ashley Roche built the station in 1912 in the wide meadow it now occupies. Surrounding it were miles of beautiful, thick timber. That would be a logical end to the story, but such is not the case. In 1926 the ranger station was moved to Spokane Meadows on Twin Creek where

Roundtop Ranger Station still had the original log cabin in the foreground and the log cookhouse, left rear, in 1951. The log cabin dated back to 1912 when the administrative site was first established. Roundtop was reduced to a seasonal work center in 1957. (Scribner)

Franklin "Judge" Girard built a warehouse, root cellar, and an office-building-bunkhouse. This was supposed to be the last word in ranger stations. And it soon *was* the last word, for after three or four years the Twin Creeks idea was scratched—along with all the mosquito bites the rangers had collected there. So it was back to Roundtop. The log cookhouse built in 1926 was replaced by three portable buildings in 1957, and the CCC constructed the present office in the 1930's. An old war prison camp from the Lochsa River made a good warehouse and residence in 1948, and bunkhouses were added in 1959. Roundtop Ranger District was disbanded in 1957-58 but the ranger station became a work center, serving as a residence for summer employees of the Avery District. It looks as if Roundtop has finally made up its mind!

Until 1928, the spokes of the Forest Service wheel ran from Avery to the northeast, the southeast, and the south. Something was missing. Then in 1927 the Slate Creek District to the northwest was formed. The Slate Creek boundary extended from the Coeur d'Alene Divide to the North Fork-Slate Creek Divide, and it included Cedar Mountain Ridge and Dunn Peak to the east and Big Creek to the west. Supplies to the new ranger station were brought in on the old Slate Creek-Wallace trail which had been converted to a wagon road. The organization of the Slate Creek District in 1930 included the following: district ranger, L.A. Williams, who wintered in Avery; an alternate ranger; packer "Mugs" Bentley, and a cook. Although the district employed about 25 men including two trail crews and firemen, its work load mainly consisted of planting trees and building trails. It had the shortest life of all the districts, being abandoned in 1932.

A BIG YEAR

One of those years of change for the Forest Service on the St. Joe was 1932. The small districts headquartered at Avery were rearranged to form large districts, and more land on the St. Joe shifted to Forest Service ownership. Fire protection, economic conditions of the times, and drastically improved transportation systems all contributed to the changes.

In 1924 Congress had passed the Clark-McNary Act which encouraged cooperative fire protection between the Forest Service and private owners. Members of the St. Joe Timber Protection Association owned land from Herrick to Hoyt Flat and paid the Forest Service for fire protection. Then came the bad fire years of 1928 and 1929 with big fires in the Calder area and around Big and Slate Creeks. When the Forest Service presented the bills for fighting the fires to the Association, the small organization couldn't pay and it disintegrated. The Forest Service took over its land in 1932 and added two new districts, Calder and Clarkia. The Slate Creek District was dissolved and divided equally between Avery and the new Calder District. Charley Scribner was transferred from Ward Peak Ranger District to organize Calder, while Dean Herrington went to Clarkia.

One of the most significant man-caused events on the Forest occurred in the early '30's when the CCC opened up the country with a network of roads. The St. Joe Forest in 1930 had only two trucks, one in Avery and the other in the Palouse Division. The truck at Avery was used to haul supplies from the railroad depot up the hill to the ranger station, replacing an old wooden sled which had been used year around. After the roads were built, many vehicles began to replace pack strings and leg power. By combining Ward Peak and Pole Mountain Districts to form Red Ives, accessibility by the new road was assured. Red Ives personnel still wintered in Avery, but Avery was no longer the base of operations for the smaller districts.

The Forest Service on the St. Joe took over protection of quite a chunk of land at this time. Private land owners, hit so hard by the Depression that they were unable to pay taxes, donated about 200,000 acres to the St. Joe National Forest. The land included nearly all of the Mica Creek drainage, parts of Marble and Falls Creeks, and sections of the St. Maries River drainage. In this same way, forest land on the Coeur

Fire burns in the background of this 1928 picture of the Slate Creek Ranger Station. This district was formed in 1927, only to be split between the Avery and Calder Districts in 1932. The site was located on the upper end of Slate Creek. (U.S.D.A., Forest Service)

d'Alene, Kaniksu, and Clearwater Forests also expanded.

Meanwhile a complicated lawsuit between the N.P. and the Forest Service was going on over land ownership that was not to be settled for nearly thirty years. When the U.S. Congress wanted transcontinental railroads in 1864, it granted the Northern Pacific Railroad every odd section of land in a strip forty miles wide on each side of its tracks. Maps showing ownership looked like checkerboards. If the

Before 1930, mules traveled a lot easier than automobiles on the St. Joe National Forest. This car, one of the earliest on the Forest, makes a trip to Roundtop shortly after the road was constructed in the mid-1930's. (Theriault)

lands fell within Indian reservations, had mineral rights, or were homesteaded, N.P. could choose unoccupied lands within an additional twenty-mile strip. This alternate choice of land was known as scrip and the land was often sold by N.P. to settlers. Most of the land belonging to N.P. was selected prior to the birth of the Forest Service, so there was no problem until 1917. Then the question arose: could the Northern Pacific choose its lieu lands from the National Forest? The court case was on.

Decisions bounced back and forth like ping pong balls. Yes, said the Supreme Court, the railroads could choose lands from the National Forests. But then the Forest Service maintained that N.P.'s selections had been questionable, if not downright fraudulent. A congressional committee investigated the issue and announced in 1929 that alienation of the National Forest could not be permitted, but that N.P. was entitled to damages suffered by the decision. More lawsuits followed. N.P. *did* have claim to the land and made its selections by 1934, involving about 870,000 acres in Region One. Back to court. In 1939 the courts decided that N.P. had the right only to *agricultural* lands, and had sold several thousand acres in error. Now it owed the government a substantial sum for that land. Finally, the whole mess was settled by the

Transportation Act passed in 1941. The railroad no longer had to haul government passengers and supplies at fifty percent fare, but all the claims against the railroad would be dropped. Certainly, all parties involved must have let out a big sigh of relief over that decision!

The postscript to the story was a big land exchange in 1947 on the St. Joe in which N.P. traded 50,000 acres in exchange for timber receipts. Okay, said the Forest Service, you give us the land; the timber purchaser gives you all the money from selling timber off of it. This tripartite (three-party) agreement covered the N.P. land north of the St. Joe River as far as Simmons Creek, north of Red Ives. And that is why land north of the river is National Forest but south of the river it is checkerboard ownership with alternate sections owned by Burlington Northern (the merged companies of Great Northern, Northern Pacific, and Burlington Railroads). A full-time position on the Avery Ranger District is devoted to cost-sharing for joint projects such as roads through the checkerboard ownership. That was the last major land exchange until the early '70's when the St. Joe Forest purchased more land from patented mining claims and acquired six miles of river frontage on the upper St. Joe considered to be prime recreation land.

RANGERS

The early day Forest Service was a colorful operation, especially in an isolated area like the St. Joe. The original rangers were usually westerners; they were outdoorsmen, former trappers, cowboys, and woodsmen. They were put aboard a horse with a rifle, six-shooter, bedroll—and told to straighten things out. Their clothing identified them only by a bronze badge while the alternate or assistant rangers wore silver ones. Their jobs required hard work, good organization, and above all, common sense. They learned their profession through apprenticeship in the woods. They came to be viewed with honor and respect by local residents. These rangers were the custodians of the forests, guarding against fire, game poachers, timber and grazing trespassers, and exploiters.

Deciding who the exploiters were was sometimes the toughest part. One story, true or not, floated around about a bad experience of one young ranger. He supposedly stopped several prostitutes along the Milwaukee right-of-way and ordered them to leave. They laughed at him and went on their very merry way. In frustration the ranger wired his supervisor: "Undesirable prostitutes occupying Nat'l Forest. Please advise." In a day and age when bureaucratic red tape is the standard procedure, it is easy to appreciate the humor in the telegraphed response: "How do you know they're undesirable? Stay away from them." Common sense, indeed.

The rangers were constantly on the go, what with fires, timber sales, mapping, and trails. The men set out on foot with blankets and supplies in a Duluth

Jake Williams, a ranger at Avery, is shown here about 1920. Early day rangers had to be proficient at packing and handling a horse, shooting, and survival. Much of their patrol work was done on foot or by horseback. (Theriault)

packsack weighing forty to sixty pounds with a 25-mile walk ahead of them. Their duties certainly weren't limited to what was written on job descriptions.

Ralph Hand discovered that. He writes: "When I started my Roundtop assignment, I wasn't fully aware of just what my job was to be but I soon found out. Although my title was Assistant Ranger, I discovered that the actual work consisted of cooking, housekeeping, assisting two lumberjacks who were building a log cabin (spare time, of course), and dispatching."

That was on Hand's way up in the world. He started his Forest Service career literally in the gutter. "I reported to Joe Mahoney at the Avery Ranger Station on the morning of June 16 (1921). Joe was the Ranger who handled the dispatching, bossed the packers and functioned generally as manager of the Avery supply Base. . . I had been assigned as look-out at Pole Mountain, but the first job that I did for the Forest Service was to help old "Dad" Propst clean out the Avery sewer system. It always became plugged after the spring rains, and it had become sort of a tradition that all newcomers take a whirl at the disagreeable task. The college student, the seasoned lumberjack and the drifter who had just dropped off from a boxcar—each took his turn and was judged according to whether he rolled up his sleeves or turned up his nose. Over a year later I was told that I had been recommended for a ranger appointment, at least partly because I had been one of those who placed personal squeamishness subordinate to the importance of getting a dirty but necessary job done. . ."

In some ways their job was simple. The office of one ranger consisted of two wooden boxes in a tent.

One box was to sit on and the other served as a desk. The filing system was so logical that today's office managers could profit by it. There were two 60-D spikes driven into a tent frame or a tree. Spike number one was for incoming mail pending action; spike number two was for work the ranger chose to ignore. Number two was never filled, however, because "its contents—always dealt with from the bottom—were used to kindle the fire each morning." How much easier the job would have been!

The qualifications for a ranger's job were determined by a ranger's examination, which in those days was both practical and difficult. Candidates had to know how to throw a diamond hitch, pack and shoe their horses, and of course, ride well. But not always. Avery's second ranger, W.H. "Bill" Daugs, had once been a German sailor until he jumped ship and came West. Someone in Montana convinced him to take the ranger test. Could he cook? Yes, he figured he could, given a frying pan and some sourdough. Could be pack a horse? He never had but he managed to throw some things on the horse and lead it around the

Pictured on the steps of the Avery Ranger Station are Forest Service employees (lower row): Alec Brebner, Tom Wurth, and Art Flemming, a native Englishman, for whom Flemming Creek is named. Standing is Ranger Bill Daugs, responsible for many of the placenames on the St. Joe National Forest. (U.S.D.A., Forest Service)

corral. Could he shoot? The gun went off. Daugs was declared a ranger: his district was the Blackfoot District which is now all of Glacier National Park. From there he came to Avery, then retired on the Palouse District, a long way from a German ship.

The Forest Service didn't exactly overpay its employees. In 1913 the Forest Supervisor made all of $1680, his assistant made $1440 (both with college degrees in forestry) while the man on the ground in Avery earned $1020 a year and paid his own board. By the early 1920's when four rangers and their families wintered in Avery, the wages had sky-rocketed to $1200 a year. By 1936 pay was $2600 for full-time employees and $2.80 a day for seasonals. Today wages are comparable to those of most other jobs.

One thing hasn't changed, though. C.S. Webb recalls, "The Forest Service in 1913 had one characteristic which it still possesses—it could never get a man placed where it wanted or needed him. And, I thing that was good, Fresh challenges developed the fellows, most of whom were natives and like myself, had no formal education."

The ranger test evolved to a full day's written examination by 1923, and then in the 1930's it was abolished. Rangers were then required to have college degrees. This meant a change from Teddy Roosevelt's rough-rider image to professional men who emphasized theory and specialties. Many of the rangers from the old school of hard knocks retained their former positions but others were relegated to lower positions.

THE PROTECTION ERA

During the two decades following the 1910 Fire, activities of the rangers were geared toward the summer fire season. One of the first developments was the construction of miles and miles of trails. The earliest trail construction by the Forest Service had been in 1908. This trail followed the Fishhook-Marble Creek Divide from the homestead of Charlie Hoyt to Breezy Point where it connected with the Forty-Nine Meadows trail put in by homesteaders. This provided a tie for the homesteaders to the railroad at Avery and allowed the Forest Service better access to its back-country. In 1911 a trail was built along Fishhook Creek for four miles, crossing Flemming Ridge to the Flemming-Marble Creek Divide. The Fishhook trail also connected with the Patricia Ranger Station, a patrol station which served for a number of years as a summer stop-over. Other early trails south of the river connected with the Old Montana Trail, including the Fishhook-Kelley Divide, Flemming Ridge, and Allen Ridge trails. The CCC continued the trail work in the 1930's to about 1940.

One trail crew member hired by the Forest Service in the late '20's would have stood out in any crowd. Johnny "Few-Clothes" did have his personality quirks. He was an Englishman who as a child felt stifled by the heavy woolen clothing worn in London. His interpretation of America's freedom meant that he would not have to wear clothes. So . . . he didn't. He batched one winter in a hollow cedar at Bird Creek with only a coat and boots on. On the trail crew during the summer the story was that "nothing's too good for Johnny," and that's just what he wore!

Trail building in 1925 was "heavy going." This trail crew on the Little North Fork Trail experimented with horses and a plow to break through the thick regeneration and brush. Trail construction opened up large areas for better fire protection. (U.S.D.A., Forest Service)

With the advent of roads, the trails were gradually abandoned. Today, however, recreationalists and backpackers have sparked a renewed interest in the St. Joe's trail system.

Communication was also improved. In the spring of 1910, Ranger Joseph Halm built telephone lines connecting Taft and Avery. The line ran by way of Grand Forks to the St. Joe Ranger Station at Falcon, and then down the North Fork to Avery.

After the fire, the line was rebuilt from Wallace to Avery with the line grounded and hung on topped trees. Messages were still hand-carried, and during the 1910 fire Harold Theriault (age twelve) and his brother Eddie ran out with the message for fire crews to evacuate. A few years later some 400 miles of line criss-crossed the Forest. Not that the communication by telephone was perfect. The Roundtop telephone was the bain of Ralph Hand's existence in the summer of 1922:

The Roundtop Telephone
(Swan Song of a Dispatcher)
By Ralph Hand

Dedicated to "Mac" McHarg, Ashley Roche, "Judge" Girard, "Shorty" Piper, Gust Miller, Andy Callahan and all of those other old timers who took part in the Battle of the Roundtop District in the summer of 1922.

———

Purple twilight shades the valley of the shadowy St. Joe
While the last rays of the setting sun sets mountain tops aglow.
A coyote splits the silence with his weird unearthly whines
And a big owl from its tree top perch sends shivers up our spines.

When the coyote's howl is silenced and the big owls' voice is still
There are other nighttime serenades, some soothing, some that thrill.
The breezes in the tree tops have a meter all their own
But there is one note that gets my goat—that blasted telephone!

"Hello Roundtop, this is Bearskull—'bout that fire in Section two,
Jack and Charlie think they'll hold it, but we're gonna' need a crew.
That old canyon's full o'broom tops; she's a nasty mess o'fuels;
Better rustle up a packer for that extra string o'mules."

Here's a call from Mac at Avery, "Have you heard from Bradner's men?
That last run took out their phone line—haven't had a word since then.
Rutledge had another blowup, lost three camps with all their tolls
Shorty's crew has Wobbly problems; Pete just rolled a couple mules."

Next it's Gust at Monumental, couldn't make his ring come through
It's a relay from the Lookout—"Foehl Creeks having trouble too.
Mushroomed out and hit the ridge top—now the whole head end is loose
They need lots o'plug tobacco and a dozen rolls o'snoose."

Then a long buzz through the howler, "It's the Horse Camp, packer Joe.
Fire crew came and stayed to dinner and our grub pile's gettin' low
We can use a hundred rations—just leave out the oatmeal mush
Gettin' awful tired o'barracks so you better mark it rush!"

Then from down in Fishhook Basin through that ragged outpost wire
Comes the news we've all been dreading—it's another logging fire.
"Somebody down in Marble Creek took chances yesterday
Lit a fire to warm his chute grease an' it must of got away!"

"We need grub an' tools an' bedding and another pump and hose
That 'sociation fire's still spreading—where she'll end God only knows!
One man's got a nasty axe cut; some stumble bum just out o'jail
Drank up all the lemon extract; cook got mad and hit the trail."

"Where's that doctor from 'the Maries'? Lots of injured—it's a fright!
Hillsides full o'widow-makers—'nother man was killed last night.
Buckskin mag hit him dead center—got him wrapped up in a tent.
All his bones that wasn't broken must be pretty badly bent."

So it goes throughout the evening—far into the lonesome night
Coyote's silent, owls' quit hooting, still the August moon is bright.
Guess I'd better get some shut-eye, but each time I settle down
It's first the bell an' then the howler; next a hungry crew from town.

Epilogue

I wonder if in some far land, asbestos forests grow
Where careless campers are unknown, where firebugs never go.
Where lightning bolts have spark arrestors; smokers always roll their smokes
In the fire resistant foliage from the tall asbestos oaks.

If there is such a spot on earth, you'll find me there to stay.
Build myself a little cabin; sleep all night and dream all day
Just forget that busted ground line and the worn out batteries too
Forget the voices I can't hear and the rings that won't come through.

Forget the time they called to say a crew was coming out
And could they get a good square meal somewhere along the route?
And after I'd prepared the food and waited all that day
They called again to tell me they'd gone out another way!

Forget that heavy lightning bolt that wrecked the Fishhook line
And the nights they called me out of bed to ask about the time.
Just relax. . .and rest. . .and listen, while the breezes sigh and moan
And forget that bloomin' torture rack, the *Roundtop Telephone.*

At strategic points along the network of tracks, patrol cabins were built. These scattered cabins constructed largely in the 'teens and 'twenties were important layover stops for the packers. Smokechasers often manned the locations during periods of high fire danger, worked neighboring trails, or maintained the miles of phone lines. Many of the cabins such as Turner's Flat and State Line were borrowed from homesteaders or prospectors, who had abandoned or sold their claims. As always, ample horsefeed and a dependable spring were necessary requirements.

The 1910 fire also focused the need for packstrings to transport men and supplies over long distances to remote camps. The Forest Service rapidly acquired horses and mules so that by the early 1920's, they had 120 head of stock stationed at Avery. The strings, nine mules per pack, were dispatched regularly to Roundtop, Pole Mountain, or Ward Peak with needed grub and supplies. Short haul strings supplied lookouts and trail crews. Because of the importance of the packstrings, the type of pack trains changed

The corral at Avery Ranger Station shows the large number of pack animals used by the Forest Service. The buildings in the background date this photo to the early 1920's, prior to the building of the large barn. (Lindow)

considerably from the days before 1910 when packs were thrown on a bunch of broncos. Selected mules were organized according to the gaits of the animals and well-supplied with the best rigging money could buy.

The Decker brothers of Kooskia, Idaho, designed a special saddle which revolutionized packing in the Northwest. An adaptation of an earlier model, this packsaddle had boards cut from green cottonwood for its base. Then two pieces of heavy canvas were sewn together and stuffed with hay, curled hair, or better yet, beargrass. One of the packsaddle's earliest runs was a grotesque trip to Storm Creek, to exhume the bodies of 28 men. The firefighters' bodies were hauled out from their shallow graves by the Deckers to a

special plot in St. Maries. The fee was fifty dollars a day plus whiskey, which was no doubt necessary to complete the work.

The pack stock was kept behind the Avery Ranger Station during the field season. A large barn and corrals were constructed in 1926. Before then, packers occasionally woke in the morning to find their string scattered for miles. Pasturing the mules after the summer field season meant a long five-day trip to Dayton, Washington, between Walla Walla and Lewiston. Some 120 to 125 head were herded down the railroad track to Marble Creek, out the Marble Creek drainage, through Clarkia to the Palouse country. In later years the strings wintered in the Ninemile area in Montana.

Managing horses and mules is an art. One former Avery packer, Hugh Peyton, observes this about mules and men: "In these days when wheels take us everywhere and where packstrings of yore have faded into oblivion in most areas, it is hard to realize that they were of great importance at one time. And we rode at the head of these strings well-aware of the importance of the jobs. In fact we maybe were an insufferable type of personnel because we did look down on the poor bipeds that had to walk from one spot on earth to another. . .We reveled in the toil that began at dawn and the trails that led toward skylines that always bore the question of what was beyond. . . In later years I have found that packers were the most difficult type of personnel to acquire. I wondered why, because to me it was easy to understand. I have often said that I probably learned more about personnel management from packing mules than any other job that I have held. . .Most people and most mules are pretty good and will accomplish much if herded in the right and reasonable direction."

That didn't apply to all mules, though. There was Raymond, a mule that was black and little and *mean*. Anytime anybody tried to convince Raymond to do anything, he was in for a battle. This mule fought the pack, he fought moving out with the string, but above all Raymond fought being shoed. Once a smithy was working at Red Ives shoeing the string, bringing in two mules at a time to work on. Raymond observed these proceedings for awhile. Then when another mule was taken to be shod, he apparently decided to join the action. He trotted up and stood politely for the blacksmith without even being tied. A total gentleman about the matter, Raymond delicately lifted each hoof to be worked on without a murmur of dissent. But when the last nail had been driven, revenge was his. Out bolted two newly shod hind feet and kicked the poor blacksmith half way down the 'Joe.

Some packers had a very special knack; they needed to be both a mother hen and a rigid old schoolmarm to adjust to the personality of each mule. For example, says George Terrien, "I don't believe that Pop Flynn had an equal as a packer. . .I have seen him take a string of twelve loaded pack mules over a big windfall that was across the trail. After jumping his horse over, he would move ahead slow, while taking each mule

Three mules pose for the camera in the corral at Twin Creek before hitting the trail on another packing job. Spokane Meadows, which surrounded the Twin Creek Ranger Station, provided ample grass for the pack stock. (Lindow)

behind him over the windfall, calling each one by name, and nary a mishap. He had absolute control over his mules at all times. They liked him and he was good to them."

In those good ol' days cookhouses and cooks were yet another institution of the Forest Service. Big work crews required big amounts of food, but there were few facilities to prepare it at the remote stations of the upper St. Joe. Facilities were often tents, especially in in the early years. Later functional cookhouses were built at the Roundtop, Calder and Avery stations. The Forest Service has discontinued these, but Red Ives still provides the service for its employees. The cooks at the various camps and stations were often characters in their own right, setting the morale of a large crew.

At Roundtop, Gust Miller was everyone's favorite. In fact, his name was given to Miller Peak. Gust made sourdough pancakes that would delight the palate of any connoisseur. When his admirers were full to the point of immobility, Gust with his heavy German accent, and pipe in hand, would announce ponderously, "Und now ve schmoke."

To guard against furry camp robbers, Gust slept with his old forty-some-odd colt six-shooter, his ear cocked for the sound of an invading bear. He set out three or four candles on a small table next to his false teeth. Then one night, wrote Ralph Hand, "Gust was aroused by a noise outside the cabin. It sounded like a bear at the screened meat cooler which was located under the eaves of the cabin porch, so he grabbed his gun and dashed for the door. He threw it open and took one step—one too many, it proved, for his bare toes came in contact with a large porcupine that had already turned in retreat.

"Now Gust had a strong accent that made him difficult to understand, but his ability at pantomime more than made up for his lack of coherence. In relating his encounter with the porcupine, Gust limped across the room, wooling his wavy gray hair with both hands and all but spilling tears down the front of his bib overalls, until I could almost feel the pain in my own toes."

Gust Miller was not the only cook beset and upset by bear troubles. At a cabin between Roundtop and Marble Mountain, one cook for a Forest Service road construction gang had to make the best use of the fourteen by eighteen floor space. As Charley Scribner tells, "When it was bed time for the cook he moved

Lawrence Deja heads out on the Snow Peak trail in 1954 to bring supplies to the lookout there. Packstrings, an integral part of the Forest Service through the 1960's, hauled supplies to lookouts, trail crews, and fire camps in the remote reaches of the St. Joe. (Lindborg)

the table against one wall, shoved the seat in as far as it would go, then unfolded his cot nearly under the table. The cook was a very quiet, slow-moving, slow-talking man with a small quiet voice, but the meals were always good and on time. The camp had been afflicted with visitations of bear and as usual practice someone sat up late to discourage such events. . .About 11:30 a small voice broke the stillness. 'Hey, fellers, hey, there's a bear in here, hey, fellers, hey.' Everyone grabbed a handful of offensive weapons—rifles, pistols, axes, clubs, anything that was handy—and advanced to the rescue, but we came to a sudden halt when we pushed the door open. The bear had his hind feet on the deacon seat and his front feet on the table, methodically cleaning up the breakfast set-up. His tummy was within less than a foot of the cook, to whom he was completely oblivious. As we opened the door, the bear calmly turned his head, looked us over critically, and returned to his labors. This presented problems.

''If we shot the bear he would have dropped on top of the cook, and if the shot was not immediately fatal, he might have been in a resentful mood. After a short consultation it was decided to block the door open so the bear could get out if he so wished, and we could observe him, and in case he decided to finish his meal on the cook, we could take preventive action. However, after leisurely cleaning the table, the bear decided to mosey out for his lair, quietly and with great dignity. When he cleared the door the artillery opened up and a few steps further, our bear troubles came to an end. All turned out to help the cook clean up the mess and again prepare for breakfast. The road crew had a lively subject for discussion for several days.''

LONELY SENTINELS

The observers on lookout towers were the key to the entire fire organization in those early years. The lonely sentinels furnished the "eyes" for the district. Many were old hands at the job, serving on a particular lookout for several years. They knew their area so well that they could pinpoint a location of a fire even in the dead of night. Others were greenhorn kids fresh out of New York City who were afraid of bears and lightning, but still gutsy and willing to tackle the job. Typically, men occupied the towers until the Second World War when women or married couples became common. One former lookout site near Calder was aptly named Maternity Hill in the 1930's after several pairs of newlyweds found themselves in the family way after a summer spent there. Yes, these sentinels of the St. Joe were a motley crew, but they performed well in safeguarding the timbered lands.

The lack of lightning protection made lookout duty hazardous indeed, and at least one lookout locally was zapped by a bolt of lightning out of the blue. The Marble Mountain observer, a St. Joe Protection

Cedar Mountain lookout north of Avery, one of the first towers built in Region One, was constructed in 1915 and destroyed in the late 1950's after several decades of service. The observer lived in the bottom of the building and climbed a ladder to the second floor to detect fires. (Saunders)

Association observer, was killed by a strike in the early 1920's. Most observers were more fortunate, but all had tales of close calls when they returned from duty in the fall. Even after towers were commonplace, strikes continued to hit those structures. The tower on Monumental Buttes was struck by a bolt of lightning in 1924, knocking the observer unconscious and making shambles of the tower. And imagine how it struck terror into the hearts of neighboring lookouts when

the abandoned tower on Wallace District's Striped Peak burned to the ground during a lightning storm in the early 1960's.

The lookouts endured a different sort of worry in the 1930's and 40's. A strange man nicknamed the Wildman of the Clearwater then roamed the backcountry of the Bitterroot, Nezperce, Clearwater, and St. Joe National Forests. The Wildman was a hermit, avoiding people and living off what he could scavenge from the land or the few people inhabiting the woods. A hunter once lost a hindquarter from his newly bagged deer to him; another hunter lost half a pot of stew. The Red Ives and Roundtop Ranger Stations were two of his favorite haunts to raid, and no lookout was immune. It was especially terrifying to lookouts to hear of his visits or to imagine his shaggy, unkempt countenance staring through the windowpanes of their lookout. Occasionally, Forest Service personnel saw his tracks in the snow. The Wildman was finally captured by the Forest Service in 1945 on the Canyon Ranger District of the Clearwater following an effort spanning several years. As it turned out, the man was Bill Moreland, a drifter who had taken to the woods in 1932. Moreland was sentenced to the state mental institution at Orofino for a short stay for breaking and entering. Following his release, Moreland was involved in a series of eccentricities including petty theft from isolated cabins where he would leave odd notes or letters. The Wildman disappeared in 1964, his whereabouts again unknown.

Lookout duty could be exciting, but not always. William Gunterman described his tour of duty on Bluebird Lookout in 1929, "A lookout job is slow part of the time, but I have lots of time to yoddle (sic)

Surveys in the 1920's and 1930's pinpointed the best locations for lookouts on the St. Joe National Forest. Areas which the lookout can directly see were plotted from each high peak, and tower sites were subsequently chosen to maximize fire detection. Stan Larson, longtime Forest Service employee, is shown in this photograph plotting the seen area. (Lindow)

Gregsons's music, to brush my teeth three times a day, to study surveying that I have forgotten, and to learn to play the mouth organ that I have. I wouldn't have time for any of it, if I were at the Ranger Station or elsewhere. I get plenty of exercise making things and carrying nine gallons of water up from my spring over a half mile away every day and keeping the main trails in good shape for two miles around me.''

The old time lookouts would probably cringe to see the changes in lookout life today. Electric lights, refrigerators, and propane stoves replace the old lanterns and woodstoves of yesterday. Televisions, stereos, and a weekly garbage and water service are additional trappings of the modern lookout. Even the food has changed. Up to the 1960's, most lookouts were supplied by the district packer. Mules carried enough grub and supplies for the entire season. Such items as fresh milk, eggs, meat, fruit and vegetables are now common fare. Only dried or condensed milk,

Bathtub Mountain built in the early 1920's was another important lookout on the St. Joe. The tower was used as the observatory with the cabin serving as housing for the lookout observer. Both were destroyed in the 1950's. (Lindow)

Hoyt Mountain typifies the interior of a typical lookout during their heyday in the 1930's and 1940's. Note the firefinder in the center of the photograph on which the observer plotted fires. (Terrien)

canned goods, staples such as flour and sugar, and huckleberries or grouse (in season) formerly tempted the oldtime lookout's palate. The flood of tourists and visitors is also a modern phenomenon. A lookout in the 1930's could anticipate only the infrequent visits by the packer with supplies or the ranger with his inspection forms. Lookout life has changed, but the romance and challenge of spending a summer on top of a mountain with the rest of the world under you has not.

The first lookout stations were crude affairs, often only a tent perched on top of a high promontory. A ladder of boards was nailed to a neighboring tree where the observer would climb periodically to check for fires. Some of these trees had platforms, or ''Crow's nests,'' in which a map and alidade (an instrument for determining direction) were placed. The

mapboard had a canvas tarp thrown over it to protect the maps from the elements. No blueprints or plans directed the observer on how to construct his site, and most sites were used from season to season. As described by one old lookout in the late 1920's, ''It sure has been a job because I have put the tent right on the peak a few feet from the mapboards and the phone. It is really solid rock, and I had to dig way into the steep slope to get a flat place big enough for my tent.''

Towers gradually replaced the earlier tents in the decades following the 1910 fire. The earliest towers (Cedar Mountain, Monumental Buttes, Quarles Peak, Fishhook Peak, and Middle Sister) were constructed by 1920. Additional lookout construction proceeded rapidly after surveys in the 1930's mapped seen areas from every knob and hill. The cheap labor of the Depression and the Civilian Conservation Corps furnished the manpower. By 1940, over eighty towers populated the forest of the Upper Joe. Lookouts were classed into primary towers, those normally manned by fire guards each summer, and secondary towers, which were maintained only during emergency fire conditions. The structures often were located so close that neighboring lookouts could hike over for an evening's visit or meet at a common point. However, where once there were many, now only a few dot the landscape. By the late sixties, only fifteen of the towers were manned, and in 1979, only four. However, with the current concern over fuel shortages and economy, the Forest Service is considering a return of lookout towers.

The main duty of the lookouts was pinpointing the location of fires upon detecting a smoke. Lookouts phoned to report to the dispatcher or ranger, who dispatched smokechasers to combat the blaze. Smokechasers were normally young men, hired during the summer months. Leaving from the ranger station or a patrol cabin, the firefighters would hike several miles, carrying their tools and rations on their back to reach some lightning-struck snag on a distant mountain ridge. The speed with which they reached their fire meant the difference between a small spot fire or a large blaze covering acres and acres of ground. Large fires could often burn for weeks before being subdued by the fall rains. The majority of the fires were ignited by lightning, even today the primary cause of forest fires on the 'Joe.

Large fires have repeatedly scarred the landscape of the St. Joe following the 1910 burn. Huge acreages in Loop Creek, Slate Creek, and Big Creek reburned in 1917, 1919, 1928, and 1929. Foehl Creek had successive fires in the teens, and a large fire on Midget Creek burned several hundred acres in 1931. The hillsides behind Avery were blackened by a 37,000 acre blaze in 1934. A spark from the locomotive at Setzer Creek set that one. The last large fire on the 'Joe was a 2000 acre fire on Sisters Creek in 1967, a result of prescribed burning operations.

PLANTING

Another cog of Forest Service work was set in motion following the 1910 fire and successive fires: the need to replant the timber. A ton and a half of walnut seed, red oak acorns and hickory nuts were sent to the Coeur d'Alene Forest in the fall of 1910 as a part of an experiment. It had mystified foresters why so few hardwood trees were found in this mountain region, so the ninety acres planted in Slate Creek the following spring were watched with interest. For a few years the little trees blazed the hillsides with autumn color before they were winter-killed.

Then, in the fall of 1912 "almost 2400 acres on the Coeur d'Alene and St. Joe Forests were seeded to white and yellow pine, the seeding being done with corn planters. . .Many a farmer's boy has used a corn planter all day where the fields are level and free from obstructions, but it is quite another thing to work steadily all day long, climbing steep hills and rockslides, and jumping over windfalls, all the time trying to keep a straight line. . .," remembers William W. Morris.

In addition, cedar, Western white pine, Eastern white pine, ponderosa pine, spruce, Douglas fir and redwood were planted. The stock came from all over the country—Arkansas, North Carolina, Pennsylvania, California, Minnesota, Michigan, New York, the Dakotas. Perhaps that is why more of the trees did not survive; they simply were not adapted to North Idaho.

Loaded with construction materials, a packstring winds up the Nelson Peak trail to build another lookout. Packer Virgil Pears heads this string. The majority of the towers were constructed in the Depression era by CCC labor. (Lindow)

Planting camps were common for many years on the St. Joe. The late Lloyd Donally who probably supervised more planting projects than anyone else in the Northern Region wrote in his memoirs of a typical planting project:

"Another fellow and I boarded a C.M. St. P & P. Ry. passenger train at Superior, Montana, destination Herrick, Idaho. On May 28, 1927, we were assigned work planting trees, mostly white pine, on the Middle Fork of Big Creek. The job location was 15 miles by trail from Herrick. Our salary was $0.53-1/8 per hour less $0.40 per meal. All supplies, camp equipment, and seedlings were brought in by mules. Quarters for the men were in brown-colored army pyramid tents; six to eight men to a tent. Bunks were made by using two six-inch poles or split cedar placed on the ground about thirty inches apart and filled with straw. Blankets and a tarp were furnished—no pillows or hand towels in those days! The work was hard; the food delicious with all you wanted to eat." The beds were nonetheless a big improvement over previous years, for in the fall of 1926 an epidemic of spinal meningitis had hit the camp on Big Creek, and two men died. The men had always slept on the ground atop boughs, ferns, grass or whatever, and this was not thought to be healthful. By 1934 folding canvas cots were issued for beds and the planting camps were more modern.

Other planting projects Donally worked on were not always thought to be healthful, either. In the Slate Creek area, there were no trails, so many windfalls, and such thick brush that the mules would get tangled up and fall with their legs in the air. "The men were offered 25¢ a day bonus, plus board and railroadfare, if they would stay until the job was finished. Not many stayed," Donally says. It rained and snowed that fall for ten days straight until the men were offered free board just to finish the work. At Ramsey Creek on the North Fork the next spring, the weather was so hot and dry that whenever the planters dug a hole, dust blew into their faces. On some of the projects the men were expected to plant 1200 trees per day. "I believe," Donally wrote, "I sent more men down the road talking to themselves who were unable to meet this quota than on any Forest Service job I was ever on. Anyone who ever worked under my supervision on tree planting never forgot how I routed them over the hills."

Besides planting on Big Creek and Slate Creek, Donally planted trees on Ramsey, Railroad, and Rougin Creeks on the North Fork; on Avery Creek; on Setzer Creek; on Beaver Creek in the Red Ives District; Marble Creek; Charlie Creek north of Baldy Mountain; and on Bond Creek near St. Joe City.

How effective was the planting? Foresters concede that the product probably did not justify the money and effort. Most of the white pine plantations were hit by the blister rust, and the large stands of Black Hills ponderosa pine did not adapt well to this area. On the bright side, Colorado blue spruce can be seen on the North Fork and some of the surviving pine has now reached dimensions large enough to log. Late in the fall of 1978, Charley Scribner made a happy discovery near Railroad Creek: a strong, healthy little redwood!

Still another result of the fire of 1910: grazing on the St. Joe. If by chance the rangers were hit by

insomnia—and even if they weren't—they could always count sheep. With the timber gone in so many areas, grass was plentiful for sheep brought in by rail. The Loop Creek grazing allotment for some 2000 head of sheep covered the area from the head of Skookum Creek to Ward Creek. Some were also brought in from Superior to St. Joe Lake to the Pole Mountain District, but the Ward Peak and Avery Districts pastured the bulk of the animals. Another large allotment was in the Monumental Buttes area. Rangers were given the job of counting noses coming off the train and heading out after summer grazing. The last sheep shipped out in 1955 after the timber and brush grew too tall for the short animals.

FOCUS: 1946

The year was 1946, and the country was recovering from the big war. Things were normal on the St. Joe Forest with forest guards clearing the trails and repairing telephone line to complete the annual preparations for the fire season. The primary lookouts were all manned: North Butte, Hoyt Mountain, Bearskull, Fishhook, etc. Most of the old hands were back, and a few women lookouts returned as a carry-over from the war years. There were some new faces—this year's crop of college boys from Montana or back East and a few recently-returned veterans seeking work in the Forest Service.

By July, a few isolated lightning fires had caused a short flurry of excitement and the setting of the Avery dump had sent a couple smokechasers scurrying there to prevent the small fire from crawling up the slope. The woods and fine fuels had gradually dried out, and it became general knowledge that another lightning storm would cause trouble. Not much later summer storms came boiling out of the Clearwater country, setting fires along their path. The phone line buzzed between the lookouts and the ranger stations with reports of fires, but the seasoned Avery, Red Ives, and

Sheep on the St. Joe? The steep timber country hardly seems like good grazing for sheep but for about twenty years the Forest Service issued several grazing permits including Loop Creek and Shefoot Mountain. The animals were shipped to Adair by rail until the mid-1950's. (Scribner)

Old meets new in this 1969 photograph. A helicopter unloads materials to repair the Arid Peak tower. Aerial reconnaissance gradually replaced lookouts during the 1950's and 1960's. (U.S.D.A., Forest Service)

Roundtop crews handily extinguished the small fires.

Meanwhile in Missoula, an experimental force of fire-fighters just had been organized as the smokejumpers of Region One. They were a highly specialized group of fire-fighting paratroopers organized by the Forest Service to combat fires in the more inaccessible reaches of the Northern Region. Memos had been sent to the Forest Supervisors and rangers, encouraging their use of the smokejumpers and touting their future importance in fire control. With this in mind, Lloyd Donally ordered these first smokejumpers to be dropped in the Little North Fork drainage. As the dozen jumpers parachuted on the fire, the lookouts on Bearskull, Snow Peak, North Butte, and Stubtoe watched the new phenomenon, without realizing that a new era of fire-fighting had begun. With new roads the St. Joe was no longer totally dependent on animals to supply its ranger stations or lookouts. Packers with their diminished strings now were needed only to supply the more inaccessible towers or to assist the trail crews. By 1950 the stock had been reduced at

This brush camp at Twin Creek housed forestry workers who piled brush and thinned timber. The Roundtop Area had been opened up to logging only a couple years before this picture was taken in 1954. (U.S.D.A., Forest Service)

Avery to one short string with seven mules and two horses. Then one nostalgic day in 1969, the last mule headed out to pasture. The patrol stations such as Patricia, Bearskull, Jug Camp, and Nugget also were gradually abandoned and later torn down.

The old telephone systems were scrapped in 1950, and replaced by radio communication. Dave Brown, longtime St. Joe employee, became the familiar Communications Officer on the Forest. Miles and miles of telephone wire are still evident on the ground with old insulators still hanging on trees along its path.

Aircraft soon proved itself invaluable in fire control activities. Most importantly, air patrol, having proved its worth in reconnaissance during the war years, replaced lookouts as the main detection force. The abandoned towers were torn down in the mid-50's and 60's. Old B-52 bombers from World War II and the Korean War attacked troublesome fires from the air

with retardant. Later helicopters spotted fires and ferried men and equipment when fire broke out.

The year 1946 also brought increased mechanization to fire-fighting. Bulldozers and other heavy equipment had been introduced into the country during the CCC road construction years. The Forest Service, however, did not start using dozers until after the two modern timber sales on Lick Creek and Wawa Creek. A dozer could construct as much fireline as 50-100 men. Fire fighting now was indeed a far cry from men and mules, pulaskis and crosscut saws.

NOW

The image of the seasonal employee for the Forest Service through the years has been altered as much as the job itself. In those early years, many of the seasonals were from skid row, using their summer work season to dry out from a winter of wine. They often worked all summer without a day off and collected their wages in Avery before boarding the train to leave at the end of the season. Sometimes they took their money with them; other times they left it in Avery after gambling sprees and much bootleg whiskey, for Avery then was a ripsnortin' town.

Today's seasonals, however, are mostly college students, many of them majoring in forestry. A growing number of workers are young women. It is not unusual to see girls wearing hard hats and work boots marking timber, surveying roads, or on the fire line.

The job is certainly different today, too. It once consisted of managing and conserving timber and range, fire protection, and patenting lands listed as agricultural. Timber management did not involve water resources, erosion control, training programs, personnel management, recreation use, information and education. There were no automobile accidents, no cost share, no environmental analysis reports (EAR's) to write. Life was simple. But the post World War II era ushered in increased home construction, urbanization, industrialization, and created a larger demand for lumber and wood products. The Forest Service was expected to tap its untouched wood resources in the Pacific Northwest. The St. Joe complied with the need by increased logging activity. Then came the age of environmental concern: disagreements over the practice of clearcutting, logging near streams, and increased interest in recreation and aesthetics. A balance must be leveled between use and abuse of our resources, and the Forest Service carries the burden of being the only guardian over much of the nation's timber land.

The growing complexity of the job has led to a larger staffing of the districts with specialists. The number of people involved in the decision-making process of timber management has multiplied by bounds. The multidisciplinary approach requires input from engineers, logging specialists, transportation planners, hydrologists, soil scientists, silviculturists, archeologists, economists, sociologists, land use planners, geologists, wildlife biologists, watershed and recreation specialists. That doesn't count the business managers, clerks, receptionists, writers, information officers—nor the entomologists, geneticists, pathologists, scientists, and chemists who work to improve stands of trees. . . Statistics have shown, however, that it still takes the average sawyer three

minutes to saw down a tree on the St. Joe.

An old Danish man, Nels Johnson, once gave some advice about work in the organization of the Forest Service: "Da vay to vork for da Forest Service is to keep da feet warm, da head cool, and learn to spell *approximate.*" Yes, times have certainly changed—or have they?

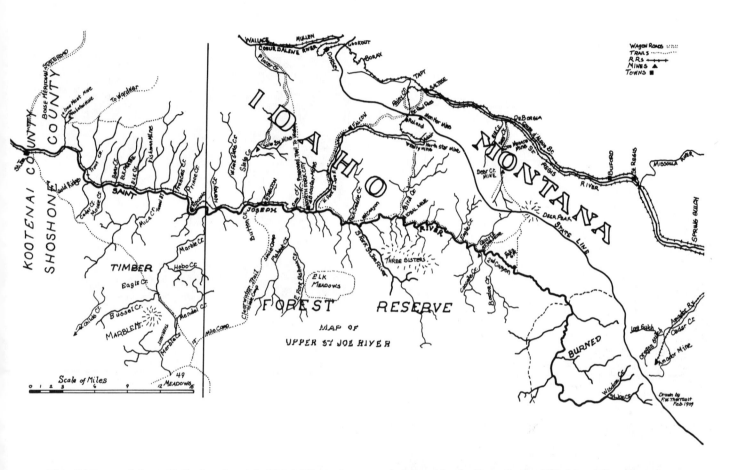

This 1909 map of the upper St. Joe, drawn by Frank Theriault, was commissioned by the Forest Service. The first trails and roads are depicted, as well as several of the earliest mines and communities of the area. (Theriault)

9 Contributions of CCC

The effect the Depression had on the St. Joe Valley was different from some parts of the United States. There were no bread lines, no broken businessmen here. Instead, the valley stepped into a whole new aspect of its development when President Franklin Roosevelt created the Civilian Conservation Corps in 1933.

One of Roosevelt's most popular "alphabetical agencies," the CCC provided employment in fresh-air government camps for about three million uniformed young men. Their work was useful—reforestation, fire-fighting, flood control, and swamp drainage. In addition to fire control work, the Corps was responsible for major road-building projects, and because of that, it probably had more of an impact than any other single agency in the history of the St. Joe.

An editorial in the *Tin Can Tamarack,* a newspaper produced at the Tin Can Camp, summed up the philosophy of the CCC. ". . .Men trained in the University of Life learn all types of trade, a measure of discipline, other fellow's rights, elimination of vicious habits and anti-social tendencies."

What the CCC meant to this area was an influx of about one thousand men in camps dotted up and down the St. Joe Valley. There were camps at Bond

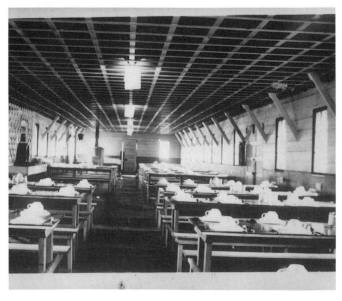

The interior of the CCC kitchen of the 120th Company in Avery was a popular place for both corpsmen and residents to watch movies, have parties, and enjoy good cooking. The cookhouse and several other CCC buildings were washed out in the 1938 flood. (Diemer)

The Avery CCC camp was located on what is now the Potlatch landing in West Avery. Camp No. 120 had its own depot (next to the track, right end), a cookhouse, PX, infirmary, and school. Nine main camps were located in the St. Joe valley. (Diemer)

Creek (St. Joe City), Falls Creek, Big Creek (Herrick), Spring Creek, Marble Creek, Hoyt Flat (a veterans' camp), Avery, Tin Can Flat, and Conrad's Crossing. Additional spike camps were set up at Bathtub, Bird Creek, Turner Flat, and Roundtop. Each camp had at least 120 men, and some had as many as 500 at their peak. They were under the jurisdiction of the U.S. Army out of Fort Wright in Spokane with an Army and Naval Reserve captain and lieutenant. The men wore olive drab fatigues left over from World War I.

Much like military bases, the camps developed their own self-sufficiency. Each camp had its own PX, infirmary and doctor, canteen, and a teacher. Each camp did its own rockwork (some still remains at Bathtub, a camp of World War I veterans), gathered its own wood supply, and even built its own additional buildings such as a large, rustic gymnasium at Tin Can Flat. The Avery camp had its own depot.

The work for the CCC boys was clear-cut. In 1931 it was impossible to travel from St. Joe to Avery by road. For over twenty years the only way in or out of the town of Avery was by rail—or by poling canoe, or by foot if one were so inclined. The CCC work projects were to be supervised by the Forest Service, a civilian contractor would supply the equipment and planning, and the CCC boys would provide the labor. So in 1934 work on the concrete bridge in Avery was started under the supervision of contractor Henry Fleming at a cost of $80,000. The CCC proudly installed a plaque signifying that the work had been done by Company 1991, F-120 (Avery camp). Downriver the men built the bridge crossing the railroad track near St. Joe City and the concrete bridge over Falls Creek.

The entire valley needed road work. The N.R.A. (National Relief Administration) workers had built the road from Avery to Packsaddle Campground in 1933-34, and the CCC took over the project from there to Red Ives Ranger Station. The entire Red Ives compound was CCC handiwork. Finally in 1938 the road connecting Avery and Red Ives was completed, a big improvement over the 57-mile Kelley Creek-Bathtub-Beaver Creek route. That hastened the end of packers and pack strings. Going downriver, the CCC broke a road from Avery to St. Maries. The valley was open at last to automobiles.

Probably the biggest project tackled by the CCC boys was the Fishhook Tunnel. Much of the time, two shifts worked on the tunnel. Some tunnel it was, too: 415 feet long, 20 feet high, 24 feet wide. The project took ten tons of blasting powder in 2,277 holes; the muck pile of 150 cubic yards a day was used for road fill. Then during the time of slack funding, the men cleared the trail to Lick Creek. It was a happy night when the boys saw moonlight at the end of the tunnel on May 23, 1939. Today the tunnel has the distinction of being the only haul road tunnel in Region One.

Responsible for most of the earliest roadwork into the upper St. Joe country, the CCC also built the Fishhook Tunnel in 1938-39. On a good day the boys could blast up to eight feet of the 415-feet hole. CCC labor was also responsible for building the Fishhook Road below the tunnel in the mid-'30's. (Scribner)

Who were these young men who came to work up the swiftwater? They came mostly to this particular area from New York, New Jersey, and Arkansas; many had names and accents foreign to northern Idaho. Young Bobby Cass sold them newspapers daily and remembers that he sometimes could not understand them. Their ages started legally at sixteen (occasionally there were some very small, thin "sixteen-year-olds" who were probably younger) and ranged clear into the thirties. Paid thirty dollars a month, the men kept only nine dollars for themselves and sent the rest home to help their families. With room, board, and clothing provided, that nine dollars during the Depression was most attractive. The enlistment period lasted from six months to five years, a choice of the boys themselves. Some stayed in long enough to become a part of the community, some left immediately, others stayed to make their home near the St. Joe. Some have returned after many years to visit, recalling their time in the CCC as the best time of their lives. Certainly many a city boy saw the rural side of life he would have missed entirely in the East or Deep South.

A few of the boys had no skills and little education, while just as many were very capable, so their jobs were planned accordingly. Their manners and attitudes varied as much as their backgrounds. A few had

A group of CCC boys pose outside their tent. Exposed to life in the Bitterroots, the CCC boys went home to New York City, New Jersey, or the backwoods of Arkansas much richer for their experience. A few stayed to call the St. Joe their home. (Diemer)

definite criminal tendencies learned off the big-city streets, and on occasion, work leaders were threatened by their charges. That was the exception rather than the rule of course, for most of the time there was a great deal of work going on. In the off-hours, there were a variety of activities. The camps had pool and ping-pong tournaments, boxing matches, horseshoe games; the boys fished, hunted, swam. Their softball leagues played against the town, other camps, and between their own barracks. They had weekly church services and invited the town to massive Christmas dinners. One enterprising young man, Charles Poindexter, was so determined to develop his hobby of photography that he created his own darkroom in the bottom of a large cedar tree on Bird Creek. He lined the ceiling with burlap, used the creek for water baths, and fought off squirrels to protect his prints. This was such an unusual thing to do that *Grit*

"Cedar tree darkroom Bird Creek Spike Camp, No. 187, Avery, Idaho. C.J.P. Photo" reads the caption on this picture taken by Charles Poindexter. Poindexter created his own darkroom in this cedar tree at the mouth of Bernier Creek, a tributary of Bird Creek. The tree is still intact. (Lindow)

This picture of the northern portal of the Fishhook Tunnel was taken in 1938. The work was largely handwork: drilling, blasting, picking, and shoveling. (Penzkover)

newspaper featured it as a human interest story in 1964.

And then the CCC boys were well-noted for another activity in Avery especially, but no doubt they pursued it whenever the opportunity arose. The *Tin Can Tamarack* explained it well in this note May, 1939: "There has been quite a bit of action downtown among the lads trying to steal the *girls* away from one another." No wonder, with so many men and the eligible girl population of Avery being somewhat limited!

When the '40's rolled around and Hitler's tanks rumbled through Europe, the Army began some calisthenics and rifle-training in the CCC camps. Then the lottery and draft calls increased, and the nation turned its eyes to threat of war. The camps were closed as their enlistees went on to defend the country. One group left behind this nostalgic verse:

> *"You are leaving Avery with lots to regret*
> *But when you get home don't ever forget*
> *To remember the 'Edol,' remember the*
>   *'Stein'*
> *Remember the fun at the old 'Canteen'."*

Somewhere, sometimes, perhaps someone still remembers the 'Edol' and the 'Stein;' but youth and time pass quickly and even the presence of the CCC in St. Joe country is a vague memory now.

10 Trapping and Wildlife

THE HARDY ONES

The popularity of beaver skin hats in London had a direct effect on the exploration of Idaho in the early 1800's as trappers were drawn out in search of beaver. Hudson Bay trappers covered much of the Northwest, penetrating thousands of streams in dugout canoes. Then after the Lewis and Clark expedition in 1805, Americans joined the lucrative trapping business. Certainly the 50,000 miles covered by David Thompson, founder of the Kullyspell House at Lake Pend Oreille, testifies to the amount of territory seen by the early trappers and traders. Because they did get into nearly every major drainage in Idaho and the rest of the Northwest, we can assume that someone at

sometime assuredly made it into the St. Joe country in the early trapping era. Unfortunately, no records verify that, and knowing that this was hostile Coeur d'Alene Indian territory may have discouraged the trappers from further exploration. Consequently, the typical mountain man did not significantly alter the history of the valley, but later trappers have definitely added drama to the saga.

Trappers cannot really be separated from homesteaders, prospectors, packers, Forest Service seasonals, or local residents, for trapping was a source of supplemental income during the winter for nearly everybody. The ones who engaged in trapping were, however, the types who were accustomed to surviving off the resources of the land. Homesteaders Black Joe Faniff, Charlie Hoyt, the Setzer brothers, and Sam "49" Williams all ran traplines. Trapper Jack Allen whose family was part of the Swiss colony downriver, left his name on Allen Ridge, eight miles east of Avery. His partner, with whom he shared the original cabin

"Three of a kind" reads the notation on the bottom of this early photograph of trapper Alec McDonald. McDonald who trapped in St. Joe country in the teens and '20's displays his furs in Avery. Trappers like McDonald lived alone for months during the winter, following their traplines. (Theriault)

Bobby Stauffer, an Avery resident who packed, prospected, and trapped, is shown here with Doris Pears on the left and an unidentified woman on the right at his cabin on the flat just east of Avery. (Lindow)

on Bird Creek, was a man named Jackson of Jacksons Knob. Swiftwater boatmen Archie Lane and Jim Peters of Marble Creek trapped during the winter months, and prospectors Con Faircloth, the Callahans, and Art Lintz added the sale of furs to their income. Bobby Stauffer, who packed, prospected, and occasionally bootlegged, worked at trapping, too, along with Fuzzy Reid (Fuzzy Peak), an iron worker on the railroad and part time saloon-keeper. The Carlson brothers, Albert,

Charlie, Frank, and Oscar, ran traplines south of Avery, and also built numerous sturdy cabins throughout the area. Wash Applegate worked as a lumberjack on Marble Creek in addition to trapping.

Of all the types of people who persisted in taming the St. Joe, trappers had to be about the hardiest. In the winter it was lonely in those woods when snow was sometimes twenty feet deep and the nearest human was two or three day's walk away. The trapper who succeeded had to thrive on solitude and use the elements to his advantage. Life was really not very complicated; either you survived or you didn't. Shelter

Gene Turner shows the bobcat he bagged on the upper St. Joe around 1912. The picture is taken just west of his homestead cabin at Turner Flat. Note the snowshoes, a necessity for checking winter traplines in the heavy snow. (Turner)

was found in one of the numerous cabins that dotted the country then, or in a small cabin the trapper built himself. If he chose to build his own, he cut down trees with a saw or hand ax and nailed the rough logs together. The structures were so small that the trapper could often light and stoke the fire without getting out of bed, which was a positive advantage on frosty winter mornings! Each man needed several shelters along his trapline, and sometimes nature provided the best ones. Wash Applegate and his partner William Dunlap trapped along the St. Joe-Clearwater Divide in the 1920's and stayed in a huge hollow cedar tree. This sanctuary was eleven feet across at the bottom, tall enough in the middle for a man to stand, and so quiet that nothing could be heard inside or out. The men installed a five-gallon drum for a stove. At another spot they found protection inside some big rocks where someone had conveniently built a rock hearth. Only at a few of the shelters did the trappers enjoy the luxury of a blanket; mostly they covered up with a bed of dried ferns and boughs, relying all night on the fire for warmth.

In the late fall trappers hired packers out of Avery or Superior to haul their grubstake to their main cabins. Applegate and his partner paid Bobby Stauffer two hundred dollars for packing in supplies, cheaper in the long run than the seventy-five dollars charged by

another outfit whose string broke up and damaged the supplies. Another sixty dollars paid for the winter's supplies. Food was simple: beans, flour and baking powder, sourdough, rice, coffee, spuds, and of course, waterproof matches which were a necessity. Sometimes the trappers ran out of food while making the rounds on their lines, especially if they got caught in a storm. They had no choice but to make the long hungry walk back to camp the next day. Applegate recalls an incident when his partner almost couldn't make those last steps to the cabin because of exposure and exhaustion.

The lines the trappers set up sometimes extended as far as sixty miles. Donning snowshoes or skis, they set out with forty-pound packs full of food, bait, and traps. With any luck at all they could anticipate a heavier load on their return trip. The lines ran high up on ridges where pine marten were readily available. Pine marten were prime furs up until the 1950's, bringing in the highest price for the least amount of work. The late Art Lintz told of trapping 38 marten at $22 each in 1938 in the Bluff Creek area, which meant good money in those years. Occasionally the poorer quality rock marten got into the traps, but more often than not, weasels were trapped. Although weasel hides were worth only a dollar, they provided the meal ticket because they were so plentiful. Beaver trapping was illegal in Idaho after the early exploitation of that fur-bearer, but that didn't stop one industrious trapper who allegedly packed thirty beaver hides from the St. Joe-Clearwater Divide all the way to Adair. There he loaded them on the train to be sold in Montana.

It took skill and determination to trap otter, a source of fascination to the trappers. Often as many as six of these playful animals romped together like kittens. They traveled up one stream, over a ridge and into another stream, and were very wise about being trapped. The trapper had to treat each trap with a kind of wax to prevent rust and disguise the smell of steel. Then the trap was set with the scent of fish oil and hidden deep in the water. After all this, if the otter was trapped, the hides were so heavy and the return so marginal that it was hardly worth the effort. Catching eight or ten marten, on the other hand, was a snap.

Although there were not many lynx around, Art Lintz devised an effective way to trap ones he knew to be available. At Quartz Creek he hung a bucket of rotten whitefish high in a tree and set four or five traps all around. The lynx, like all fur-bearers, were drawn to the odor of fish and walked into the traps.

Of all the trappers on the St. Joe, Paddy McIntyre stood out as the legend. During the labor problems in the Coeur d'Alene mines at the turn of the century, Paddy left his home in Arkansas for a job as a strike-breaker. When the Northern Pacific train on which he was riding got as far as Deborgia, he and a friend jumped off but never got to the mines. He stayed on the Montana side of the mountains for awhile before coming to Avery during the teens. Soon he was established as the seasonal observer for the Forest Service at Needle Peak Lookout, and during the winter he made his rounds trapping. A tiny cabin he built at Bathtub served as home base where his grub was packed in, but on his rounds he slept in a hollow cedar at Foehl Creek or even made himself a hole in a snowbank.

Paddy, who stood all of 5'3" in his dirty socks, could not read or write. His favorite statement was, "Brains is the cheapest thing ya' can buy." He held soap and washing in even lower esteem. He had one set of underwear that he put on in the fall to last all winter; a quick dip in the creek solved his laundry problem. Bob Cass as a young boy was terribly impressed with Paddy's cooking—bacon, eggs, fried potatoes like you wouldn't believe—and Paddy never even had to wash his hands after skinning hides! Over the stove in his cabin he hung a quarter of venison with the hide still on it. When it was time to eat, the portion closest to the stove had thawed enough so that all he had to do was hack a steak off and drop it in the pan. Guests sometimes declined a dinner invitation with him after observing rats scampering over the hardened grease on the stew. The eight or ten skinned animal carcasses sitting forlornly outside the door also did little to enhance one's appetite.

After a winter of trapping (and not washing) Paddy could be seen on a March day making his way out of the woods. On his small back were piles of hides, for he was a darn good trapper, and surrounding him was the aroma that comes from months without a bath or change of clothes. But after a bath at the roundhouse in Avery, he was socially acceptable and once again Avery's own endearing little character. One of the hardy ones.

NATURE'S OWN SECRET—WILDLIFE

Secret of Winter Morning
It was early this morning
*   even before light brightened the snow.*
The quiet spread over the world
*   like a warm woolen blanket;*
The only sound was the ppfft
*   of new flakes falling*
*   and the cub-crunch crunch*
*   of my boots breaking a new pattern,*
Snow shimmering around each print.

There, suddenly was the deer.
*   Sleek, elegant,*
*   and unafraid.*
It watched.
*   Big ears powdered by puffs of white.*
Still. Pensive.
Then
*   with a flick of white tail*
It was gone,
*   carrying over the bank*
*   the silent mystery*
Of Winter Morning on the 'Joe. . .

poem written by
Sandra Crowell,
January, 1979

Anyone who knows St. Joe country from trapper to recreationist cannot help but be touched by its wildlife. In fact, today more visitors are drawn to the area by the game and fish than by any other factor. Since the first white men came up swiftwater and the first trapper sold his catch, wildlife patterns have changed considerably.

Take the story of Knut Glover, a saloon-keeper from St. Joe City. He had some big news in 1908. He shot a bull elk near the mouth of Slate Creek! Everyone in the valley was talking about it, but that was not a reflection on Glover's marksmanship. It was the novelty of a bull elk on the St. Joe, an occurrence rare enough that it gave people something to talk about.

The growth of the mighty elk population in the last fifty years is an interesting story. Longtime hunter Bill Robinson recalls that in his first years on the St. Joe there were just a few deer and fewer elk. Some elk had been spotted around Nelson Peak, Eagle Creek, and Simmons Creek, but their total numbers probably never exceeded one hundred animals. Although deer were more abundant than elk, their populations were small compared to later years. Then two major events worked to change things. The first was the 1910 fire

Avery residents (left to right) John Cass, Jasper Jones, Elmer Jones, Paddy McIntyre, and Coleman Allen pose outside the cabin on Mallard Peak with their freshly bagged mountain goats. Paddy McIntyre, a local legend on the St. Joe, built this cabin as a line-cabin for his trapping expeditions. (Theriault)

and the subsequent fires in the 1920's and '30's. These fires denuded the lower elevations of heavy timber and opened the land for massive brush fields, which served as important winter forage. Willow, redstem ceanothus, mountain maple, serviceberry, and chokecherry spread for miles; the valley was like an overladen dinner table waiting for hungry guests. Then in 1928 the guests arrived. Two carloads of elk, 36 in all, came to Marble Creek by rail, their fare from Yellowstone National Park paid by a group of local sportsmen. In 1938 the Idaho Fish and Game brought 61 more and another 74 to Kellogg. The elk herds then grew by leaps: a wildlife report by the U.S. Forest Service in 1932-34 indicated a population increase of eighteen per cent. At that time there was no hunting season allowed for the elk, although limited weekend hunting for deer and "anytime" hunting during the Depression did occur near Avery and off the railroad tracks. By the late 1930's hunters would bag their first official elk. Bill Robinson, who had previously seen so few elk, led hunting parties into the St. Joe, and in 1951 built the St. Joe Lodge for hunters near the Spruce Tree Campground.

Today the resident elk population in the St. Joe drainage is estimated to number between three and four thousand animals. The question still remains in the minds of the wildlife experts: was the growth of the elk herd the result of a spurt in the small resident herds or the result of the transplants? Many old-timers attribute some of the increase to a migration of elk from the Selway River, south of the St. Joe. Elk are a naturally mobile animal, and some migrations into this area cannot be ruled out. Others note the higher numbers following the logging operations. Although these reasons help to explain the phenomenon, the increase of elk is still nature's own secret.

Deer are very much a part of life on the St. Joe. In winters of heavy snowfall, the graceful animals flock close to the river and into the yards of Avery residents. Their population has changed in the last century too. Following the large wildfires the corresponding increase in forage, deer numbers increased for a couple of decades. At one time mule deer numbered in the hundreds and formed a migratory path across Simmons Creek and into Montana for winter range. Railroaders recall hills blackened with deer returning in the springtime during the 1930's. Their numbers probably reached a peak in the early '40's, generally declining since then because the rising elk herds out-compete deer for winter forage. Long-time residents recall the careless slaughter of deer; that too may have affected the deer population.

Modern game management is geared at maintaining and increasing the numbers of deer and elk. If history teaches anything, it is that the future of the animals depends on the quality and quantity of winter forage. Efforts of forest and wildlife managers center on maintaining the all-important, low elevation brush fields, says Mark Orme, Avery wildlife biologist. Prescribed fires under carefully controlled conditions are now used to maintain brushfields on major winter ranges.

The elk herds of the St. Joe grew quickly in the decades following the 1910 fire and successive fires which created thousands of acres of browse. Pictured with a bull elk they shot in 1948 near Simmons Creek are: Red ———, Dooley Cramp, Billy Williams, Bill Robinson (who built the St. Joe Lodge), and Jack Shaner. (Cramp)

Deer have been common visitors into Avery during several winters. In one particularly harsh winter, residents fed deer in the downtown square near the fishpond. (Lindow)

A mountain goat surveys his St. Joe domain from the top of Snow Peak. Once a common sight at several locations, goats now stay in areas far from roads. (Scribner)

In addition to elk and deer, a small population of mountain lions; bobcats, mountain goats, and moose make the St. Joe their home. Mountain lions do inhabit the area and bobcats can be seen regularly. Canada lynx appear to have been more common in the early 1900's, however, judging from trappers' stories. One thing trappers today can count on—the bobcat population is always highest when the deer population is up, and bobcat pelts bring a good price. As for mountain goats, those on top of Snow Peak have had a large enough herd at various times to provide transplants for places in Washington and Oregon. No hunting is allowed for the Snow Peak goats, though limited permits are given for hunting goats on the Little North Fork of the Clearwater. Enough moose wander the area so that the first controlled hunt was held in the 1950's.

Dooley and Thelma Cramp tell of an amusing encounter with a moose. They were driving from their home at Camp 44 on a snow-banked road in a brand new 1954 Pontiac. "A bull moose apparently considered the car a flashing rival and was about to settle its hash," wrote Thelma, "when Dooley leaped out of the car and charged right back at him. The moose felt defeated when he saw his rival multiply like vermin by dividing. He fled in astonishment!"

Occasionally a rare predator, the fierce wolverine, has been seen in the valley. Wolverines are so disagreeable they can't even stand each other; therefore the territory of each one is about 300 miles. The wolverine and fisher have been considered for the rare and endangered species list.

The black bear population has apparently remained stable throughout the history of the area. In fact, the Northern Region of the Forest Service of which the St. Joe is a part, has one-fourth of all the nation's bears. Bear season is open from September to May with the spring season open on boars and females without cubs. Black bears are their own worst enemy; with no natural predators, the boars kill the cubs. Hunting helps to maintain a natural balance in the bear population.

Furbearers found near the swiftwater include beaver, muskrat, coyote, badger, red fox, weasel, and pine marten. The river otter population is currently high, for the animals which once were trapped are now protected by law. Trapping is permitted on most of the furbearers, and while it is regulated stringently by Idaho game laws, trapping provides extra money and an interest for a few local residents. If by chance they get a coyote, they won't get a bounty; however, coyote hides are valued at about fifty dollars, the lighter the color, the better.

The 560 miles of fishable streams and the seventeen lakes that make up the St. Joe River country have attracted fishermen for many years. Anglers once came from everywhere to what was known as one of the finest trout streams in America, "abounding in so many fish they almost crowded themselves out of the river." Ruth Lindow, a life-long Avery fisherman, fished for an hour and caught enough fish to feed six members of her family in her youth. Another fisherman caught a phenomenal 35 pounds of fish in one hour. The *St. Maries Courier* between 1901 and 1905 frequently reported catches of seven- to nine-pound trout and fishing trips where anglers landed

Avid fisherman Ruth Lindow is on her way to another afternoon of angling. Ruth has spent over sixty years catching her suppers on the 'Joe. (Lindow)

of the Little North Fork of the Clearwater. Until the construction of the Dvorshak Dam at Ahsahka, salmon runs were an annual occurrence in the drainage. The Little North Fork is still well-known for good catches of cutthroat, Dolly Varden, and kokanee.

In spite of changing patterns, the St. Joe River is still classified as a blue ribbon fishing stream for over one-third of its water. The rating given by the Idaho Fish and Game is based on unique fish resources, use, access, and aesthetics.

Early St. Joe fishermen had no trouble earning a day's catch. Jess Turner (left) and a friend show off their strings caught near their Turner Flat homestead. Fish was a main staple in their diet in 1910 when this photograph was taken. (Turner)

nearly a hundred "speckled trout," (i.e. cutthroat).

The fishing story has changed somewhat with the decline of the cutthroat. Various theories explain its low numbers. Overfishing due to increased access no doubt had its effect. Minor siltation of the river may have hurt the cutthroat as it did the fresh water clams in the river above Avery. The opening of small spawning streams for fishing could have had its effect; another possibility is the introduction of other fish species. Cutthroat still remain the fisherman's favorite, however: 88 per cent of the 292 anglers interviewed in 1972 chose to restrict fishing in order to save the native cutthroat. Other native fish to be enjoyed are the Dolly Varden, whitefish, and occasionally the Eastern brook trout. While the rainbow trout is not a native fish, it is now abundant from artificial stocking by the Idaho Department of Fish and Game. Steelhead and salmon have never made runs up the swiftwater because of natural barriers in the Spokane River, but west slope Kokanee salmon are a new addition to the fishing scene. Kokanee, also known as bluebacks, are a land-locked sock-eye salmon that grow to maturity in Lake Coeur d'Alene and migrate up the rivers and streams to spawn. Following a plant near Big Creek, these fish have expanded as far upriver as Red Ives, some fifty miles away.

Long before white men entered the area, bands of Nez Perce and Coeur d'Alene Indians fished the waters

Birds cannot be overlooked as part of the St. Joe's wildlife. Over 185 species of birds reside at least part of the year in the valley. The spruce, blue, and ruffed grouse provide excellent hunting, along with ducks and geese. On occasion, bald and golden eagles soar majestically overhead. Many of these birds are only transients, but some nests have been located in the St. Joe valley. The largest woodpecker in Idaho and the second largest in North America is found in the St. Joe valley. This bird, pileated woodpecker, has a unique role in that its large nest cavities provide homes for some ten other species of birds and mammals, including screech owls, saw-whet owls, and pine martens. The woodpecker's environment is dependent on a mature forest canopy.

It should be remembered that each species of birds has its own unique characteristics and habits, and some species command more attention than others. Take, for example, the relatively unknown bird, the water ouzel or dipper. Once called the teeter-ass because of its dipping motion, the dipper is truly a swiftwater bird. The more turbulent the water the better for it—in fact, the face of a waterfall is its favorite nesting place. It has oil glands ten times the size of its close relative, the wren, to protect it in water. Sometimes the dipper can be seen walking on the bottom of the St. Joe River searching for food. Just one little creature filling an ecological niche. . .

Wildlife makes the St. Joe a special place for residents, recreationists, and hunters. With nature's own wisdom and the help of wildlife management, future generations will be able to enjoy the presence of everything from the imposing elk to that happy little swiftwater bird dipping in the river.

Wildlife viewing and photography is another popular pastime of both residents and visitors to the St. Joe. Here, several elk wind their way up a small stream near Avery. (Schoeppach)

11 Logs Down the 'Joe

Happy Van Luben, a Dutchman, was a lumberjack who worked on the upper landing out of Avery. He had one set of clothes to wear all week before heading home to Missoula each weekend on the evening train. They say he changed clothes every weekend whether he needed to or not. Anyway, Happy hopped on the evening train for home one Friday as usual. The only seat on the train was next to a buxom, well-dressed young lady. Happy realized that his clothes were pretty dirty, so he was willing to stand. "Sit here!" urged the young lady. He declined but she insisted. As the train passed over the mountains, she asked him his occupation. "I'm a hooker, Ma'am." "Oh," she answered brightly, "so am I! But tell me, how did you get so dirty?"

Logging camps on the 'Joe have generated many colorful (and off-color) stories, for the epoch of logging has been varied and vivid.

The story started far away from the St. Joe with the decline of the eastern forests and the diminishing stands of white pine in New England and the Lake States. As the land had been cleared for settlement by the latter part of the nineteenth century, the white pine had nearly been wiped out. The nation needed wood. Timber cruisers were sent to the woods of North Idaho as the new century dawned, and they liked what they saw. They saw forests containing a large percentage of high quality white pine, plus an endless supply of western red cedar which could be used for poles, pilings, shingles, and lumber. They saw timber-laden drainages favored by a relatively good climate, and they noted the rivers which could be navigated by steamboats and tugboats with protected bays for log storage. The rivers could be sources for hydroelectric power, and the area was accessible to a transcontinental railroad. A ready market existed for wood products; cattle and wheat ranches west of the Rockies and the new agricultural business east of the Cascades needed building materials. Mines in the Coeur d'Alene mining district needed timbers for their growing underground operations, and new railroads needed rails. People would surely want to settle in a spot such as this with its natural beauty and abundant wildlife, and they would need lumber too. Soon entire towns of people migrated to the timber country of the West, and it was not uncommon for former neighbors to meet in their new locale. After the miners had made their rush for what was *in* the hills, homesteaders and timber barons made a rush for what was *on* the hills.

Much land on the public domain was available to

them in spite of previous withdrawals for forest reserves. Settlers could claim homesteads under the Homestead Acts of 1862 and 1906 and the Timber and Stone Act of 1878 to take advantage of the timber. The Northern Pacific Railway also offered land for sale that had been granted to them. Some state land, granted when Idaho achieved statehood in 1890 to support its public institutions, could sometimes be purchased. Entrepreneurs, such as Fred Weyerhaeuser and the Milwaukee Land Company bought up hundreds of thousands of acres of timber land in Idaho. For a few years after 1900 large stands of virgin timber were taken from public lands. . . and by 1910 many homesteaders had proved up on their claims and sold them to large lumber companies. Except for the National Forest, these companies owned most of the sawtimber.

The land on the St. Joe was covered with what was recognized as "the largest body of standing white pine in the country." And no wonder. The tremendous giants towered high everywhere. In fact, the largest white pine on record stood near Theodore Fohl's homestead in Section 10, T41N, R1W, west of Bovill. It was estimated to have had 18,000 board feet (the average house requires about 10,000 board feet), but when it was cut in 1911, it scaled 28,900 board feet, enough for three houses! The tree stood 227 feet tall, had a 10-foot diameter and was 425 years old. Its successor for the world's record was also a product of the St. Joe Forest, standing on Rocky Run Creek with a 96-inch diameter. This giant was uprooted by the terrific windstorm of 1949.

Timber of that size lit up dollar signs in the eyes of mill operators and company owners. The first sawmill in the immediate area was opened by John, Jess, and Hogue Fisher in St. Maries in 1887 to meet the growing demand for lumber to replace original log cabins. It later supplied lumber for the railroad bridge at Chatcolet. Another mill was built at Rose Lake in 1889, the same year that St. Maries had its first shingle mill at the mouth of the St. Maries River. Most logs cut on the St. Joe found their way further downstream to a mill at Coeur d'Alene or to Post Falls where Frederick Post had been sawing timber since 1880. Some seven million board feet had already been cut on the lower St. Joe by 1892 and sent to mills. By 1906, a larger mill was built at Potlatch and another at St. Joe City, started by A.L. Flewelling for Monarch Lumber Company. After the construction of that mill, the Milwaukee Land Company bought it and retained

Flewelling as manager. Avery even had a small mill in 1911, built by W.W. Ferrell who set it up right next to the depot, and another mill opened in Fernwood in 1913. Indeed, mills were cropping up like a new growth of trees.

Then, with the construction of the railroad, a further incentive excited mill owners—the need for railroad ties. The railroad lines required some 2500 ties per

Some mighty giants grew in the forests of the St. Joe, attracting homesteaders and timber barons alike. Charley Scribner poses by this cedar in Fishhook Basin in 1924. (Scribner)

mile or something like ten million ties for a transcontinental line. Mills opened in the area for that purpose alone. One operated a mile east of Pocono near Marble Creek in 1911 and 1912, and another on Clear Creek, a tributary of Loop Creek in 1908-1909. In 1914 the Valentine-Clark Pole Company harvested poles for the Milwaukee electrification project. In addition to using timber for ties and poles, the railroad provided the all-important transportation of logs from the hills to the mills.

Big hopes for the timber bonanza were turned to ashes in the year of 1910. The great Idaho Fire ravaged much of the timber on the St. Joe that year; what wasn't burned was blown down by the hurricane winds that preceded the fire. However, much of the timber was still merchantable, choice, old-growth white pine, but it had to be logged as soon as possible before the sapwood turned blue and the wood checked. No market existed for the blued wood at that time, and the price was much lower for the deteriorating wood. It required a major effort to cruise and salvage what remained of the vast forest. Timber survey crews and appraisers were organized quickly so that areas could be cruised, appraised, advertised, and logged within the time span of a few months. During the years of major salvage operations from 1911 to 1914, the lumber companies of Idaho and Montana transferred their entire operations to the fire-killed timber. Spruce deteriorated first and was logged through 1912. White pine lasted until 1915, then fir and larch were logged for mine timbers up until 1918. Although no record shows the exact amount, fire-damaged timber accounted for about two-thirds of the 539 million board feet logged in Region One during the first years.

Early logging was carried out on Big Creek by Fred Herrick's Milwaukee Lumber Company, on the North Fork of the St. Joe by Mike Bogle and Jerry Callahan, and on Slate Creek by the McGoldrick Lumber Company. When most of the fire-damaged timber had been removed, Oscar Hopkins cut green logs at Roundhouse Gulch in 1915, C.H. Gregory at Adair on Loop Creek, and George Ripley at Turner Creek. Marble Creek became a major logging site in the early teens with the Dave Dollar and Valentine-Clark logging camps. Later in that decade and during the 1920's, Martin and Lewis Olson logged in the Fishhook drainage.

In country as rugged and isolated as parts of North Idaho, a way had to be devised to transport the valuable timber to the mills. It would be years before roads, trucks, or caterpillars entered the timberlands, but in the Coeur d'Alene and Bitterroot Mountains, the system of rivers made a natural course for floating the logs out during spring runoff. So began the big river log drives each spring on the Kootenai, Pack, Priest, Coeur d'Alene, and St. Joe Rivers. Starting about 1907 and lasting until the early years of the Depression, each runoff ushered some forty million board feet of logs down the St. Joe River alone. In the wide, lower valleys they were sorted and stored before being moved to various mills. Most of the drives employed about fifty men.

"THE DRIVE'S ON!"

"Bank beaver, married men and valley cats, best go home—the drive's on!" yelled French Louie, stuffing his shirt with snow in excitement. And thus, the first of many log drives started on Marble Creek. But this drive on the Marble meant the end of French Louie, who drowned the following year. His grave along the banks of Marble Creek was solemnly marked by river pigs each spring as they made their way to the woods. His death came to symbolize their death; his grave, a reminder of the hazards the 'jacks faced herding the round stuff out of St. Joe country, but his cry marking the start of the drive somehow signaled the thrill of it all.

The upper dam on Marble Creek with its gates open in 1913. Splash dams such as this controlled the flow of water in order to shoot logs downstream. Note the logging camp on the right of picture. (Gem State Tavern)

"First Bateau taken accross (sic) St. Maries Bridge 1901." Bateaus were specially designed swiftwater boats for use in river drives. The boats were pointed at both ends to negotiate the current more easily. Note the sleigh and matched teams. The sign reads, "5$ Fine-Rideing-Driving Across Bridge Faster . . ." (Gem State Tavern)

The river drives did call upon the skills of the hearty, that was for sure. Getting logs out of the remote country was a challenge to be met. First of all, streams had to be cleared of natural log jams and large rocks before anything could happen. Then splash dams were built to dam up the water and the logs. The area chosen for the dam was dug out so that thick timber could line the bottom of the dam. Logs were set about thirty feet apart parallel to the river, then crossed with more logs sloped at an angle to relieve the pressure on the dam. Two high walls were built with a gate edged in rubber set solidly between them. A big wheel with a spool on the top controlled the gate; two men wound up the gear to open the gate. Gates were closed until the water built up behind the dam. A telephone connection told each pair of operators when to release the water and logs while big booms on the back side of the dam guided logs into the sluice gate. As the water and logs rushed through the gate, men worked behind the dam to break up the log jam with peaveys (spiked poles with a hook-like device made to grip and guide logs in the river drives). Five of these splash dams were built on Marble Creek, one on Fishhook, and several on Slate Creek.

Once the logs began heading down the river, specially designed boats named bateaus were used. These swiftwater boats, as long as 34 feet, could carry a dozen men. They were pointed at both ends to move better with the current, and rather than using oars, the boatmen used pike poles for guiding. The boats were stopped by being snubbed into eddies in the river. As the logs moved down, men in bateaus pushed to the wings (where the logs piled against the banks) and then the most skilled crew went to "brick the center," to roll logs loose to drift with the current. Bateaus were used on the St. Joe up until the late 1940's.

Sometimes the logs jammed—four of five million board feet scattered like a box of spilled toothpicks. These "jackpots" had to be broken up and headed downriver, a struggle sometimes requiring months. On the Coeur d'Alene River, long-time lumberjack Dooley Cramp recalls, sometimes logs were jammed purposely until the creek ran low so that logs would not be lost in the numerous channels. On Marble Creek, jams were planned for spring runoff and high water because of the narrow, rough riverbed. One record pile on the banks of the Marble stood sixty or seventy feet high and over a hundred feet long. If the jammed logs were not piled too high, the whole jam sometimes moved out en masse. Even when the creek in front was nearly dry, the force of the moving logs pushed them faster and faster until a man could not run as fast. The more adventuresome river pigs jumped aboard for a ride downriver. "It was sure fun!" Cramp says, his eyes twinkling with the memory of a ride on the moving mountain of wood.

Transporting the logs downhill to the rivers required the use of chutes on small tributaries and flumes on major streams. Chutes were constructed of logs whereas the more expensive flumes were built of lumber and filled with water. Jacks, who spent their lives on the river in the spring and summer, hand-logged to the chutes in the fall and winter when the chutes were iced down. The V-shaped troughs were made of logs with 12-inch tops laid side by side horizontally down the hill. These logs were "scored" or chopped out, then smoothly hewn by a broadax. It took a special skill to prepare the chutes so that no

"Drive hung on Marble Creek . . . 1914. 6,000,000 ft. of white pine." "Jackpots" as large as this one often took many long, hard weeks of manpower and horsepower to break up. (Gem State Tavern)

This log chute was across from Rocky Riffle on Harry Harrison's homestead, three miles downriver from Avery. The chute was built by logger Oscar Hopkins in 1916 or 1917. Horses pulled logs from the woods to the top of the 2,000-foot long chute. (Theriault)

rough spots or bumps slowed the sliding logs. Sometimes the chutes were greased so that the logs would slide easily. Not that there was that much problem on the steep hills of the St. Joe; sometimes the logs went so fast they actually smoked from the friction. Cold-sanding, putting cold sand on the chute, slowed their course, as did hot-sanding on the iced chutes. Special hooks known as goosenecks were put in some chutes, especially those in Marble Creek, to slow the logs down, and piles of shavings along the chutes testified to the damage to the logs. In fact, logs chuted from the Marble were damaged so much by the creekbed that the Rutledge Mill hired someone just to chop the rocks out of the ends of them, and logs were cut extra long to allow for the damage. Remains of chutes as long as a mile and a half can still be seen at Chute Creek (named for obvious reasons), Roundhouse Gulch, Rocky Riffle, and Theriault Creek.

The construction of flumes was a more involved process. Some contractors such as Carey and Harper in Marble Creek specialized in their building. Little sawmills were often set up at the head of the flumes producing about 10,000 feet a day for the sole purpose of construction. As the lumber was sawed, it was floated down the flume to the portion being built. Each flume absorbed a quarter of a million board feet of lumber in addition to hand-hewn foundations and cross ties for support. Low-valued species like spruce and fir were used. In 1920 the cost of the flume was

seven thousand dollars a mile—pretty expensive, especially for those times when the cost of labor was cheap. However, the size of the sales and the price of lumber were attractive enough to make flumes and river driving cheap transportation.

The most spectacular flume in the area was built in 1915 by C.H. Gregory, a corpulent lumberman who could "walk the legs off a jackrabbit." His flume above Adair, near the mouth of Ward Creek, flowed around the contours of the hillside and anchored itself into the side slopes. It passed over the railroad tunnel and carried logs over a mile before depositing them for pickup near the railroad siding. Remains of the flume can still be seen.

Let's look at one early day logging operation at Slate Creek. An early reconnaissance of the Slate Creek basin revealed an estimated 300 million board feet of timber with six to eight million on the sections closest to the stream. Most of the timber was white pine with stumpage rates of $3.50 per thousand, while the mixed timber sold for fifty cents. At one point a wagon haul to Wallace and a logging railroad were considered. It would cost about $20,000 to improve Slate Creek for log drives, but that did not deter the McGoldrick Lumber Company from buying the timber and floating it out.

To construct flumes, the company put in a mill at the head of Slate Creek in 1915 and built trail chutes to carry logs into two small splash dams on Dam and Flume Creeks. Then 'jacks opened the gates of the dams daily and flumed the logs down Slate Creek. A larger dam further down on Slate Creek periodically splashed logs to the St. Joe; from there they rolled to

Lake Coeur d'Alene to be towed by steam across the lake. At that point they were loaded on cars and shipped by rail to the McGoldrick mill in Spokane.

An interesting story floated out of the McGoldrick operations one winter. It seems that a snowslide had filled the canyon on Dam Creek with over fifty feet of snow. With three million board feet cut and decked above the dam, the crew was befuddled. How were they to get the cut out for the spring run? They noticed that the unfrozen creek had made a tunnel through the slide. Maybe a few logs could be shot through. Voila! It worked! By sluicing a few through at a time, the entire deck of logs passed under the snowslide.

Sometimes more than logs floated down the river. One spring the manager of the Slate Creek drive, Ira Fleming, set up a log raft at the mouth of the creek. On it was the cook camp made up of several tents where the men from the drive came to eat their meals. When it came time for the logs to roll out of the stream, the crew moved the cook camp a half mile down the river out of the way. Or at least that was the plan. The behavior of the St. Joe River in the spring is not always just what a person can plan on—and the

men on board found themselves at Herrick after a very wild river ride. The only way they had found to stop their exciting voyage was to get the raft on top of a big uprooted cedar tree. Otherwise, they might have ended up at Coeur d'Alene. As it was, the rest of the party got fed at two o'clock in the morning and the whole "maryann" made everyone unhappy.

Before the logs from the river drive were stopped at the sorting gap near St. Joe City, they were branded on the end by a sledgehammer. Each owner had his distinguishing mark, an identification that assured payment for the log. At the sorting gap logs were organized according to the mill that was their destination. The Dollar logs out of Marble Creek were appropriately branded "$." Martin and Louis Olson stamped their logs with a fishhook brand for their Fishhook Creek operation.

In the early days, horses pulled their share of the load in the steep timber country, skidding logs just as dozers do today. Big horses, such as Percherons, that worked in the woods weighed nearly a ton. Tow paths for teams often followed the chutes, and horses skidded and decked logs to the chutes. Trail dogs—pieces of metal with a chain—were attached to

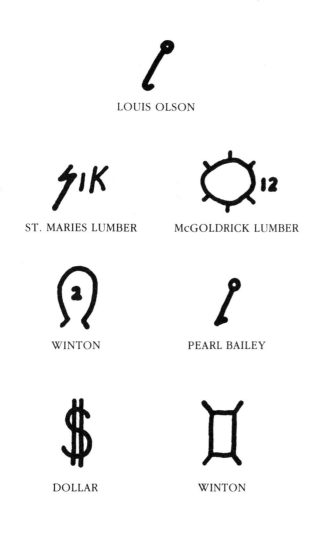

LOUIS OLSON

ST. MARIES LUMBER   McGOLDRICK LUMBER

WINTON   PEARL BAILEY

DOLLAR   WINTON

The white-water of Fishhook Creek ushered out logs each spring as shown in this 1927 photograph. Released from the splash dam up the creek the logs rushed downstream narrowly missing Olsons' logging camp near the mouth of the stream. (Scribner)

the logs to hold them while allowing them to roll. Twelve logs to a load, eleven loads of logs a day was the average work load for a team. Sometimes the horses pulled the bateaus up the river along the rough and rocky shore. That was grueling punishment for the animals, and ten years in the woods left a horse broken and disabled. Horses could be seen in logging at George Ripley's camp on Bird Creek, Oscar Hopkins' camp at Roundhouse Gulch and on Fishhook. They were used as pack animals in nearly all the camps. The LaVigne Brothers developed their string of pack horses just for packing and the Buells packed into camps on Mica Creek. Camps were set up near good grazing spots, and corrals and barns were built for the horses. The services of veterinarians, blacksmiths, and trainers were also needed.

"18-mile move up Marble Creek . . . Year of 1913. First steam donkey in Idaho," reads the caption on this photograph. "Ol' Betsy," the 20-ton steam donkey, took over a month on its trek up the Marble. These machines largely were used to skid logs out of the woods. (Gem State Tavern)

It was a horse of a different color that pushed its way up Marble Creek swiftwater in 1913. It wasn't a horse at all but a twenty-ton steam donkey just like ones used in coastal logging. Moving a half mile a day, "Old Betsy's" eighteen-mile trek to the Dave Dollar camp was not easy. A special sled forty feet long with cross-ties carried the cumbersome machine, though the wooden shoes had to be replaced after a day or so. The crew almost lost her in the spot known as Big Gorge where the water is twenty feet deep and the canyon walls are just as high. But on she went! Was it worth the effort? Huge stands of trees stood untouched up the creek. Along the way, 500,000 board feet could be harvested, plus any other trees that just might cause a jam—yes, it was worth it. Old Betsy later rode a barge named the Bumblebee up and down the Marble, continuing to yard the round stuff off the banks.

The steam donkeys, their cables extending a mile and a quarter, were generally an efficient method of logging. On a good day the donkeys brought out 100,000 board feet, besides preventing and untangling jams. That led Rutledge Lumber Company to bring in seven or eight huge donkeys to Marble Creek from the

Clarkia side. Teams pulled up the first donkey, then it pulled the second, the second pulled the third, and so on. The cost of getting these puffing monsters to the woods outweighed their efficiency, however, and they were not used for long.

When the iron horse entered the picture, railroads became a major part of transporting logs. This particular horse did not have to be fed; it did not rely on the seasons, and logs shipped out on it were not damaged or lost on the rivers. Soon the accessibility of the Milwaukee Road to the timber stands led to the construction of several railroad logging spurs. Timber magnate Fred Herrick had purchased a large timber sale on Big Creek prior to the 1910 fire. He was building an eighteen-mile track when the blaze damaged much of the timber and the track as well, but in spite of the damage, plans continued. Under contractor George Branson, some 500 men logged on Big Creek and shipped out the logs by rail. The most dramatic logging railroad in the area was built by Rutledge Lumber Company over the Marble Creek-Elk Basin Divide in 1922. This seventy percent gradient on Incline Ridge plunged breathlessly down the slope to Clarkia. During the season of 1923, 21 million feet of logs went out over the incline, but in spite of that impressive figure, the operation was thought to be unprofitable.

Clyde S. Webb scaling loads of fire-salvage logs in the summer of 1914 at Bogle's Spur at the junction of Loop Creek and the North Fork. Thirty carloads a day were loaded out of the spur for several years. Scaling was Webb's first job after joining the Forest Service in 1913. The co-author of White Pine: King of Many Waters *was later to become Forest Supervisor on the St. Joe National Forest, and Acting Regional Forest until his retirement in 1949. (Theriault)*

Placenames in the upper North Fork drainage tell the story of the logging railroad in that part of the country. Mike Bogle and Jerry Callahan (Bogle Spur and Callahan Creek), contract loggers for the St. Maries Lumber Company, harvested fire-killed timber off several spurs. Loggers camping at Show Falls named the adjacent creek Rougin after a card game they played. From the head of Rougin Creek a chute shot timber to two ponds where jammers loaded the logs onto the railroad. Railroad Creek carried an additional spur a mile up its banks. Both Heisler and Shay locomotives, noted for their ability to make sharp turns, were used in the drainage. They puffed the large volume of logs to Bogle Spur to be scaled for passage out on the Milwaukee Road. In its prime in 1915, thirty carloads of logs a day were shipped out of the Bogle Spur where four sidetracks stored the cars. This spot prospered as a tiny settlement. It even had its own school and company store for several years, but by 1916, the timber was gone and Oscar Hopkins dismantled the chute on Rougin Creek.

Another logging railroad was planned up Fishhook Creek in the fall of 1927. "This is a tough job," wrote Harley A. Harkins. "Above the forks it was steep mountain work, and below the forks we were working in ice cold water most of the time." The toughness of the job and the expense had something to do with the fact that the Fishhook railroad was never built, despite the fact that it was thought to be one of the best railroad chances. A similar scheme led to the construction of a tunnel and part of a railbed up Marble Creek that was never used.

However, a system much like a railroad was used by Martin and Louis Olson on a bench west of Fishhook Creek. In 1916 to 1918 they used polecars, so named because the heavy log-hauling cars had concave-rimmed wheels which ran on round pole tracks supported by cross-ties. These tracks, much like a railroad, sloped gently to the creek. A team of horses pulled the polecars, hauling 7500 to 8000 feet daily. The cost of the pole road was low compared to other means of transportation—about 500 dollars a mile in Idaho. That system was short-lived, however, because the ground was steep and polecars all too often jumped their tracks.

Logging was much more than the means, though. It was also the men.

A Bad Day on the Marble
I says, Be sharp, boys!
Be on your toes.
The jam is about to go!
Then she twisted her tail
And with vengeance she did roar,
And the next day we found young Foreman
 McKolski's guts
Scattered along the shore.

—Old lumberjack's poem
author unknown

It took a special breed of man to be a lumberjack. Men worked all day, ten to sixteen hours, in icy rivers from early spring to late fall, no matter what the weather. Wet up to their waists constantly, they never changed their damp clothes. It was amazing that so many of them survived. They wore Wright's black wool underwear, overalls, caulked ("cork") shoes, and wool socks. At night they pulled their soggy, weary

Lumberjacks spent much of their working lives in icy water, often putting in 10 to 16 hours a day, from early spring to late fall. Notice their use of peaveys (poles with hook devices) to guide these logs down Fishhook Creek. (Scribner)

bodies out of the creeks and hiked the mile or so to their camps. They always counted on a hot meal, and hopefully it would be a good one, for a good cook was a necessary drawing card in the camps. Good cooks put out such goodies as baking powder biscuits, bread, and pies baked in a reflector oven and did fancy things with huckleberries in season. After eating, the men could dry their wool socks over an open fire. Stakes set back from the fire held up their shoes to dry overnight. If the shoes were frozen solid in fall or spring mornings, a dipper full of boiling water thawed them out for a day's labor in the river. The bunkhouses, a rare sight in those days, had no floors, no springs or mattresses. The double bunks were lined with three inches of boughs or hay—though sometimes the horses would beat the tired men out of that. The 'jacks spent many a night on a bale of straw spread out on the wet ground. Everybody had his own blanket and by unwritten law no one else dared touch it. Those blankets gave a small comfort to men who sawed logs all night as hard as they drove them during the day. A noxious odor often wafted from the bunkhouses.

The 'jacks who worked the north woods were all types of men, working stiffs with good and bad luck. They came from everywhere: Michigan, Minnesota, Wisconsin, Arkansas, New York State, Italy, Sweden, France, Russia. Each one developed his own speciality. Russians Alec Lulchuck and Harry Boscki were good peavey men; Pete Madison and Dick McPike handled a bateau better than anyone; the three LaVoie brothers were good river drivers; Two-Gun Gunderson was a fine sawyer. Greenhorns to the woods studied the moves of the experienced men until their peaveys could manage the Saginaw flip, an old Mick Spin, or a St. Croix, all special peavey maneuvers used to break logs loose. Or their broadax could smooth a chute to a perfection. Interestingly, the same nationalities often chose the same specialities. Frenchmen were log drivers, Russians were peavey men, Swedes were sawyers. Many Swedish men worked the woods on the 'Joe, speaking their native tongue and demanding only that plenty of snuff be kept on hand.

In logging camps "Underclothing should be washed each week," warns a 1914 book entitled *Logging,* "since by doing so the men are kept in better health and the danger of wound infection from cuts is greatly lessened." The book recommends hiring a man to do the laundry, "because Sunday, which is the only day for washing, is needed by the men for recreation and rest." That was a great idea, but the lumberjacks on the St. Joe boiled their own black underwear over an open fire in a five-gallon drum with a bar of Fels Napa soap every Sunday. While their undies boiled, the men fished. Fishing was good, too. When the splash dams backed water up and the streams were low, they could almost catch big fish by hand in the low pools.

Of course, everybody had to go to town sometimes, especially over the Fourth. The 'jacks collected their stakes and headed over the hump to "Clarkee" (Clarkia) and its five bustling saloons, or to the 'Maries. St. Maries, at one time labeled as "the largest logging camp in Northern Idaho," drew lumberjacks to its many bars like bears to honey. They'd wallow in the sweetness of high living, often until their entire stake was gone—then lumber soberly back to hibernate in the camps again until Labor Day. Sometimes they'd return so broke they'd have to search through the scrap pile for a pair of caulked shoes. But what a time they had! The *St. Maries Gazette* in April of 1906 carried this editorial: "Although we would not like for the lumberjacks to be arrested after spending his earnings in town, yet it might be suggested that they be prohibited from sleeping off their jags on sidewalks and along the docks." Occasionally, in a town a disagreement popped up, and the fight had to be settled with the "Kalispell hop." That meant that the unlucky fellow on the bottom got stomped by a caulked boot.

A trip to town generated lots of good stories, like what happened to old Johnny Bedore on his trip out from Marble Creek.

Johnny got a great start with his big roll of money in the 'Maries. He bought himself new fancy city clothes and a bright red shirt. All decked out, he set off for the Davenport Hotel in Spokane in style for once in his life. He had a big hankering for ham and eggs, so he ordered 25 dollars worth. Now, in those days fifty cents bought a nice portion of ham and eggs, so the waitress brought him one order. He blew up, said if he couldn't get what he wanted there, he'd go somewhere else. The manager asked if he could pay for it. Ol' Johnny pulled out that big roll and threw it down on the table and told the guy to get his pay out of that, and to hurry, since he was getting mighty hungry.

Everybody started jumping, cooks and waitresses piling ham and eggs on the table, customers watching

John shovel it in. He couldn't quite make it, but when he had done his best, he tilted back in his chair and purred and grinned at his audience.

Now the chairs at the Davenport were delicate little things. He tilted back a little too far in his, and over backwards he went, grabbing only the tablecloth. Johnny sat there, dishes, ham and eggs, and tablecloth right on top of him. He shook his head and grinned. "Paintin' ol' Jesus, she's a self feeder!" Then he hauled his roll out to pay for all the damages, which were considerable. They say Old Johnny didn't mind, though. It had always been his life's ambition to have all the ham and eggs he could eat in one sitting!

There's another story they tell about Old Johnny heading down the street one day on another trip to town. He came face to face with a lady. He stepped to one side to let her by; she stepped the same way. He stepped the other way. So did the lady. Finally, after zigzagging back and forth for awhile, Johnny let out his favorite expletive, "Paintin' ol' Jesus, Madame. Stand still and I'll leap over ya!"

Wages were high enough that men could get a pretty good roll built up to take to town, though by today's standards the wages may not look so good. A yarding hook tender earned $3.50 to $4.00 per day in Idaho in 1911; chasers and head fallers earned $2.00 to $2.75; a cook netted $65 to $90 a month, and board was $5.00 a week. In 1923 a skilled river driver could earn $3500 a year. Mansfield Shepherd, a St. Joe lumberjack, reportedly started work one January at Marble Creek for $3.00 a day. At the end of the season, his wages completely paid for a house in St. Maries. *That* was good money—or was it low-priced real estate?

The men in the camps were usually single, often drifting from camp to camp. Their real names may not have been known even to their closest fellow workers, for everyone had a nickname. Cooks especially had some monikers that would set your teeth on edge. There was Gut Robber White, Greasy Pete Carmen, Prune Joe McClennan, Oatmeal Johnny, Burn Tom, Terrible Tom Kits, Ptomaine Dick, Poison Tom Lay, and Burn-'em-up Brown who cooked in white gloves and a derby hat. In the woods you'd hear of Wood 'em up George (who encouraged big loads by telling his crew, "Wood 'em up, boys! Wood 'em up!") You'd run into Ax-Handle Dennis and Over-Haul Bill, Hairless Joe, Pretty Boy, the Baby-Face Kid, Hell-Roarin' Jack, Dublin Dan, and Michigan Bill. Moosehead Dutch got his handle (and a helluva headache) from having a moosehead fall off the wall in a bar and hit him in the head. As for Runaway Johnny, he hardly had time to earn his name because he never spent more than a few days at a time in one camp. While loggers today don't get tagged with as many nicknames, one local legend is "Dimmer" Whipple who earned his name in his youth by hitting a power pole with his rig and dimming the lights in the whole town of St. Maries.

The camps did not always attract the most honest

sort of folks. The three Gates brothers who worked the Marble had a reputation for stealing everything that was loose. Two old-timers were discussing this seamy family recently. One explained that the first brother got shot in the wrong bedroom, the second was in the pen for armed robbery, and the third was preaching. "Goddamn!" exclaimed the other, "They'd do *anything!*"

Some pretty slick types also worked the camps. Dressed as 'jacks, these men took jobs in camps just for a place to stay. Maybe some like Old Silver Fox on the Coeur d'Alene River would work as watchmen on the dams or hold some minor job. At night, they'd haul out the cards and begin the poker games. As soon as they cleaned out one camp, they'd go on to the next, for there was a lot of money in the camps in those days. Several made enough money to avoid hard woods work permanently. It's even said that one St. Joe City man actually netted enough to finance the bank in St. Joe. "Just fancy it—a fella making enough to start a bank!" remarked long-time resident Lloyd Buell. However, the odds worked against this financier after all. He bought a pair of new shoes a size too small, and from the sores they made, he contracted an infection and died.

One man always managed to be around to give guidance and support in time of trouble, and how he did it, only the good Lord knew. Reverend Dick Ferrell, known as the "Sky-Pilot of the Lumberjacks," claimed as his parish the woods of Oregon, eastern Washington, western Montana and the Idaho Panhandle. He traveled 19,000 miles, gave 217 sermons, made 222 visits to the camps and hospitals, called on 902 families and wrote 380 letters—all in one year! When Reverend Ferrell dropped in on logging camps to preach, he filled in as a blacksmith, cook, or in any job that needed to be finished. He was cited as "the self-appointed employee of every logging company in the Inland Empire." If that and his good connections with the Man Upstairs didn't earn him the respect of the lumberjacks, his boxing experience did. Hardly a typical, "book-larned" man in black, Ferrell had left school after the eighth grade in Illinois to work in the coal mines and to become a blacksmith. Then he became a boxer and contender for his state's welterweight championship. Boxing was not to be his calling though, and in 1914 he came West to preach. Fred Herrick, the wealthy lumberman, held Reverend Ferrell in such esteem that he had Ferrell choose his tombstone off Marble Mountain. Ferrell saw to it that the stone was engraved and shipped to Michigan, so that when Herrick's time came, everything would be in order. Life for everyone in the woods fell into a little more order, thanks to their Sky-Pilot.

The lumberjacks were always close to crossing "the Great Divide." Driving logs in white water is a dangerous occupation. But it was part of the glamour and excitement of the job. Highly respected was the man who had worked the Marble, such a rough turbulent stream that at its crest even the best swimmer didn't stand a chance. As for accidents, they were not viewed with sympathy by fellow workers. "If you broke a leg, it was your own damn fault," observed Dooley Cramp. The sympathy went instead to the poor devils who had to carry the injured person those long hard miles out of camp.

A man made only one major mistake in that kind of job, and he was gone, "just another 'jack who made his last play and went out on white water." It happened frequently. The *St. Maries Record* on August 15, 1916, carried these headlines, "Marble Creek Claims Third Victim—L.M. Young Accidentally Loses Life—was Working on Carey and Harper's Log Drive—Funeral Here Monday." In this particular instance, the victim was at work on the rear when he slipped from a log and was carried under the roaring creek. Sometimes river drivers whose names or faces were not even known would be walking along the trail to a camp, possibly half-drunk. The white water appeared to snatch them from the trail, leaving behind a lonely hat on the trail as evidence that they had even been there. Bodies in those fast-moving streams as well as the St. Joe were often never recovered. The water wasn't selective about whom it grabbed, and familiar faces went under as well. In 1927 Louis Olson, partner in the Olson Fishhook Logging Company, lost his life driving logs down Fishhook Creek.

The river drivers viewed the danger philosophically. "Damn good way to check out, if you ask me. Go with your caulked boots on, in the face of a jam, on a white water stream like the Marble. Damn good place to plant a slough pig, too, right here on the bank, where you can sit up high on a mossy bank and watch the rear go by," remarked Oscar Blake. That was preferable to dying alone on skid row as many of the old lumberjacks did.

The good ol' days were exciting; there were thrills on the rivers and a certain glamour about the work. But the 'jacks put in long days, suffered on poor bedding and food, worked for low wages, had no sanitary or laundry facilities—and those conditions led to labor problems in the logging camps. An organization to promote better conditions for all laborers, The International Workers of the World (Wobblies) was formed in 1905 and extended red cards to scattered lumbermen throughout the Northwest. The October, 1907, edition of the *St. Maries Gazette* reported that rumors of a strike were brewing in the lumber camps of the upper St. Joe and that several buildings had been burned. "The trouble has grown out of the recent reduction in the wages of the men, and many of whom refused to work at the scale established by the lumber companies and the latter, in retaliation, are bringing in cheap Italians. The trouble is likely to spread to all lumber camps. . ." the paper noted. Trouble did indeed spread. Before the 1920's industrial violence became a common occurrence in mills and occasionally in the camps. A major strike in 1917 brought over a hundred traveling Wobblies from Seattle, Portland, Spokane, and Butte to the mouth of Marble Creek where they set up a large camp. Near "Ol' Betsy," the donkey engine at the

Dollar camp, 24-hour guards were posted to discourage saboteurs. In St. Maries, workers were incarcerated in two different bull pens under martial law. The violence was not pleasant, but the formation of the unions did lead to some definite changes for the better. They forced management to build bunkhouses with real beds and floors, and to provide better laundry and cooking facilities.

Fires, floods, and the Depression hit the St. Joe logging business like a kick in the stomach with caulked boots. The 1910 fire at Big Creek, the severe flood of 1917-1918, hurricane winds, and the depressed economy all crippled Fred Herrick's logging empire. His four large plants at Coeur d'Alene and the St. Maries Lumber Company went "belly-up" at the very beginning of the Depression. In 1928 the large mill and two planing mills at St. Joe City, owned since 1920 by Winton-Rosenberry Lumber Company, burned to the ground. That was when St. Joe City became another ghost in Idaho history. The logging industry, that in its peak had shipped 300 million board feet annually down the St. Joe, sunk to its low point in the years from 1929 to 1940.

A ghost of a logging camp from those days still haunts the memory of area logger "Dimmer" Whipple. In the fall of 1950 Whipple and his father went into the Marble Creek drainage near Delaney Creek. It was a dark, dreary day when they found the old camp. The lines from the machines were still strung out, just as the day the workers had left them. The old blacksmith shop stood intact, complete with hand-made rigging and 500 pounds of horseshoes. Trees had cropped up in front of doors and next to walls. Through the windows, Whipple saw tables with dishes set upside down over silverware, waiting thirty years for a hungry crew as the buildings around them deteriorated. "It was like somebody'd come and taken 'em away, just like a fantasy show on TV," says Whipple. But the Depression and hard times were no fantasy—and no one ever came back.

TODAY'S LOGS

The face of logging has been transformed since the days of horses, steam donkeys, cross-cut saws, and river drives. Part of the associated romance of logging is gone also. The mechanical whine of chainsaws and the toot-toot of the "talkie tooter" (radio signals) are the noises of the woods now, replacing the slow dragging of logs along the forest floors. The spring river drive to transport logs has given way to growling log trucks, while the advent of the caterpillar has changed the work style of the man in the woods. The caulked shoes of the old-time lumberjack have been filled by the modern logger.

Of course, not everything from the early days ended abruptly. The cross-cut saw was a carry-over from the past for a long time, used by Swedish sawyers up until the late 1940's or early '50's. The reason was obvious. The first Homelite chainsaws weighed about 140 pounds each, a bit hefty to carry around in the woods.

The days of the old-time river drives have been replaced by modern logging methods. This early caterpillar and jammer are decking and loading logs in the Fishhook drainage in the 1950's. (Lindow)

Besides, the new-fangled gadgets got hung up in trees and lowered efficiency. A good sawyer with a cross-cut saw cut 15,000 to 20,000 board feet daily, but the first chainsaws cut only 7,000 or 8,000. They were improved with time, and the cross-cut saw fell by the wayside of progress. As Dooley Cramp once observed, "We used to outsmart the trees, but these fellas nowadays just overpower them."

Modern logging made its debut with the brightened economic prospects of World War II and a bustling war economy. While mill construction reached its peak in Benewah and Kootenai Counties between 1900 and 1910, Shoshone County's mills flourished during and after the second war. The biggest block of timber ever sold by Region One of the U.S. Forest Service went up for bid on the Avery District in 1947. Such stimulation and government war contracts encouraged Erling Moe to open seven different log camps on the Coeur d'Alene and St. Joe rivers. With help from George Moody, round stuff again floated down the 'Joe. After

Pictured are the forlorn remains of Erling Moe's Spring Creek Mill shortly before it was torn down in the early 1970's. The mill was the largest ever to be constructed along the swiftwater of the Joe. (Ruff)

working Trout Creek, Daveggio and Marble Creeks, Moe got financial backing from Ohio Match Company and built a mill by Spring Creek in 1951. The Milwaukee Railroad recognized the siding at the mill by the name Erlmo. The valley had high hopes for its success, but it folded after less than two years of operation. The lack of timber close by along with marketing and management problems probably led to its closure. Moe, a mighty brick of a man, stood five feet seven and weighed 265 pounds in clothes especially made by Spokane Tent and Awning. After his mill closed, Moe ran the Big Eddy restaurant for many years.

Steady operation of most of the mills in North Idaho was the exception rather than the rule. In Calder, for example, mills came and went. Lloyd and Carl Buell opened the first one in 1943 which functioned until 1948. The Calder Lumber Company with J.R. Edson in charge operated from 1950 to 1953, followed by Shepherd and Barden in 1954 through 1960. That mill burned and was rebuilt in 1955. Chase and Shepherd Lumber ran a mill from 1954 to 1961, and the Forest Lumber Company started in 1961 but was destroyed by fire in 1965. Charlie Harpole now owns a shake mill in Calder.

Additional mills have operated throughout the area at different times. Three different operators had mills in Clarkia: F.J. Rooney (1936 to 1938), Leslie Mallory (1949 and 1950), and Smith and Eddy in 1960. Closer to Avery, Harry Petroff set up a small cedar mill near the mouth of Setzer Creek in the early 1970's, and currently Tom McQuade has a mill at Marble Creek.

The big companies have played a part in local logging history, either in contracting the work out to gypos or more directly as owner/managers. Names that come to mind are Atlas Tie, Ohio Match (later to merge with Diamond Match), Plum Creek Lumber, Rutledge, McGoldrick, and St. Maries Lumber.

The Weyerhaeuser Company had investments in the area since the turn of the century. Among other activities, the company owned the Potlatch Lumber Company and had controlling interest in the Edward Rutledge Timber Company, which relied heavily on Marble Creek timber. In 1930 Weyerhaeuser's board of directors voted to merge the Rutledge, Potlatch and Clearwater plants into one management unit. Its name was to be Potlatch Forests, Inc. The combined interests of Weyerhaeuser and P.F.I. have since been divided by anti-trust laws, but both companies share some members on their boards of directors and some major stockholders. P.F.I. has changed its name once again and is now known as the Potlatch Corporation. Potlatch's first sale on the Avery District was on Lick Creek (Section 14) in 1944. More than any other event, that seems to have marked the beginning of a new era of logging as business improved and many more sales were harvested.

It has been said that windstorms are good for business. A severe windstorm in 1949 proved that statement to be true, blowing down eleven million board feet. It weakened large stands of trees and

provided a source of incubation for a huge epidemic of spruce beetles. The beetles were so thick in the woods in 1952 as to be nearly blinding, recalls Dooley Cramp. Whole sections of land, belonging to both Northern Pacific and the Forest Service, had to be logged. Potlatch alone tallied 55 million board feet of bug-killed timber for several seasons in the mid-'50's from sales on the East Fork of Fishhook, the Little North Fork of the Clearwater, and on Outlaw and Lick Creeks. To reach the timber, the Avery Timber Creek Road to Bluff Saddle was built. Ohio Match also logged extensive areas during this time.

It was also in 1944 that Potlatch set up a camp for its employees on Lick creek (it later was moved to the West Fork of Fishhook Creek), coincidentally named Camp 44. Because the employees wintered in Bovill, the camp remained a seasonal residence until the logging peak of the '50's. Then the camp housed a

Camp 44 on the West Fork of Fishhook Creek housed 100 families at one time. Built in 1944, it was heavily used until the 1960's by Potlatch Forest Industries. (U.S.D.A., Forest Service)

hundred men and their families. It was a completely modern camp, boasting two bathhouses, laundry facilities, a drying house, cookhouse, and oil-heated bunkhouses. Camp 44 was in use for eighteen years before being dismantled in 1962. Four years later, highly respected Potlatch superintendent Dooley Cramp retired from a long life in the woods and river drives of North Idaho.

During the height of logging activity, Potlatch added seventeen buildings at the mouth of Fishhook and a family camp of trailers above the present Burlington Northern camp. Another camp, active during the 1960's, was owned by J.E. Hall near the mouth of Jungle Creek. Hall, who had other camps on the Clearwater, employed about fifty men on the St. Joe until he was forced to declare bankruptcy.

To accommodate all the logs piling up from the

Logs from the St. Joe are transferred from truck to train in this 1950s photograph to head downriver by rail from the landing on the west edge of Avery. (Piccinini)

woods, Potlatch also established the lower landing in Avery in 1944. That was expanded to its present size in 1966 by removing a bar from the river for fill. Logs at first were scaled right on the cars, all 39 cars per day. Today the landing is still in use, as the Potlatch Corporation hauls out over 1200 cars annually. The upper landing just east of Avery was built with the plan in mind that a road up Sisters Creek would wedge an opening into more timberland. Facetiously called the St. Joe & Eastern Railroad, the railroad spur was used only intermittently by several companies. Other more practical roads provided access to the woods, and the upper landing has not been used a great deal.

The history of logging would not be complete without mentioning the important part various gypos have played in getting wood out of the 'Joe. Gypos, who should more correctly be called contract loggers, contract with various employers and mills to do certain jobs. By definition they start out small with the resources of one or more people involved. Take the story of the Robinson Brothers, Aaron and Skip, who chose to follow in the footsteps up the 'Joe of their father, Bill Robinson. Bill had logged on the Marble, Bond Creek and Emerald Creek on the St. Maries River during river driving days, in addition to building roads and the St. Joe Lodge. Aaron started logging in this country before 1940. He later formed a partnership with his brother Skip when he returned from World War II. Equipment for the two consisted of a team of horses and a gin pole, a pole set up with guy lines for loading tracks. Now, after nearly forty years of logging, there aren't many places on the St. Joe that the Robinson Brothers have not been. They have logged upriver from Avery on Tourist creek, Turner Creek, and Bluff Creek; they've skidded out trees on Sisters Creek, Rutledge Creek, Bearskull, and on Fishhook. Their cats and jammers have worked in Marble, Daveggio, and Boulder Creeks. For many years

now, the livelihood of fifty or sixty men has depended on their company. Among the companies that have contracted their services are Russell and Pugh Lumber, Atlas Tie, St. Maries Lumber Company, Potlatch, and most recently Diamond International. Robinson camps have been set up on Tom McQuade's property at the mouth of Marble Creek, across from the Log Cabin Inn in Avery, and at Spring Creek, which they took over from Diamond International in 1965. Additional camps were manned at White Rock near Clarkia, at Floodwood, and on the Coeur d'Alene River. Certainly when the Robinson brothers retired in 1979, they had literally logged one of the most impressive records on the St. Joe.

Another logger, Henry Sindt, came to the St. Joe area from Oregon in 1952. His sole equipment was an old, battered D-7 cat. Finally, he convinced the bank to loan him the money to get more machinery, though he still did everything himself.

Now Henry Sindt's contracting company has acquired nearly twenty pieces of heavy equipment, including two Skagit Skyline yarders, and the efforts of fifty-plus men.

The Sverdsten Company also started small but has grown into one of the area's successful businesses. Trucking companies specializing in hauling logs have also grown prosperous on St. Joe timber. Richard Crandall is the owner of a trucking operation based in Avery, while the Jack H. Buell Company now runs about fifty log trucks in the area.

Idaho jammers have been the main yarding machines in the woods of the St. Joe, until an entirely different method of logging caught everyone's attention in the 1960's. In fact, if you happened to be traveling upriver from Avery, you couldn't miss paying attention to it. The Wyssen Skycrane logging system had cables strung two or three hundred feet over the road and

The Wyssen Skycrane logging system was designed in Switzerland and used successfully on the St. Joe to log steep slopes in the early 1960's. The motor was located on the top of a hill to utilize power more efficiently. Its line often spanned out over a half-mile long. (U.S.D.A., Forest Service)

Modern logging on the St. Joe makes use of high-lead logging machines such as Henry Sindt's pictured here. The Skagit, introduced to the St. Joe in the 1970's, decks logs to a landing where the loader (in front) operates. This 1979 sale is on Turner Peak. (Crowell)

river to yard out the logs. The easily accessible country in the area had been logged first, leaving the steep slopes untouched. Designed and used in the steep mountains of Switzerland, the system was especially effective on the steep slopes. Its lines that extended out half a mile eliminated the need for many damaging roads or skid trails, and its motor was located on the top of the hill to utilize power more efficiently. The lines carried a carriage with chokers; by radio connection, the operator dropped the chokers to the hook tenders on the ground. Up the logs went, high over the ground to the landing, without damaging a single tree around them. The Wyssen worked on settings at Bird Creek, Lick Creek, and across from Turner Creek Campground. To prove how successful this method was, hardly any signs remain in those areas to show that logging even took place.

The Swiss-made machinery and system needed Swiss men to operate it. About a dozen came to Avery from Switzerland, speaking French, Italian, and German. The men were exceptionally strong, and their ability to run up the mountains became legendary. One man could carry eight or ten chokers over his broad shoulders without a flinch. Some of the men lived in a camp at Tourist Creek, while others lived in Avery and became a part of the community. Ben Linder, Fritz Zahler, and Johann Nadig married local girls, and some such as Johann Nadig have made the United States their home, retaining ties with friends in Avery.

Today's logger on the St. Joe is a different sort of person from his predecessor, the lumberjack. Most loggers now are family men who live elsewhere. They commute daily from other towns in their own pick-ups, rather than hiking in and out a couple of times a season. Those who do stay in the woods live in small camp trailers; gone forever are the large camps. The days of specialization are over as today's logger

becomes diverse in many woods jobs. Even the jokes they tell are updated. The story is told of a new kind of chainsaw using a laser beam—but the loggers on the 'Joe had to stop using it because they kept looking to see if the light was on!

The woods are still there, maybe not as magnificent as they were before the large fires, but growing nonetheless. Islands of trees that did not burn in the 1910 fire were logged until recently, fire-killed cedar is being salvaged, and now entire stands grown since the big fire are approaching maturity. In addition, some of those first sales logged selectively in 1944 are ready to harvest once again. The wood from the area is used for a variety of things: pulp, sawtimber, cedar shakes, house logs, and firewood. These markets have placed the St. Joe high on the list of timber-producing forests of Region One. The key to maintaining the future supply of logs lies in careful forest management; the large clearcut that was standard practice in the 1960's has been replaced by more selective cutting today as environmental awareness has grown. The future of logging on the St. Joe looks bright as better utilization of wood fiber becomes a reality and as the nation searches for more energy sources.

As for the past, the places of some of those wild times on Marble Creek may be preserved by their nomination as National Historic Sites. And the spot where the once innovative locomotives hauled out "the round stuff" is now looking at another innovation. The Ramsey-Railroad area has a new crop of trees to be harvested, but this time a new mode of transportation is used. For the first time on the St. Joe, helicopters are lifting logs off the steep hillsides.

The forests of the 'Joe have survived fire, wind, bugs, logging, and they still provide a livelihood for many. They are indeed our renewable resource.

The Wyssen System, used on Bird Creek, Turner Creek, and Lick Creek, yarded logs out of the woods without building roads and skid trails. Operators for the equipment were mainly native-born Swisslanders. (U.S.D.A., Forest Service)

The last log drive on the St. Joe occurred in May, 1951. This photograph was taken near the old bridge just upriver from Falls Creek, with the railroad grade in the background. All three transportation systems—water, rail, and road—moved millions and millions of board feet of timber down the 'Joe. (Stewart)

EPILOGUE

Each day when the trains came
the old timer at the window waved his flashlight:
I am fine I am here I have always been here
I am he said.
He was here (by the river) when the first train came;
A boy thrilled with boats and adventure and
Black engines puffing excitement into the air.
New town! New lumber! New track!
A whole future to bite into
like a crisp apple!

The trains came the years came
His loves came the town stayed and
he lived
savoring the apple (that ripened by the river).
And the locomotives!
Proud the best the biggest
HIS train came its mighty rhythm
pounding in his veins
pulsating across the nation
through wars and hard times—
Over the mountains each time!
The trains came
And one day his little-boy-turned-to-man
got aboard too.
The apples mellowed.
Through the tunnels
(down the river) on to the sea
The trains. . . .

Gone now his family (makers of the town)
The proud hotels the caring wife
the brothers the son. The town dwindles.
Friends pass through with only a whistle in the night.
He gives the apples to others.

The last train came through last night
Bankrupt broken tired
The end of the line.
The old trainman put away his flashlight
and stared down the track
for a long time

(But the town stayed and the river ran.)

S.C.
March, 1980

Bibliography

Books

Anastasio, Angelo. *The Southern Plateau - An Ecological Analysis of Intergroup Relations.* Moscow: University of Idaho Laboratory of Anthropology, 1975. (Chapter 1)

Andrews, Ralph W. *Glory Days of Logging.* Seattle: Superior Publishing Company, 1956. (Chapter 11)

Bailey, Thomas A. *The American Pageant, A History of the Republic.* Lexington, Massachusetts: D. C. Heath and Company, 1975. (Chapters 5, 9)

Blake, Oscar. *Timber Down the Hill.* St. Maries, Idaho: (By the Author), 1969. (Chapters 3, 11)

Brosnan, C. J. *History of the State of Idaho.* New York: Charles Scribner's Sons, 1918 and 1926. (Chapter 10)

Bryant, Ralph Clement. *Logging.* New York: John Wiley & Sons, Inc., 1914. (Chapter 11)

Chalfant, Stuart A. *Aboriginal Territory of the Nez Perce Indians.* New York: Garland Publishing, Inc., 1974. (Chapters 1, 3)

Defenbash, Byron. *Idaho, The Place and Its People: A History of the State From Prehistoric to Present Days, Vol. III.* New York: The American Historical Society, Inc., 1938. (Chapter 3)

Dictionary of the Chinook Jargon, 7th Edition. Portland, Oregon: L. McCormick, 1879. (Chapter 1)

Gibbs, Rafe. *Beckoning the Bold.* Portland, Oregon: Durham and Downey, Inc., 1976. (Chapter 2)

Goetzmann, William H. *Exploration and Empire.* New York: Vintage Books, 1966. (Chapter 5)

Hebard, Grace R., and E. A. Brininstool. *The Bozeman Trail,* Vol. I. Cleveland: The Arthur H. Clark Company, 1922. (Chapter 1)

Holbrook, Stewart H. *Burning an Empire.* New York: Macmillan Company, 1943. (Chapter 7)

_____. *Rocky Mountain Revolution.* New York: Henry Holt and Company, 1956. (Chapter 6)

Horr, David Agee, Editor. *Interior Salish and Eastern Washington Indians,* I. New York: Garland Publishing Co., 1974. (Chapters 1, 3)

Hult, Ruby El. *Northwest Disaster.* Portland, Oregon: Binfords and Mort, 1973. (Chapter 7)

_____. *Steamboats in the Timber.* Portland, Oregon: Binfords and Mort, 1968. (Chapters 1, 3)

Magnuson, Richard G. *Coeur d'Alene Diary.* Portland: Metropolitan Press, 1968. (Chapters 2, 3, 6)

Miller, Merle. *Plain Speaking.* New York: Berkley Medallion Books, 1964. (Chapter 4)

Miller, John B. *The Trees Grew Tall.* Moscow, Idaho: News-Review Publishing Company, 1972. (Preface, Chapter 1)

Palladino, L. B., S. J. *Indian and White in the Northwest.* Lancaster, Pennsylvania: Wickersham Publishing Company, 1922. (Chapter 1)

Peltier, Jerome. *Manners and Customs of the Coeur d'Alene Indians.* Moscow, Idaho: Peltier Publications, 1975. (Chapter 1)

Pough, Richard. *Audubon Western Bird Guide.* Doubleday & Company, 1957. (Chapter 10)

Schussler, Edith M. *Doctors, Dynamite and Dogs.* Caldwell, Idaho: Caxton Printers, Ltd., 1956. (Chapter 5)

Scott, Orland A. *Pioneer Days on the Shadowy St. Joe.* Coeur d'Alene, Idaho: The Caxton Printers, 1967. (Chapters 1, 3, 5, 10)

Shawley, Stephen D. *Nez Perce Trails.* Moscow, Idaho: University of Idaho Laboratory of Anthropology, 1977. (Chapter 1)

Space, Ralph S. *Pioneer Timbermen, A History of Clearwater Timber and Timbermen.* Lewiston, Idaho: Printcraft Printing, 1972. (Chapter 3)

Spencer, Betty Goodwin. *The Big Blow-Up.* Caldwell, Idaho: Caxton Printers, 1956. (Chapters 3, 7)

Strong, Clarence C. and Webb, Clyde S. *White Pine: King of Many Waters.* Missoula, Montana: Mountain Press Publishing Co., 1970. (Chapters 3, 11)

Teit, James A. *The Salish Tribes of the Western Plateaus.* Bureau of American Ethnology, 45th Annual Report. Washington: U.S. Government Printing Office, 1930. (Chapter 1)

Walker, Deward E., Jr. *Indians of Idaho.* Moscow, Idaho: University Press of Idaho, 1978. (Chapter 1)

Wolff, Ernest. *Handbook for the Alaskan Prospector.* Ann Arbor, Michigan: Edwards Brothers, Inc., 1969. (Chapter 2)

Wood, Charles R. and Dorothy M. *Milwaukee Road West.* Seattle, Washington: Superior Publishing Company, 1972. (Chapter 5)

Zimmerman, Karl R. *The Milwaukee Road Under Wire.* New York: Quadrant Press, Inc., 1973. (Chapter 5)

Government Documents

Avery Ranger District. Avery, Idaho. Historical Files. (Chapters 1 through 11)

Greeson, David R. "U.S. Forest Service Lookout, Life and Habits." (Chapter 8)

Idaho Panhandle National Forest. Coeur d'Alene, Idaho. Historical Files. (Chapters 1 through 11)

Mullan, John. *Report on the Construction of a Military Road from Fort Walla Walla to Fort Benton.* 1863. (Chapters 1, 2)

Red Ives Ranger District. St. Maries, Idaho. Historical Files. (Chapters 1, 8)

Region One, Forest Service. Missoula, Montana. Historical Files. (Chapter 8)

Roundtop Ranger District, "Wildlife Management Plan." (Chapter 10)

St. Maries, Ranger District. St. Maries, Idaho. Historical Files. (Chapter 8)

U.S., Congress. Senate. Hearing Before the Subcommittee on Parks and Recreation on the Classification. Statement of Dr. Ruthann Knudson, 95th Congress. August 28, 1978. (Chapter 1)

U.S., Department of Agriculture. Forest Service, Northern Region. *An Introduction to the St. Joe National Forest.* Missoula, Montana. 1972. (Chapters 2, 10)

_____. *Early Days in the Forest Service,* Vol. I-IV. Missoula, Montana.

   Donaldson, Walter A. Vol. III. (Chapters 3, 5, 7, 8)
   Donally, Lloyd V. "My Experience on Reforestation (Tree Planting) All on the St. Joe National Forest." Vol. III. (Chapter 8)
   _____. "Other St. Joe National Forest History." Vol. IV. (Chapter 8)
   _____. "Tree Planting Projects on the St. Joe." Vol. IV. (Chapter 8)
   Fickes, Clyde P. "The Decker Saddle." Vol. IV. (Chapter 8)
   _____. "The Story of the Remount Depot." (Chapter 8)
   _____. "Some of the Highlights of My Career in the Forest Service." Vol. I. (Chapters 7, 8)
   Gunterman, William F. "Letters to Folks Back Home." Vol. IV. (Chapter 8)

Hand, Ralph L. "Anecdotes and Fireline Philosophies."
Vol. IV. (Chapter 8)
Harrington, Dean. "The Beginning of the United States
Forest Service As I Remember It." Vol. III. (Chapter 8)
_____. "The First Years Were the Toughest."
Vol. III. (Chapter 8)
Koch, Elers. "Early Ranger Examinations in Montana."
Vol. I. (Chapter 8)
_____. "My Closet Shave on a Fire." Vol. I.
(Chapter 8)
_____. "Region One in the Pre-Regional Days."
Vol. I. (Chapter 6, 7, 8)
Landsdale, O. O. Vol. I. (Chapter 1, 3, 8)
Morris, William W. "Experiences on a National Forest."
Vol. I. (Chapter 8)
Olson, Donald S. Vol. III. (Chapter 8)
Samsel, W. K. "The Lookout." Vol. IV. (Chapter 8)
Weigle, William G. "William G. Weigle Reminisces."
Vol. II. (Chapter 6, 7, 8)
_____. *Fire Report on the Coeur d'Alene National
Forest.* Missoula, Montana. 1910. (Chapter 7)
_____. *St. Joe River, A Summary Report of Inventories.*
Missoula, Montana. 1979. (Chapters 1, 2, 10)
_____. *When the Mountains Roared: Stories of the 1910
Fire.* Missoula, Montana. (Chapter 7)
U.S., Department of Agriculture. Washington Office. *100 Years of
Federal Forestry.* Washington, D.C.: Government Printing Office,
1976. (Chapter 8)
U.S., Department of Interior. Geological Survey. *Channeled
Scablands of Eastern Washington—the Geological Story of the
Spokane Flood.* Washington, D.C.: Government Printing Office,
1976. (Prologue)
U.S., Department of Interior. Land Office. "Brief for Transferee,
Clearwater Timber Company in U.S. vs. Cornelius Willis,
Entryman, and Clearwater Timber Company, Transferee."
Lewiston, Idaho, 1914. H.F. 92809. (Chapter 3)
_____. "Brief on Behalf of Entrywoman, Luella Durham,
in U.S. vs. Luella Durham." Coeur d'Alene, 1914. H. F. No.
01777. (Chapter 3)

Interviews

Iona Adair, Moscow, Idaho, 1977 (Chapters 3 and 7); Wash
Applegate, St. Maries, Idaho, 1979 (Chapter 10); Felix Aripa,
Avery and Plummer, Idaho, 1979 (Chapter 1); Annetta Kellom
Bellows, Avery, 1979 (Chapters 3 and 4); Lloyd Buell, St. Maries,
1979 (Chapters 3 and 10); Bob Cass, Avery, 1978 and 1979 (Chapters
4 and 9); Dooley Cramp, Avery, 1978 and 1979 (Chapters 10 and
11); Thelma Cramp, Avery, 1978 (Chapters 3 through 11); Olive
Ferrell, Calder, (Chapter 8); Ray Hilding, Coeur d'Alene, Idaho, 1978
(Chapter 8); Ruth Lindow, Avery, 1976 through 1979 (Chapters 4, 8,
and 10); Art Lintz, St. Maries, 1979 (Chapter 10); Tom McQuade,
Avery, 1980 (Chapters 3, 10); James Northrup, St. Maries, 1979
(Prologue); Mark Orme, Avery, 1978 (Chapter 10); Aaron Robinson,
St. Maries, 1979 (Chapter 11); Bill Robinson, St. Maries, 1977
(Chapters 3, 8, and 10); Nile Saunders, Peshastin, Washington, 1976
(Chapter 4); Mrs. Henry Sindt, St. Maries, 1979 (Chapter 11); Charley
Scribner, St. Maries, 1978 and 1979 (Chapters 1 through 11); Mrs.
Mabel Scribner, St. Maries, 1978 and 1979 (Chapters 4 and 8); Harold
Theriault, Avery, 1976 through 1980 (Chapters 1 through 11); Bob
"Dimmer" Whipple, Avery and St. Maries, 1979 (Chapter 11);
Larnerd Williams, St. Maries, 1977 (Chapter 8); Mrs. Mary Wurth,
Spokane, Washington, 1978 (Chapter 4).

Magazines

Clark, Rodney A. "The Milwaukee Electrification—A Proud Era
Passes." Special Supplement to *The Milwaukee Road Magazine,*
July-August, 1973. (Chapter 5)
Cox, Thomas R. "Tribal Leadership in Transition: Chief Peter
Moctolme of the Coeur d'Alenes." *Idaho Yesterdays,* Spring,
1979. (Chapter 1)
Fletcher, Marvin. "Army Fire Fighters." *The Quarterly Journal of
the Idaho Historical Society,* Summer, 1972. (Chapter 7)
Geoffroy, William. "The Coeur d'Alene Tribe." *Idaho Heritage,*
October, 1977. (Chapter 1)
Griswold, Gillett. "Aboriginal Patterns of Trade Between the
Columbian Basin and the Northern Plains." *Archeology in
Montana, II,* April-September, 1970. (Chapter 1)
Lewis, William S. "The Camel Pack Trains in the Mining Camps of
the West." *Washington Historical Quarterly,* 1928. (Chapter 1)
McClenahan, Judith. "Call and See the Elephant." *Idaho Yesterdays,*
Volume III, 1967. (Chapter 6)
McClusky, Thorp. "Timberland Parish." *Presbyterian Life,*
September 17, 1949. (Chapters 4, 11)
Morgan, David P. "The Lost Promise of 1950." *Trains,* August,
1979. (Chapter 5)
Pratt, Grace Raffey. "Timber Thieves." *True West,* August, 1973.
(Chapter 3)
Ogden, G. W. "A World Afire; Heroes in the Burning of the
Northwestern Forests." *Everybody's Magazine,* December,
1910. (Chapter 7)
Sims, Don. "Milwaukee Electrics and the Avery Yard." *Railroad
Modeler,* February, 1974. (Chapter 5)
Watt, James W. "Experiences of a Packer in the Washington
Territory Mining Camps During the Sixties." *Washington
Historical Quarterly,* 1929. (Chapter 1)

Newspapers

Daily Idaho Press (Wallace), August 22 to September 2, 1910.
(Chapter 7)
St. Maries Courier, March 12, 1901 to August 13, 1901. (Chapter 3)
March 12, 1912. (Chapter 4)
St. Maries Gazette, March 30, 1906 to May 18, 1906. (Chapter 3)
St. Maries Gazette-Record, Avery news by Ruth Lindow, 1963-
1965. (Chapter 4)
Silver State Post (Deer Lodge), September 11, 1953. (Chapter 7)
Spokesman-Review (Spokane), August 22, 1910. (Chapter 7)
The Wallace Times, August 22 to August 30, 1910. (Chapter 7)
Wallace Press, December 20, 1890. (Chapter 1)

Unpublished Documents and Papers

Avery Hi' Gra' Booster. Avery School Newspaper. March 29, 1940.
(Chapter 4)
Avery School District No. 10. Minutes of School Board Meetings,
1910 to 1956. (Chapter 4)
Avery Sportsmen's Club. Records, minutes, correspondence, 1950
to 1962. (Chapter 4)
Koch, Elers. "Derivation of Geographic Names for Montana and
Idaho." (Unpublished article, U.S. Forest Service). (Chapter 1)
Latah County Historical Society. Oral History Collection. Interview
with Carol Ryrie Brink. Moscow, Idaho: Latah County Historical
Society, 1976. (Chapter 3)
Latah County Historical Society. Oral History Collection. Interview
with Iona Adair. Moscow, Idaho: Latah County Historical
Society, 1976. (Chapters 3 and 7)
Rankel, Gary L. "An Appraisal of the Cutthroat Trout Fishery of
the Joe River." Master's Thesis. Moscow: University of Idaho,
1971. (Chapter 10)
Red Collar Lines, Advertising Brochure, 1909. (Chapter 4)
Red Eyes Bulletin. Red Ives Ranger Station Newspaper, Avery,
Idaho. June, 1938. (Chapter 8)
Ross Hall Studio. Postcard Historic Taft Hotel. Sandpoint, Idaho.
(Chapter 5)
Scribner, Charles. "Historical Data—Trails." (Unpublished article,
U.S.D.A., Forest Service). (Chapter 1)
Scribner, Charles. "Sparks of St. Joe History." (Unpublished
article, U.S.D.A., Forest Service). (Chapter 2)
Tin Can Tamarack. CCC Newspaper, Tin Can Flat, Avery, Idaho.
May, 1939. (Chapter 9)
Turner, Mary Elizabeth. Private Diary Written at Turner's Flat eight
miles upriver from Avery, 1912. (Chapter 3)
"Valuation Section Montana 4." Historical files of the Chicago,
Milwaukee, St. Paul & Pacific Railroad. (Chapter 5)

Index